THE ONLY TAX BOOK
YOU'LL EVER NEED

THE ONLY TAX BOOK YOU'LL EVER NEED

by Robert A. Garber

HARMONY BOOKS/NEW YORK

Copyright © 1983 by Robert A. Garber

Published by Harmony Books, a division of Crown Publishers, Inc., One Park Avenue, New York, New York 10016, and simultaneously in Canada by General Publishing Company Limited

HARMONY BOOKS and colophon are trademarks of Crown Publishers, Inc.

Manufactured in the United States of America

Library of Congress Cataloging in Publication Data

Garber, Robert A.
  The only tax book you'll ever need.

  Includes index.
  1. Income tax—Law and legislation—United States—Popular works. I. Title.

KF6369.6.G36 1982   343.7305′2   82-11681
ISBN 0-517-54627-2   347.30352

10 9 8 7 6 5 4 3 2 1

First Edition

"Tell me not, in mournful numbers..."
A Psalm of Life, H. W. Longfellow

Contents

PART IV · TAX CREATURES

PART V · TAX PLANNING

APPENDICES

What This Book Can Do for You

For better or worse, richer or poorer, taxes are part of our lives. It doesn't seem possible for us to go about the world without the ominous accompaniment of the Internal Revenue Service. Perhaps this text will ease that enforced relationship a bit. It provides a coherent explanation of the current Internal Revenue Code. Tax ignorance isn't merely ignominious. It's expensive.

Whether or not you have an avid interest in the tax law or accounting, this book will be useful to you. It's designed to do more than hold your hand and walk you through this year's tax return. It presents a clear translation of the Internal Revenue Code into English—into a language that the ordinary taxpayer can understand and benefit from. The tax law isn't called the Code for nothing. If knowledge isn't power after all, maybe it's money, which is pretty close.

After reading this book, you will be able to put the tax laws to work for *your* advantage. You will also understand what the tax lawyers, accountants, and Internal Revenue Service agents are saying and be able to ask them the right questions. Of course, the more you understand about the federal income tax, the easier the preparation of your returns will be; but filling out a tax form is much like completing an application for a job or a bank loan. What happens *before* you put your pencil to the paper is what really counts. Tax planning beats tax paying every time, and this book will help you plan ahead.

We will also go over a bit of tax theory and explain some of the buried logic in the law. Although it's complicated, the basic tax law is not as difficult as you have been led to believe. Once you understand what the Code says, you can put it to work for you.

If a particular tax topic insistently claims your attention, by all means read the chapter devoted to it independently. Or just read the book straight through. The plan is relatively simple. After an introductory word or two about the Code and how it got that way, we get down to essential points regarding income—what is subject to tax, what isn't; capital gains and other special kinds of income. Next we talk about what can be subtracted from taxable income—expenses, contributions, taxes, and other deductions. After that, we make sense of the basic tax return—including computations, credits, estimates, and withholding. Since individuals are not the only taxpayers, we also discuss the rules under which business entities, charities, and other tax creatures operate, and we focus on estate planning. Then we will be ready for some fundamental precepts of general tax planning and, finally, some information about the government's management of your return and audits. Appended is an extensive glossary for quick reference, as well as tax rate schedules, forms, a list of publications, and, if all else fails, a short list of tax havens. Also included is a tax data organizer to help with your year-round tax planning and preparation.

This handbook is founded on the following proposition: whether or not you have a competent tax adviser, you—like every other taxpayer—ought to know as much as you can about the law that takes your money. It's your right.

The Code

The tax law pervades our every activity, from the birth of a little exemption to death and the estate tax. Over 140 million federal tax returns are filed in a good year. There are nearly 90,000 Internal Revenue Service (IRS) employees (and more to come), yet the IRS started in its present incarnation just about seventy years ago.

"Taxes are what we pay for civilization," said the redoubtable Oliver Wendell Holmes, but ever since the halcyon days of the pharaohs, taxes have been imposed or increased to pay for war, at hand or anticipated. Our Revolution and the War of 1812 were supported in large measure by excise taxes, and the first real federal income tax was imposed by the Revenue Act of 1861, in time for the Civil War. That tax, last collected in 1872, was held to be unconstitutional. Various tax laws were tried again at the jingoistic turn of the century, just before the Spanish-American War. Unconstitutional again. It took the Sixteenth Amendment to make the income tax permanent. Philander C. Knox, secretary of state with the most euphonious name, tacked the national seal onto the amendment in late February 1913, a few days before Woodrow Wilson became our twenty-eighth president. The law we all think we know and love to hate took effect on March 1, 1913. The Great War began in Europe the next year, of course.

Here's what the first page (of four) looked like of a 1916 Form 1040. (If you recently retired at age sixty-five, this form may have been the one your folks used the year you were born.)

TO BE FILLED IN BY COLLECTOR.	Form 1040 (Revised October, 1916).	TO BE FILLED IN BY INTERNAL REVENUE BUREAU.
Assessment List 23-B .... (Month.)	**INCOME TAX.**	File No. ....
Folio .... Line	**THE PENALTY**	Audited by ....

FOR FAILURE TO HAVE THIS RETURN IN THE HANDS OF THE COLLECTOR OF INTERNAL REVENUE ON OR BEFORE MARCH 1 IS $20 TO $1,000.

(SEE INSTRUCTIONS ON PAGE 4.)

IMPORTANT.
Read this form through carefully. Fill in pages 2 and 3 before making entries on first page. Write legibly, using typewriter if possible.

Above space to be stamped by Collector, showing district and date received.

UNITED STATES INTERNAL REVENUE.

RETURN OF ANNUAL NET INCOME OF INDIVIDUALS.
(As provided by Act of Congress approved September 8, 1916.)

FOR YEAR 1916.

Filed by (or for) ...., of ....
(Street and number.)

....
(Post-office addr. s.)   (State.)

		Millions	Thousands	Hundreds	Cents
1. Gross Income (brought from line 31)	$				
2. General Deductions (brought from line 40)	$				
3. Net Income	$				

Dividends and personal exemption to be deducted in computing income subject to normal tax.

		Millions	Thousands	Hundreds	Cents
4. Dividends brought from line 30	$				
5. Personal exemption (single, $3,000; married or head of family, $4,000).	$				
6. Total dividends and personal exemption (Items 4 and 5)	$				
7. Amount of Income subject to normal tax	$				
8. Amount of Normal Tax at rate of 2 per cent on income shown on line 7	$				
9. Credit by amount of normal tax paid or to be paid at source (1 per cent of amount of income shown on line 25, Column A)	$				
10. Balance of normal tax due	$				

NOTE.—When the net income shown above on line 3 exceeds $20,000 the additional tax thereon must be calculated as per schedule below.

	Income.				Tax.			
	Millions	Thousands	Hundreds	Cents	Millions	Thousands	Hundreds	Cents
One per cent on amount over $20,000 and not exceeding $40,000	$				$			
Two per cent on amount over $40,000 and not exceeding $60,000	$				$			
Three per cent on amount over $60,000 and not exceeding $80,000	$				$			
Four per cent on amount over $80,000 and not exceeding $100,000	$				$			
Five per cent on amount over $100,000 and not exceeding $150,000	$				$			
Six per cent on amount over $150,000 and not exceeding $200,000	$				$			
Seven per cent on amount over $200,000 and not exceeding $250,000	$				$			
Eight per cent on amount over $250,000 and not exceeding $300,000	$				$			
Nine per cent on amount over $300,000 and not exceeding $500,000	$				$			
Ten per cent on amount over $500,000 and not exceeding $1,000,000	$				$			
Eleven per cent on amount over $1,000,000 and not exceeding $1,500,000	$				$			
Twelve per cent on amount over $1,500,000 and not exceeding $2,000,000	$				$			
Thirteen per cent on amount over $2,000,000	$				$			
11. Total additional tax					$			
12. Balance of normal tax due, as shown on line 10					$			
13. Total Tax Due					$			

There were just seven paragraphs of instruction. The "normal" tax was 2 percent. Note the additional rates on amounts over $20,000—a princely sum in those days. The highest marginal bracket, on amounts over $2 million, was 13 percent!

Despite what you may think, our tax law was not fabricated

by the Marquis de Sade; neither was it designed by Mortimer Snerd. Hardworking, serious people did it.

Though revenue measures, in theory, are born in the House of Representatives, a tax bill, often proposed by the current administration, is hammered into shape by committees of both houses of Congress. They do it with considerable help, or hindrance, from interested folk in what some call "the private sector"; others call them "lobbyists." Monumental technical aid is rendered by earnest Treasury experts and the skilled staffs of the House Ways and Means Committee and the Senate Finance Committee before the bills reach the legislative floors. Bills are knocked about and "marked up" after committee hearings, and eventually a Joint Committee produces the final version. If it's passed, the bill is signed into law by the Chief Executive in time for the six o'clock news. It is then part of the Internal Revenue Code of 1954. (The last time the Code was rewritten from cover to cover was 1954, when it replaced the 1939 Code.)

That's not all. The Code, 2,000 complex pages of it, is supported and explained by detailed and even more copious Treasury regulations. The "regs," as tax folk call them, are often founded on legislative committee reports, but are more detailed. They are proposed, discussed, reproposed, and promulgated. Cases are tried that augment the body of tax law. Rulings, public and private, are published. The weekly *Internal Revenue Bulletin* announces lively developments—for example, "one adjustment factor in Rev. Rul. 51–57 is corrected with respect to defined benefit plans for self-employed individuals," or "amounts received by an electing small business corporation from the 'dry' lease of an aircraft are rents within the meaning of section 1372 (e) (5) (c) of the...." Well, you get the idea. But don't think *that's* all. There are multivolume loose-leaf tax reporting services and comprehensive texts on various aspects of the law. There are the lectures and seminars for the professionals. There are journals, instructions, forms, manuals; there are expert lawyers, accountants, insurance folk, and corporate tax managers all instructing one another.

The IRS even teaches foreign jurisdictions—from El Salvador to Jordan, from Sierra Leone to the Northern Mariana Islands—how it's done. Tax administrators from 134 countries have taken Washington's instruction. The Code has spread around the world.

Hereinbelow, as lawyers say, there will be little legal citation and few references to case law. Federal taxes are complicated enough. Worse, the rules change all the time. In August 1981, the largest tax reduction in history (from Uncle Sam's point of view, at least) was enacted, along with the usual complex alterations in existing law. Within a year, Congress was at it again, with a gigantic tax increase this time—and more changes in the law.

Changes are not necessarily the fault of an avaricious Congress or the foxy Internal Revenue Service. Often the law is adjusted to suit taxpayers themselves. Perhaps only a few taxpayers with peculiar problems need "relief." There's a hoary provision in the Code dealing with capital gains that was tailored to fit the late Sam Goldwyn. No one else seems to have been able to have used it. The Economic Recovery Tax Act of 1981 followed the tradition of the Code in its peculiarities. It permitted qualified fishing-boat owners to exclude the wages of their sternmen from certain unemployment taxes. Unless you are a movie mogul or a sternman employer, these provisions probably won't be of immediate interest. The Tax Equity and Fiscal Responsibility Act of 1982 was no better.

Perhaps, on the other hand, some general public policy, like the need to find more hydrocarbons or to increase low-income housing, can be furthered with some tinkering to the Code. Admittedly, other changes are made to prevent inventive uses (here read "tax shelters") by taxpayers and their clever advisers.

But rely on it—the law, the regulations under it, the rulings, the cases, and the commentary often appear to be written in sand. This book is up-to-date, but if you are considering a major transaction that depends on favorable tax treatment, check with a tax professional regarding the currency of the tax rules, their application to your situation, and the possible impact of state or local rules.

"What makes sense," said a wise federal court judge once, "does not necessarily dictate the definitive answer in the tax area; apparent conceptual niceties often must give way to the hard realities of statutory requirements." That's a proper thought with which to start.

PART · I

INCOME

1
Gross Income

"Gross income" means the receipts from labor, capital, and the sale of assets. For purposes of taxation, the Code says flatly that gross income means "all income from whatever source derived," *unless* that income is specifically excluded from gross income. The *unless* is important because the Code grants some significant exclusions, such as municipal bond interest, gifts and inheritances, and certain other types of receipts that don't have to be reckoned as income.

Gross income is the starting point from which adjusted gross income, taxable income, and, eventually, your tax payments are calculated.

What Is Income?

Gross income includes gambling winnings and dog catchers' wages, rents and royalties, jury fees and directors' fees, tips and embezzlement loot, farming profits and the proceeds from poetry. Many kinds of income, though, are subject to special rules, which account for some of the more interesting chapters to follow. Here are some common forms of income about which questions often arise.

Compensation for Services. Under this heading put wages, professional fees, bonuses, commissions, tips, awards, most fringe benefits, and whatever else you earn by mental craft or elbow grease. An employee must, for example, include

3

the value of the shares of stock in his or her company that are paid as compensation.

Normally cash is involved. If service or property is received instead, the fair market value of the service or property is included in gross income—that's barter and it's taxable. The IRS is not at all pleased with the mistaken notion that barter is not a taxable event. The case of canned tuna the grocer gives his dentist for extraction of an impacted wisdom tooth is, simply, income to the dentist (and perhaps a deductible medical expense for the grocer). When merchandise or services are received, there may be a problem, because taxation is a cash-and-carry business. The IRS wants money when tax time arrives and the Service won't take some of the employer's securities or half a case of tuna.

Some bargain purchases come under the same rule. If an employee buys property from the boss for less than fair market value, the IRS man is liable to claim that the difference between the value and the bargain price goes into gross income. The cost basis of the property would be increased accordingly for purposes of computing gain or loss on a subsequent sale. (We will be talking about cost basis a good bit because it is an integral part of taxation. For now, it can be thought of simply as the true cost of an asset.)

Pensions and Annuities. Except for Social Security payments, pensions are normally included in gross income. They are forms of delayed income. If the retiree didn't contribute to his or her pension, it's all includable as received. If the worker contributed to its cost, the portion of the pension payment received each year, in the form of an annuity that represents his or her contribution, is excluded. If the employee's contribution will be recovered within the first three years, and the employer also contributed, all payments received during those first three years, up to the employee's cost, may be excluded. (There are certain types of retirement plans that receive favored tax treatment. These are discussed in Chapter 20.)

An annuity is a type of insurance policy or retirement plan that pays a fixed return each year to the annuitant for life or a stated number of years. The part of the payment representing the purchaser's cost is tax-free. The rest of the payment, which may consist substantially of interest on the investment, is gross income.

EXAMPLE: Bob Cratchit invests $22,500 in an annuity which, starting at age sixty-five, makes variable annual payments to him. His life expectancy at sixty-five, based on actuarial tables, is another fifteen golden years. The annual exclusion will be $1,500 ($22,500 ÷ 15) no matter how long he lives, or how much he gets each year. If Bob gets $2,000, he'll report $500 as income; if he gets $2,500, he'll report $1,000. (If he gets $1,000, though, he may refigure the excludable portion for future years.)

Because an annuity isn't taxed at all until payments are received, the interest earned isn't taxed during the accumulation period, and the tax money ordinarily payable on the earnings during that period may compound and earn still more interest.

Alimony. Alimony is deductible by the spouse who pays it (this text forswears any hint of sexism), but only if it is first considered income to the spouse who receives it. This tax connection, of course, doesn't assist delicate negotiations when a marriage founders. Payments are generally taxable to the recipient (and deductible by the payer) when they are "periodic" payments made under

- a decree of divorce or separation founded on marital obligations of support,
- a written separation agreement, or
- a support decree.

In any event, the payments must be "periodic," by which the law means payments in a fixed amount for an indefinite time (for example, until the death of either spouse or the remarriage of the recipient spouse), or of an indefinite amount for a fixed or indeterminate period. If a set sum is to be paid in installments, the installments must be designed to stretch over ten years or more; if so, up to 10 percent of the sum will qualify as periodic each year.

Under the rules, then, a lump-sum payment will not be income to the recipient because it isn't periodic. A property settlement may not be income because it's not made under the obligation of support or under a proper agreement or decree. Payments received because of a handshake promise will not be income, either. The same handshake can't be brought to an audit; something in writing is needed.

Child support, normally segregated from other payments, simply doesn't qualify as income. That's a different obligation of the supporting parent, which is not deductible as alimony, and the payment of child support comes first.

> EXAMPLE: Archy is obliged to pay Mehitabel $1,000 each month; $500 is designated as alimony and $500 as child support. If Archy pays only $750 each month, the first $500 is considered child support—not income to Mehitabel—and the rest—$250—is treated as alimony income.

Sometimes a trust is established, or an insurance policy is purchased to meet alimony obligations. The income under such an arrangement is usually taxable to the recipient, even if the spouse who sets it up does not get a corresponding deduction because it doesn't fit within the rules.

Winnings. The value of a prize or an award won in a competition is included in gross income. Gambling winnings are income if they exceed losses (but don't try to deduct losses in excess of winnings). A television set won in a sales contest or on a game show is taxable, and the IRS is notified if a valuable prize is awarded. Only if the winner doesn't ever have to do a thing to get the bonanza is it tax-free—a rare event, according to the IRS. Thus, because a fish had to be caught, a $25,000 prize won in a fishing contest was taxable. But a Pulitzer Prize is tax-free because it's awarded in recognition of past achievement or present distinction. It's an honor and a gift.

Scholarship and Fellowship Grants. A scholarship is a grant in aid to a pupil at a recognized institution, while a fellowship grant does not require an educational institution if it's made to conduct research or pursue a particular course of study. True scholarship and fellowship grants, including the value of tuition, room, board, fees, laundry, travel expenses, and related research costs which are actually expended are tax-free. Even living expenses paid for the student's family are exempt from taxation.

Of course, such payments are subject to strict scrutiny. It first makes a difference whether the studious recipient is a candidate for a degree. Those who are not are limited in the kinds of grants and the amounts that may be received tax-free. Generally, the granting organization must itself qualify. Further, the student who isn't a degree candidate can't receive, tax-free, more than $300 a month, and, even then, is limited to no more than thirty-six months' worth during his or her life.

Amounts really paid as compensation for services or primarily for the benefit of the grantor are not tax-free. Thus, scholarships won in beauty contests are taxable. The IRS knows that being Miss America is a job. Stipends received by medical interns or nurses in training are likewise taxable.

Sometimes it's a close call. One ruling held that the value of an athletic scholarship (tuition, fees, supplies, liniment) is excludable from an agile student's taxable income when it is awarded by a university—but only if the university cannot demand participation by the athlete-scholar in a particular activity and cannot cancel the scholarship if the student doesn't join the fun.

Tip Income. In 1983 and thereafter, restaurants (other than fast food emporiums) with more than ten workers generally may be required to report 8 percent of gross receipts from food and drink sales as tips to employees on an allocable basis. (If a service charge of at least 10 percent is imposed on customers, the 8 percent rule won't apply.) Tip allocations are to be reported on Forms W-2 for each worker if the total amount of tips reported to the boss doesn't equal 8 percent.

What Is Not Income?

It's an axiom of taxation that where there's a rule, there's an exception, and of course, there are exceptions to the rule that virtually all receipts are income.

The receipt of an inheritance or a gift is not reportable as income. Unless it has been previously written off as a loss or bad debt on an earlier tax return, a repayment of capital isn't income to the lender. Mere appreciation in the value of an asset, without a taxable event such as a sale or exchange, is not income. Nonevents don't, by themselves, reach the status of income in the first place.

The law specifically excludes some receipts from gross income. One notable example, certainly, is interest on municipal or state, or federally backed bonds of local authorities.

There are a variety of other exclusions, including

- Social Security and Medicare benefits
- Employer-provided health and accident insurance
- Federal income tax refunds
- Damage, other than punitive, awarded for personal injury or libel
- Meals and housing provided for the benefit of the employer, rather than the employee.

Disability income payments made as compensation to a worker, under a qualified disability plan or as the result of a lawsuit, are free from tax. Such exempt payments may also be received by way of a health and accident insurance policy or a life insurance policy. Insurance payments to replace income lost because of illness or bodily injury are also not taxable.

A taxpayer who retires on full, permanent disability before age sixty-five may exclude amounts received in lieu of wages up to $100 a week. But if the disabled worker's adjusted gross income (together with that of his or her loyal spouse) exceeds $15,000, each dollar above that figure reduces the amount excludable as disability pay, dollar for dollar. The exclusion ends the year the disabled taxpayer reaches sixty-five. If the taxpayer and spouse lived together anytime during the year, they must file jointly to exclude amounts as disability payments.

Insurance is subject to several special rules. Life insurance proceeds are not considered gross income if they are received because of the death of the insured.

The cost of the first $50,000 of coverage of an employee's group term life insurance provided by his or her employer is excluded from gross income, but the premium on coverage over $50,000 is considered includable compensation. A detailed low cost table with this information is buried in the IRS regulations.

EXAMPLE: Mr. Bigley is forty-seven years old and is employed by Bigley & Co., which provides group term life insurance coverage. Mr. Bigley's coverage is $100,000. The excess $50,000 of coverage is valued, for purposes of calculating his additional gross income, at 40 cents per thousand per month, or $240 a year, even if the coverage costs the company more or would cost the insured more if it were purchased independently.

The estate or beneficiary that receives an employee's death benefit may exclude up to $5,000 paid by the departed worker's employer. A benefit paid to two or more beneficiaries must be allocated among them if it is over $5,000.

The first $1,000 of interest received on life insurance proceeds by a surviving spouse is tax-free each year. Such interest is very often part of a regular insurance payment. No matter how many policies there may have been, the rule allows one $1,000 exclusion per decedent. (On the other hand, if a surviving spouse receives interest on life insurance proceeds after the sequential deaths of several unfortunate mates, several exclusions may be available.)

Who Owns the Income?

Tax lawyers are fond of pithy maxims. "You can't separate the fruit from the tree" is one of them. By this they mean that a taxpayer normally can't give away income without also giving away the source of that income. To do so would surely be a valuable tax scheme. Why not allow children, in low tax brackets, to report the income of their parents who are in high brackets? The law is emphatic that, while gifts may be made anytime, to be unburdened of gross income a taxpayer must give away not only the right to the income but the origin of the income as well. Property transferred to children under *Uniform Gifts to Minors Acts,* for example, becomes the property of the minors, rather than reverting to the donor or the custodian when the minors reach their majority.

Of course, there's an exception. A formal trust arrangement may be used to relieve a taxpayer of gross income. The principal—the source of the income—must stay in trust more than ten years, for the life of the beneficiary, or until the occurrence of an event that reasonably shouldn't happen for a decade. In that case, the income will be taxed to the beneficiary, not the grantor of the trust. (Capital gains and losses of the trust, however, are reportable by the grantor because the principal will revert to that interested party.)

EXAMPLE: In 1981, Charlie Noble set up a trust for the benefit of his Aunt Mary. The trust will last for the life of Mary, but no later than 1995, even if she lives until then. The Noble Trust is funded with stocks and bonds that can be expected to yield $15,000 a year. The stocks and bonds—the "principal" of the trust— will revert to Charlie's ownership when the trust termi- nates. The income of the trust is not taxed to Charlie. Mary, presumably in a lower bracket, will bear the tax on the trust's distributions to her. If the trust were simply scheduled to end after five years, Charlie would be taxed on all the trust's income.

It may happen that a child receives income for services performed. (Think of the road-company casts of *Annie*.) Even if a parent signs the employment contract, the income belongs to the child. Separate accounts ought to be kept for children, and custodian accounts are convenient for this purpose.

Remember that the child's services must actually be ren- dered. A family business may want to put the kids on the payroll. That way, the business gets a deduction, and the income is taxed in significantly lower brackets. If this appeals to you, be ready to substantiate that youthful services were rendered. The IRS is quite ready to admit that a child may have an investment in a business, but may not be so quick to allow the siphoning of income for their "services."

2
Interest and Dividends

Interest and dividends—basic investment income—is meat and potatoes for the workaday tax collector. An abundance of tax rules have evolved regarding such investment income. Interest and dividend income is reported to you by the payers, and after June 30, 1983, such income is subject to a flat 10 percent withholding of tax. (More about that later.)

What Is Taxable Interest?

All interest except municipal bond interest and, up to a limit, interest on the new All Saver's Certificates is taxable. Every other kind of interest, even if it isn't so designated, is taxable, though special rules may apply. Include, for example, in the list of reportable interest

- Corporate bond income
- Series E or H bond income
- Mortgage interest received
- Savings bank interest—and premiums
- Savings and loan company and mutual savings bank "dividends"
- Interest on tax refunds or condemnation awards

Even though tax rates may go down the next year, a cash-basis taxpayer (one who must report actual receipts and expenses during the tax year) may not postpone the receipt of interest—or any other kind of income—by simply not cashing a check or turning in a bond coupon for payment. Income is taxable in the year it is under the taxpayer's control.

When a saver has funds in a long-term savings account or Certificate of Deposit that are withdrawn prematurely, the full amount of credited income is reportable. If a penalty is also imposed by the bank because of the early withdrawal, the penalty may be taken as a deduction.

Imputed Interest. Property sales often provide for deferred payment. The tax rules may consider a portion of each payment to be interest received by the creditor if: (a) the payments are to extend beyond a year after the sale, (b) the sale price is over $3,000, and (c) the sale agreement doesn't provide for interest or the interest agreed upon is too low. (Currently, the threshold rate to be provided is 9 percent, but that is subject to occasional change.) If interest is imputed under these tests, a part of each payment is considered to be interest, reducing the portion more advantageously taxed as capital gains. (Imputed interest is currently calculated at 10 percent, compounded semiannually, but that rate is also subject to change.) The rule simply requires provision for adequate interest in covered transactions.

Original Issue Discount. OID (tax practitioners love acronyms even better than maxims) is the difference between the reduced issue price of a bond and its stated price of redemption at maturity. If the difference is less than .25 percent for each year from the bond's issue to its maturity, it's *de minimis*—which means it's too small to fool with—and it is not considered OID.

If there is OID, it's taxed as interest, not as part of capital gain (or reduction of a loss) on the sale or redemption of the bond. The rule is applicable to all holders, including buyers after the original issue. For certain bonds, the recognition of OID is postponed until disposition. But others, primarily corporate bonds issued at a discount after May 1969, cause OID income to be recognized each year.

The discount on these issues is calculated and added to the interest payments on the bond. Previously reported OID is added to the bond's cost basis so that the interest isn't taxed twice.

EXAMPLE: On January 1, 1981, Mr. D. Ben Shores paid $760 for a bond newly issued by Plotz, Ltd. The Plotz bond will mature in 1992 at a redemption price of $1,000 and pays 10 percent on its coupons. The OID each month is $2—face amount of $1,000, less purchase price of $760, or $240, divided by 120 months to maturity. In 1982, D. Ben Shores will report interest from the Plotz bond of $124—coupon interest of $100 plus OID of $24. (If he sells the bond at the end of the first year, by the way, the cost basis will be $784.) OID on a bond issued after 1982 would be calculated on a compounded basis.

Interest Exclusions. Beginning in 1985, the law will provide a 15 percent interest exclusion up to a maximum of $450 on a single return or $900 on a joint return. The limit equals 15 percent of $3,000 (or, for joint filers, $6,000) of interest received to the extent it is in excess of interest expense from which the taxpayer received a tax benefit (but mortgage interest, interest incurred in a trade or business, or forfeitures on premature CD redemptions will not have to be deducted from the amount on which the exclusion is calculated).

The 1981 $200 exclusion for interest and dividends reverted to $100 for dividends only in 1982, rather than 1983 as originally scheduled.

All Saver's Certificates. Special one-year savings certificates have been offered by many commercial and savings banks and other thrift institutions during the fifteen-month period ending December 31, 1982. Thus, one-year certificates will be maturing from October 1, 1982, to the last day of 1983. Under the law, All Saver's Certificates will yield tax-exempt interest up to $1,000 for each taxpayer or $2,000 for joint filers. The limit is a lifetime ceiling. The certificates are to yield no more than 70 percent of the fifty-two-week Treasury bill rate for the same issue period. If, for example, taxable T-bills are yielding 14 percent, an All Saver's Certificate will yield tax-exempt interest at 9.8 percent.

Clearly, for taxpayers in at least the 30 percent marginal tax bracket, such certificates have a better after-tax yield than comparable T-bills—at least up to the $1,000 (or $2,000) limit.

Municipals. There is a constitutional restraint on the federal government's power to impede the full faith and credit of the states. To put it on a more mundane level, interest paid on the obligations of a state, possession, or any political subdivision, the District of Columbia, a territory, or a federally sponsored project is not taxable by Uncle Sam. (The states, though, may tax such interest—the restriction applies only to federal taxation.)

Thus, your Hometown Sewer Revenue Bonds, issued as it is by a "political subdivision," is a tax-free municipal, and Drover's Mills Civil War Veteran's Housing Authority 4¼s, due in 2001, as a federally sponsored housing authority, will yield federally tax-exempt interest. Such investments, and investments in funds that hold municipals only, have always stirred the blood of taxpayers in elevated tax brackets. At the pre-1982 70 percent tax bracket, a municipal paying 7½ percent was equal to a taxable 25 percent. The chart below displays the before-tax yield taxable investments would have to pay to match the equivalent income from municipals at selected marginal tax brackets:

At Marginal	A Municipal Yielding:				
	6%	6½%	7%	7½%	8%
Tax Bracket:	Is Equivalent to:				
30%	8.57	9.29	10.00	10.71	11.43
39%	9.84	10.66	11.48	12.30	13.11
44%	10.71	11.61	12.50	13.39	14.29
50%	12.00	13.00	14.00	15.00	16.00

Government Issues. Interest on federal savings bonds is taxable by the federal government, but not by state or local jurisdictions. The reporting of interest on Series E bonds and their alter ego, Series EE bonds, may be deferred until the bonds mature or are redeemed. (It's up to the taxpayer whether to defer, but the decision may not be altered.) The interest on Series H bonds or Series HH bonds is taxable in the year the interest is received.

Adjustments for Interest on Purchase or Sale. For a bond bought "flat" (that is, without adjustment for any inherent interest in its price), the cost includes principal and any unpaid accrued interest. The full cost is a capital investment. There is no adjustment for interest. If a bond bought flat while it is in arrears on interest payments finally makes payment of interest accrued before purchase, the payment is treated as a return of capital. That's not a taxable event. If the cost basis is exceeded by payments of arrears, the excess arrearage receipts will be considered capital gains. On the other hand, interest earned or accrued after purchase is considered normal interest income.

EXAMPLE: On April 15, 1980, Mr. Jarndyce bought a $1,000 Plotz bond for $400. There was interest in arrears to the tune of $500 on the bond at the time of purchase. Wonderful as it seemed, on November 15, 1981, Plotz, Ltd., paid the $500 of accrued interest in arrears. Jarndyce received $100 more than he paid for the bond. That's a long-term capital gain. On January 15, 1982, the Plotz bond paid another $50. That's 1982 interest. On February 15, 1982, if Jarndyce sells the magic bond for $850, that sale price is *all* long-term gain.

When taxable bonds are sold, interest accrued between dates designated for the payment of interest is allocated between the buyer and seller, based on the settlement date of the transaction. Interest earned, though not paid, *from* the date of sale belongs to the buyer; interest *to* the sale date belongs to the seller. However, the annual information return (the 1099) made out by the paying agent will not reflect the allocation. The amount reported should be adjusted on the tax return.

EXAMPLE: Last year, Chick Pease bought a $1,000 Fitz and Starz, Inc., bond at face value, with interest to be paid at the annual rate of 8 percent each January 1 and July 1. Each semiannual interest payment is, in other words, $40. On May 1, Chick sold the bond to Clay Crock for $1,026.67. The $26.67 represented accrued interest.

Chick will report $66.67 as interest income. That's the $40 received on January 1 and the $26.67 that accrued until May 1, the date of sale.

By June 1, the next payment date, Clay will have $13.37 of reportable net interest. The Fitz and Starz,

Inc., information return, however, will show Clay as having received $40. On his 1040, Clay Crock should show receipt of the $40 and subtract the $26.67 that went to Chick Pease, thus reporting the net of $13.37.

Chick, of course, should report the full $66.67 on his own return, even though his information return will indicate only $40 received. He should, at the same time, reduce the amount received for the bond correspondingly, since he really sold it for $1,000, plus accrued interest.

What Is a Taxable Dividend?

Dividend receipts are taxable if they are distributed from a corporation's earnings and profits account, either for the current year or accumulated in prior years since February 28, 1913 (when the whole odious thing started, you recall).

To be taxable, dividends need not necessarily be paid in cash. If a noncash dividend is paid, the fair market value of the property or services received is the amount reportable as a dividend. While it is not likely that Exxon will ship barrels of SAE 20 to each shareholder as an extra dividend, it is not uncommon that the proprietor-shareholder of a small corporate business enterprise is thought by an audit agent to have received a dividend in the form of property or services. Remember, a dividend payment isn't normally deductible by a corporation, even if its receipt by the shareholder is taxable; business expenses are deductible.

Some distributions, called "dividends," are misnamed for tax purposes and are not taxed in that category. For example, mutual life insurance "dividends" may be simply returns of premiums paid. And savings bank and savings and loan "dividends" are really payments of interest, and should be so reported.

A stock split—common or uncommon—is not a dividend. Cash received in lieu of fractional shares on a split may be either capital gain or an ordinary dividend, though. Either way, the payer will notify its shareholders.

If a shareholder has a choice as to receipt of cash or stock in a split, however, the transaction is taxable (except for certain public utility dividends described below). A distribution of stock in a different corporation is generally taxable in full as a dividend.

"Tax-Free" Dividends. Dividends flow from corporate earnings and profits. If distributions are from sources other than earnings or profits, they are said to be "tax-free" because they are merely returns of invested capital, which reduces the taxpayer's cost basis of the stock in the distributing company. When that basis reaches zero, further distributions will be taxed as capital gains.

Information regarding nontaxability of a dividend, subject to later correction by the IRS, is sent to each recipient by the payer, so that a timely tax return can be prepared. A dividend may be designated either wholly or partially tax-free, and distributions from particular corporations may vary in taxability from year to year.

Companies that customarily pay partially or wholly tax-free dividends should be of particular interest to taxpayers in elevated marginal tax brackets. The tax on part or all of each dividend is delayed and subsequently taxed at salutary capital gains rates.

EXAMPLE: Suppose Onendaga-Cayuga-Hadassa Power Co. common stock had a cost basis of $5 per share in your hands and in 1981 it paid a dividend of $1.50 per share, one-third of which was tax-free:

1981 dividend	$1.50 per share
Less: Taxable portion	1.00
Nontaxable portion	.50
Cost basis of O-C-H	5.00
Less: Reduction	.50
Your adjusted cost basis	4.50

If O-C-H Power is then sold for $5 per share, the $.50 nontaxable portion of the dividend would be taxed at capital gains rates, rather than as ordinary income.

Public Utility Dividends. The general rule that applies ordinary income treatment to distributions that may, at the shareholder's option, be taken in stock or in cash is subject to a special exception for 1982 through 1985. Dividends from qualifying public utilities that are not received in cash, but rather are reinvested in additional common stock, will be specially taxed. They will qualify for capital gains, rather than immediate ordinary income treatment, if the new stock or its equivalent is sold after one year. This advantage is limited to $750 per year for single taxpayers and $1,500 for joint filers.

Capital Gains Dividends. Certain distributions from mutual funds, regulated investment companies, or real estate investment trusts may really be distributions of gains rather than simple earnings and profits earned by less favored organizations. Capital gains dividends, so designated by the payer, are reported as long-term gains on the recipient's tax return, no matter what the holding period of the investor in the fund.

Liquidating Dividends. When corporations go out of business, either a little bit at a time or all at once, they may redeem part or all of their shareholders' interest in the company. A liquidating dividend, essentially a redemption of such interests, is treated as a capital transaction.

Dividend Exclusion. Though the law has eliminated the $200 per taxpayer exclusion for interest and dividends received for years after 1981, taxpayers are entitled, for 1982 and after, to exclude the first $100 of regular dividends received.

Withholding on Your Dividends and Interest

Somehow the Treasury Department had an inkling all along that a lot of taxable income in the form of dividends and interest was never reported. The tax collectors have long urged that there ought to be withholding on such payments before taxpayers got their hands on them. They've finally persuaded Congress.

Starting July 1, 1983, withholding at the flat rate of 10 percent will apply to most interest and dividend payments made directly or indirectly by corporations.

It's not a new tax. It is a new method of *collecting* tax, somewhat like withholding on wages. Like amounts withheld from paychecks, withholding on dividend or interest checks are simply prepayments, for which credit is claimed on the taxpayer's return. The payer who withholds the 10 percent is obliged to furnish the information necessary to claim the credit.

There are certain exemptions. Individuals are not required to withhold on interest they pay to others. Don't keep back 10 percent when you pay interest on your home mortgage.

Banks and other entities who pay interest may decide not to withhold if they make payments of not more than $150 a year to you. But don't bother splitting up your account into smaller ones so that they don't reach the threshold. Payments to the same payee have to be aggregated.

What if you don't expect to owe any tax in the first place? Payers of amounts normally subject to the withholding rules need not withhold on payments to:

- individuals whose tax bill in the preceding year was no more than $600 (or $1,000 in the case of a joint return), or
- taxpayers who have attained the age of sixty-five whose tax liability for the preceding year was no more than $1,500 (or $2,500 on a joint return if either spouse is sixty-five or more).

In either case, an exemption certificate must be filed with each payer by the taxpayer who wants to be excused, please, from withholding. (A bit of your personal tax business, therefore, may, for the first time, become known to a stranger when you file an exemption certificate.)

EXAMPLE: Telly Gramm and his wife, Millie, are both over sixty-five. In 1984 their gross income totals $27,600. They are entitled to four exemptions because of their senior status and each exemption is worth $1,000. The standard "zero bracket" deduction is worth another $3,400. That's $7,400 taken from their gross income, leaving $20,200 subject to tax. In 1984 the tax on that is $2,497. That is less than the $2,500 joint ceiling for exemption, so the Gramms may file certificates in 1985 that will relieve them from withholding.

If you are thinking that the yearly paperwork after Thursday, June 30, 1983, will come to resemble an Alp, you are right.

Without electronic data processing neither the payers of dividends and interest nor the Internal Revenue Service could cope. You may want to get a little home computer yourself.

3
Buying, Selling, and Exchanging

Good tax news! For individuals, only 40 percent of long-term gains on capital assets is subject to taxation at regular rates. And, for sales after June 9, 1981, the highest rate applicable to such favored income is 20 percent, which is 40 percent of the top marginal tax bracket of 50 percent. These rates don't apply to corporations; we'll discuss them later in Chapter 15.

The theory behind reduced taxes on capital gains is that the existence of inflation is recognized, investment is fostered, and the special treatment protects long-range earnings from the ravages of taxation when a capital asset is sold.

In the world of taxable transactions, a long-term capital gain—that gain realized on property held, under current rules, for more than a year—rates a "10." Next to tax freedom, it's tops in tax. However, the beneficial quality of "cap gains" (by which practitioners usually mean long-term capital gains) may not always droppeth as the gentle rain from heaven—which explains why so many tax lawyers are so diligently trying to contrive machinery so that current transactions will, in the fullness of time, crank out long-term gains.

Conversely, a capital loss is not as tax efficient as an ordinary loss. When a long-term loss looms, tax gears are shifted. Capital losses are better than losses with no tax recognition at all, of course. They are available, however, only for property held for the production of income or for investment.

21

That's why the loss on the old family Studebaker never interested Uncle Sam.

If you made a profit on that unsightly old clothes press you sold at last year's garage sale, that's a capital gain. Pay tax on it. More likely, you lost money, in which case, the IRS doesn't care. The loss on the transaction, albeit capital in nature, is a personal, not a national, loss.

What Is a Capital Asset? A capital gain or loss can happen only to a capital asset. Such assets include such things as stocks and bonds (including municipal bonds), options and interests in partnerships, real estate and works of art. An asset that qualifies for special treatment upon sale or exchange is just about any property, with (as you may have anticipated) certain significant exceptions. It's really simpler to say what doesn't meet the definition. These types of property are *not* capital assets:

- Assets normally considered inventory (such as goldfish in a pet store, or stocks and bonds for a securities dealer).
- Property held primarily for sale in the normal course of business.
- Depreciable business property (which may be subject to other tax benefits).
- Business real estate (also subject to other rules).
- Accounts receivable or notes derived from business operations.
- Copyrights, literary, musical, or artistic works sold by the creator.
- Government publications, like the *Congressional Record*, are likewise not usually capital assets (and may not even be Capitol assets, but that's another matter).

Sales or Exchanges. If the rules regarding capital gains and losses are to operate, there must be a taxable event in the form of a sale or exchange of a capital asset. The Supreme Court has given some attention to the matter.

A sale is the transfer of property for a price. The price can be in the form of cash or an undertaking to pay in the future. A stock redemption, for example, meets the definition of a sale. An exchange is the transfer of property in return for some other property, instead of money. Sometimes an exchange is accompanied by cash in order to balance the value of the assets exchanged (and such a cash difference is called "boot" by those in the tax business).

Nontaxable Exchanges. There are, happily, certain situations in which exchanges of property are not immediately taxed but postponed instead (and the postponement may be rather protracted). No gain or loss is usually reportable, for example, when common stock in a corporation is exchanged for other common stock in the same firm. The cost basis of the exchanged property is substituted for the basis in the new.

One popular method of postponing reporting involves business or investment property that is exchanged for "like-kind" property. Inventory or securities qualifies under the like-kind exchange rules, and many swaps (such as the trade-in of an old jalopy for new wheels) well might too.

Like-kind is a reference to types of property, not to quality or location. Old computers may be traded for new computers. Real estate may be exchanged for other real estate. A vacant lot may even be exchanged for an apartment house. The lot won't meet the test if it is exchanged for a yacht, however, nor are Guatemalan quetzals like Namibian rands, either, and bulls are not the same as cows, the IRS has noted.

If money (or other property that doesn't qualify under the rules) is received in an otherwise nontaxable exchange, that's boot, and boot is taxable if it represents gain. On the proverbial other hand, if cash (or other nonqualified property) is *paid* in an otherwise sanctioned nontaxable exchange, no gain will be recognized by the payer.

By exchanging something more valuable for like-kind property, it's possible to reinvest all the noncash receipts without using part of it to pay taxes.

Finding an owner of property one wants who is ready to make the swap is sometimes difficult. You, like other clever operators, therefore may utilize a three-way deal instead of the simple two-way exchange. A buyer who wants your property and a seller who owns the property you covet are required to take part with you in the transaction. Suppose you operate a commercial playground for which there is a buyer. The buyer has no property you'd be willing to take in exchange. There is, though, a parking lot in town you would like to have. But the owner wants money instead of property. Simply arrange for the one who wants your playground to buy the parking lot and then exchange it for your property. The buyer has no tax on his purchase. The seller of the parking lot has his money. You have exchanged your playground for the real estate you wanted in the first place. (It could work the opposite way, with you swapping the playground for the parking lot and having the seller transfer the vacant land to your buyer for cash.)

Of course, such a financial *ménage à trois* is usually more complicated than that. It's not common for values to be equal and, therefore, payments have to be arranged to make the deal go.

Tax triangles may become a bit complex, and it's not useful to have one side of the deal go through while the other fails. Therefore, agreements are necessary by which each corner of the transaction is hitched to the other two.

Accounting for Capital Gains and Losses

Holding Period. For many practical purposes, a capital gain has no distinctive advantage unless it's long-term. That means that the holding period must be more than one year. One year or less equals short-term. The calendar count normally starts on the day after acquisition and ends on the day of sale or exchange.

Assets acquired on the last day of any month must be held on the first of the following thirteenth month to qualify as long-term.

EXAMPLE: Fran Tichleigh acquired Shelf Co. stock on January 5, 1982. The first day the Shelf Co. holding will go long-term will be January 6, 1983.

The trade date is generally the one used for calculation of the holding period for securities, not the delivery date or settlement date. (Special rules: the holding period of a commodity taken by exercise of a futures contract starts on the day the contract is purchased, and on the exercise of stock rights, the holding period includes the day of exercise.)

Sometimes property may be received in a transfer that is not recognized as taxable for income tax purposes, such as a transfer by gift or the placing of property into trust. The holding period of the previous owner is, in such cases, added to that of the current owner. Sometimes one asset replaces another, tax-free, and the holding period of the old asset is added to the new one. Tax folk call this addition of holding periods "tacking."

For inherited property, acquired from a decedent, the long-term holding period is assumed to be met in all cases.

Identifying Securities. An investor may not want to sell all of the holdings of a security, and the holdings of the particular security may have been purchased in different lots at different times and at different prices. The shares sold to reduce a position should be selected and identified so that the maximum benefit may be obtained. The holding period and the size of the gain or loss to be recognized can be selected to fit the year's tax situation.

If specific identification is not made, or can't be made because records are insufficient, the first lot purchased is deemed to be sold first. A first-in, first-out rule applies, but specific identification can supplant it.

To make tax-wise identification, an investor should keep full documentation of certificate numbers, costs, and dates of purchase. Brokers' confirmations act as appropriate identification. If the taxpayer holds the securities, or they are registered in his or her name, the certificates to be sold should be plainly indicated; if they are held in "street name" by a broker, instructions should be clear so that the broker's confirmation will be conclusive.

It may seem like a bit of bother, but once a transaction is completed, the shares actually delivered will be the ones used in calculating the tax effect.

Computations. Short-term transactions are set off against each other; long-term transactions are too. If there's a gain in one category and a loss in the other, the short-term and long-term figures are combined to find the net gain or loss (which itself may be short or long).

- If there's a *net long-term gain,* fine. Only 40 percent is included in ordinary income. That can happen when there's a net long-term gain that exceeds short-term transactions, or when there's a net long-term as well as short-term gain.
- If there's a *net short-term gain,* after all the figures

are in, the whole gain is treated as ordinary income.

- If there's a *net capital loss, long or short,* special rules apply that limit the deductibility. We'll get to those rules in a minute. A net loss can happen when there are net long-term losses that exceed any short-term gains, net short-term losses that exceed any long-term gains, or both net long- and short-term losses.

EXAMPLES:

Net short-term gain	$14,000
Net long-term loss	(10,000)
Net short-term gain	$ 4,000
Net short-term gain	$ 6,000
Net long-term loss	(14,000)
Net long-term loss	($ 8,000)

We've learned that a net long-term gain is includable only to the extent of 40 percent of the gain. Net short-term gain? It's all ordinary income.

A net capital loss is deducted from ordinary income, with certain limitations. In any event, no more than $3,000 of capital losses may be deducted in any single year. (This figure is the same for single or joint returns, but if a married couple files separately, they are limited to $1,500 each.)

It's important to keep losses short-term, if possible. If it is short-term, the net loss is deductible, dollar for dollar, up to the $3,000 limit.

If the net loss is long-term, only half of the loss is allowed, so it takes a dollar of long-term loss to offset 50 cents of ordinary income. (This is after losses are fully set off against gains, of course.)

If there are both long- and short-term losses, the short-term loss is applied against ordinary income first.

EXAMPLE: Tab Lloyd has a short-term loss of $1,000 and a long-term loss of $4,000. The $1,000 short-term loss is used before the long-term loss, of which only half is available as a deduction. Thus, Tab's $2,000 long-term loss (after deduction) is added to the short-term. There's a $3,000 deductible loss. There is no carryover. If Tab's short-term losses were $2,000, he would have to use it first. Because of the $3,000 limit on capital loss deductions, Lloyd would have to carry over the excess as long-term loss to a later year, and use only half of it then.

Once you know these basic rules, certain strategies will surely come to mind. For example, if an investor has realized short-term gains, it might be advisable to realize enough long-term losses that are available in the same year so the full benefit of the losses, rather than half, can be obtained. If a gift of property is contemplated, the prospective donor should consider whether the property bears a built-in gain or loss. If there's a gain, the property itself should be given, so gain isn't recognized. (The donee will do that eventually.) If there's a loss, however, it might be better to sell the property and give away the proceeds. That way the donor can take the loss himself, offsetting capital gains or deducting it against ordinary income, to the limit of $3,000.

Carry-overs. The excess of losses over $3,000, not used in one tax year, is carried over to a succeeding year. It is carried over, subject to the $3,000 limit each year, until it is used up or until the taxpayer dies. It's not elective. The carry-over must be used when available, not when the taxpayer wants to use it.

The carry-over retains its short- or long-term character in subsequent years, so that carry-overs of long-term losses will continue to be cut in half to the extent that there are no gains to offset it.

Basis. Obviously, the differentiation between gain or loss depends in any transaction on the cost basis of the property sold or exchanged. If an adjusted cost basis can't be determined by a taxpayer, the IRS will assert a very low basis, or even no basis at all, thus increasing the gain to be recognized until it approaches the entire sale price. It's the taxpayer's obligation to maintain records that are adequate to support the adjusted cost basis of a capital asset.

The starting point of the cost basis, naturally, is the original cost at the time of acquisition. But that may be subject to adjustment before gain or loss can be calculated.

For assets bought by the taxpayer, the basis is normally the original purchase price, plus commissions paid on the purchase. Security purchase tickets, incidentally, contain all the necessary information. Occasionally, securities are purchased as part of a package of notes, common stock, and convertible bonds. In that case, relative values must be assigned or appropriately allocated to each type of security.

When an exchange is recognized for tax purposes, the cost basis of the new property received is its fair market value.

Sometimes an asset is received in a tax-free exchange. Then a "substituted basis" is employed. The basis for the new property received is the basis of the old asset that is surrendered.

> EXAMPLE: Anna Purnah owns one hundred shares of Crowbar Corp. common, for which she paid $2,000. Crowbar undergoes a tax-free reorganization. It issues one hundred shares of its new class A convertible preferred to Anna, which at the time of the exchange are worth $2,500. Under the terms of the exchange, Anna's gain isn't recognized, so her basis in the class A convertible shares is still $2,000.

Often, an asset that bears a debt obligation with it is acquired. Tax shelters often involve property that carry a debt. A mortgage on realty is a common example of "leverage" that fits the rule. The debt obligation, at full value, is added to the cash paid to calculate the cost basis. (This is not a loophole. When the leveraged property is disposed of, the value, at that time, of the obligation from which the taxpayer has been delivered is added to the cash received.)

> EXAMPLE: Tor K. Mahdegh buys a house, for $14,500 cash and the assumption of a mortgage of $85,000. Tor's basis in the building is $99,500. He later sells for $25,000 in cash and the buyer's assumption of the mortgage, which is then down to $84,500. His gain is $10,000 ($99,500 basis less $25,000 and $84,500).

When property is received as a gift and has appreciated in value, the cost basis for the donee is usually the donor's basis, which, as a substituted basis, goes along with the gift. (If a gift tax was paid by the donor, an adjustment may be necessary.) For gift property on which there is a loss, the donee's basis is either the donor's basis or the fair market value at the time of the gift, whichever is lower. (If the sale price is between the two possible bases, no gain or loss is recognized.)

The rule is different for inherited property. Assets received by inheritance receive a "stepped-up" basis. The basis of property owned as a result of the death of the previous owner is either the fair market value at the date of the decedent's death or the fair market value six months later. The decision is made by the decedent's personal representative, or "fiduciary," on an estate tax return. If no return is necessary, the date-of-death value applies.

This step-up in basis has, from time to time, been perceived by some students of the subject as an egregious loophole. Why, they ask, should the decedent's cost basis be ignored and the increased value of his or her property go untouched by income tax? Death, they claimed, was a gratuitous, though decisive, tax advantage for the rich. For a while, "carry-over basis at death" was part of the law (and there may be the odd estate still subject to it). Carry-over was not at all popular, though, and it was soon repealed. *Vox populi.*

There are other, technical, basis adjustments. Nontaxable stock rights may require an allocation of the basis of the underlying shares if the rights are worth, on the market, at least 15 percent of the value of the shares on which the rights are distributed. If the market value is under 15 percent, the allocation is elective. Other adjustments may be necessary for "wash sales," the claiming of depreciation, amortization, depletion, and certain partnership transactions. Tax accountants don't like such computations any more than you do, but they get paid for such toil.

And don't forget, for property owned before the current tax law was enacted, the adjusted cost basis starts with the fair market value on March 1, 1913.

4
Home Sales, Short Sales, Wash Sales, and Disallowed Losses

The rules regarding the tax on sales of property summarized in the previous chapter are fundamental. But by now, it's plain that the tax law thrives on exceptions to fundamental rules. Some of the major ones are gathered here. Others—notably special pension plan exceptions—will make their appearances later.

Sale of a Residence

A personal residence is indisputably a capital asset. It's probably the most important one most of us will ever own. On the sale of a residence that isn't used for business purposes Uncle Sam is your partner only if there's a gain.

It's nice to report that the Code contains two special maneuvers that may be resorted to if there's a gain on the sale of a personal residence.

Replacing a Home. Gain realized on the sale or exchange of a principal residence (and there's only one of those at a time per taxpayer) is taxable when it's sold only so far as the sales price, less fixing-up costs, exceeds the cost of a replacement. Thus, if a taxpayer sells his or her home and reinvests at least the amount received in another principal residence, he or she may postpone reporting the gain until the new dwelling is sold. If it is never resold, the gain need never be reported. The cost

31

basis of the new dwelling is adjusted so that, in effect, it takes the cost basis of the old place. The replacement must be made in time.

The law has recently extended the time limit for replacement of the old residence from eighteen months to twenty-four months for sales taking place after July 20, 1981. The two-year period also applies to sales before then, if the prior law's eighteen-month time limit expired after that date.

> EXAMPLE: Mr. and Mrs. Wynn D. Hill have owned their home in the valley since 1962, when they paid $20,000 for it. On January 1, 1981, they sold it for $90,000, and on December 1, 1981, the Hills bought a new home for $100,000 and happily moved in. Their $70,000 gain is not reported as income in 1981. The basis of the Hills' new home, by the way, is $100,000 less the gain of $70,000 realized on the old place, or $30,000. (That's the same as the cost of their old place plus the extra amount invested in the new one.)

Either residence may be a co-op or a condo (though there is some restriction on going from condo to condo). The postponement of gain can, under normal circumstances, be used only once during the two-year period.

Sales by Adults. Taxpayers who have reached the age of fifty-five by the time they sell their homes may elect a once-in-a-lifetime tax exclusion. Under the most recent rules (effective after July 20, 1981), up to $125,000 of gain can be received tax-free—*tax-free*—if the property sold was used as the principal residence by the taxpayer (or the deceased spouse of the taxpayer) for a total of at least three years out of the last five.

> EXAMPLE: On November 1, 1981, when he was sixty years old, George Gibbs and his wife, Emmy, age fifty-seven, sold their residence in Grover's Corners for $250,000. They had bought their home thirty years before for $65,000. That basis, together with selling expenses of $10,000, equals $75,000. The Gibbses' gain, therefore, is $175,000 ($250,000 less $75,000). If they elect to use the full exclusion, their taxable gain

on the transaction is only $50,000. The other $125,000 of gain is tax-free.

It isn't necessary to replace a home to obtain this bounty, but if another is purchased, there may be a chance to choose which is more beneficial, the "roll-over" provision or the "over fifty-five" break—or they may be used in combination. Taxpayers may exclude $125,000 of gain and defer the rest. Remember, however, that it's a one-time bonanza, and married taxpayers must jointly make the election. If a person elects to use the exlusion on a joint return and later remarries, the newlyweds are precluded from making another such election. And even if the gain is below $125,000, it can't be used more than once in order to reach the full amount allowed. Therefore, the election should be carefully considered so that it is used to maximum advantage.

Short Sales

Ever since Grandpa purchased the Brooklyn Bridge from the feller in the derby hat, you've believed that selling something you don't own is wicked. Don't be naïve. In the stock market, it's done all the time. It's called "selling short," and selling short is perfectly permissible.

A short sale is the sale of stock or other securities borrowed for the occasion. The short sale may be for securities the seller doesn't yet own. That's a "naked" sale. Or it may be for more securities that are identical to those he or she does own, but doesn't want to deliver, at least not just yet. That's going "short against the box." Later, whether he or she is naked or short against the box, the seller must, of course, "cover" the sale by delivering the property he or she sold.

If the property used to cover is a capital asset, the gain or loss on a short sale is a capital gain or loss, which normally takes place when the sale is closed, or covered.

Whether the sale is long- or short-term depends on some complex rules. Basically, because of the standard terms of a short sale, if the sale is made naked, the one-year holding period requirement cannot be met. For long-term treatment, therefore, the sale must be covered by long-term stock in the box. Selling short simply can't extend a short-term gain to long-term.

EXAMPLE: Rosemary Ann Teime, a sage investor, purchased one hundred shares of Fitz and Starz Co. at $2 a share on December 15, 1979. On January 15, 1981, she sold one hundred shares of Fitz and Starz short at $2.50, and on March 1, 1981, she delivered the shares bought in 1979 to cover her short sale. Rosemary had a long-term gain of $50 (before commissions, of course). The stock delivered was held long-term before she went short against the box.

On February 15, 1980, sagacious Rosemary Ann Teime bought one hundred shares of Plotz Corp. at $1 per share. She sold one hundred shares of Plotz short on December 15, 1980, for $1.50 per share. Rosemary closed out the short sale on March 15, 1981, by covering with the shares purchased in February of the previous year. There was a gain of $50, and that gain was short-term. When she entered the short position, the stock used to cover was held less than a year. It was to no avail, as far as the holding period is concerned, that the Plotz position was held over a year when Rosemary covered the short sale.

A short sale cannot be used to convert a long-term loss to a short-term loss, either.

However, what can be done with short sales is guaranteeing long-term gains by locking in a profit and postponing recognition of gain.

EXAMPLE: Dr. Pangloss bought one hundred shares of Suture Self and Lye Kit, Inc., at $10 a share on December 1, 1980. Suture stock rose, and Dr. Pangloss wanted to insure his profit. After a year, on December 15, 1981, he sold the stock short at $17.50 a share. Tax rates, he knew, would drop in 1982. Pangloss waited until the new year to cover the short sale so the taxable event would occur in 1982. His profit of $750, locked up in 1981, is taxable in 1982.

Remember, these neat transactions incur trading expenses. And the value of dividends received while short in the distributing company may have to be paid by the short seller to the lender. Their value is deductible if the dividends are ordinary cash dividends and the short seller itemizes his or her deductions.

Wash Sales

Suppose, now, you hold a security that has—temporarily, you believe—dropped below its cost basis. Why not sell it and immediately buy it back so the "loss" can be recognized and claimed as a deduction? Because it's a "wash sale," and the rules say the loss simply won't be recognized. (The IRS is older than most of us; it wasn't born yesterday.)

A wash sale results in a nonrecognized loss on the sale of a security. If the same security—or a security "substantially identical" to it—is bought within a sixty-one-day period that begins thirty days before the sale and ends thirty days after it, that's a wash sale.

Gains are recognized whenever they happen; only *losses* are subject to the wash-sale rules. Inherited securities and those received by gift are not subject to the wash-sale rules, since they were not bought by the seller. The rules are operative only for securities that are purchased, or received in a taxable exchange.

In a wash sale, the disallowed loss isn't lost. Recognition of the loss is delayed. The cost basis of the securities bought during the proscribed period is increased by the amount of unrecognized loss. For purposes of calculating holding period, the time the sold securities were held is added, or "tacked," to the holding period of the newly purchased security.

EXAMPLE: On October 1, 1981, Mr. de Charlus purchased one hundred shares of Quarr & Teen, Inc., common at $15 per share. On December 7, 1981, Charlus bought an additional one hundred shares at $10, and on December 21, 1981, he sold at $10 the shares he bought in October. Mr. de Charlus could not claim a loss of $500, because he has purchased the same security, Quarr & Teen common, within thirty days before the year-end sale. His acquisition date of the stock he bought on December 7 is considered to be October 1, and his cost basis is $15 per share.

Note that the rule applies to the same or substantially identical securities. It's a nice question. What is "substantially identical" to something else? Clearly, one may swap General Electric for Westinghouse. A different security in the same industry doesn't run into the rule. This accounts for the "tax swapping" perennially popular at year-end. Even securities of the same issuer may differ in some material ways. For example, if the value of bond coupons differs by at least 25 percent, or maturities differ by at least three years and five months (based on litigated cases), bonds of the same issuer probably won't be considered substantially identical. But sometimes it's a delicate determination, and a prudent investor would probably seek qualified counsel in a close situation.

Some clever folks have used the wash-sale rule to advantage. Suppose, for example, Mr. D. Harum takes a licking in Fritter Co. stock late in December, so he sells. Just after New Year's Day, Harum discovers that taking the loss won't be very helpful from a tax point of view. He simply moves the loss into the new year by repurchasing Fritter stock within thirty days of the sale, and sells later.

A final word regarding wash sales: no one seems to know for sure how to report them. It's a curious lapse by the Service. You should post the proper information to tie into future transactions. It might be well to make a memo entry on Schedule D, the capital gains schedule, of the return for the year the wash sale takes place.

Lost Losses

If the wash-sale rules operate to prevent a taxpayer from recognizing a loss when buying and selling at the same time, can the taxpayer recognize a loss by selling to a related party? No! Another section of the law simply disallows losses on such sales, whether made person to person or in the open market. Related parties for this purpose include

- members of the taxpayer's family—spouse, brothers and sisters, ancestors and descendants;
- corporations and those who own more than half of their value in outstanding stock—partners, other corporations, family members, and others who own

shares are, for this purpose, considered to own the taxpayer's stock, too;
- exempt organizations and those who control them, or whose families control them; and
- trusts and their beneficiaries—including fiduciaries or others in any way interested in the trusts.

(For sales made in the marketplace, not directly between related parties, there is no specified time limit for the rule that disallows losses. Certainly a legitimate loss on the market, rather than person to person, ought to be recognized if it is outside the period set for wash sales. It might be accepted even if it takes place within that period, depending on the facts and circumstances, and assuming, of course, that there is no repurchase by the taxpayer personally within the sixty-one-day period. But if it's essentially a device merely to gain recognition, such a loss even on the market will *never* be recognized. The related-party prohibition is not related to the wash-sale rule. It's simply a good friend.)

There's no "tacking" of holding period or cost basis for a loss that is disallowed because it results from a transaction between related parties. If there's no gain in the future, the loss disappears.

EXAMPLE: Marston Moore sold 1,000 shares of Kulpable Corp. to his wife for $2,000. He had bought the shares ten years before for $3,000. The indicated loss is $1,000, but it's simply disallowed. Mrs. Moore's acquisition date is the date her husband sold her the stock. The ten years before are disregarded. Her cost basis is her purchase price of $2,000. The disallowed loss, by the way, of $1,000 can be used only to offset any *gains* she may realize on the Kulpable shares in the future. If she sells for $2,000 someday, there will be no gain or loss. If she sells for $1,500, the loss will be limited to $500.

Remember, finally, that the rule that disallows losses between related parties applies to the sale of any kind of property. It is not, like the wash-sale rule, restricted to stock or other securities.

5
Puts, Calls, and Futures

Admittedly, this chapter offers the rudiments of some tax esoterica. It's not a facile subject and not really essential, but there may be a lesson here about how the tax rules have wrought overblown inventiveness. The part about puts and calls is an introduction to sophisticated techniques to which some unique terminology and special tax rules apply. Commodity futures, having enjoyed what the IRS claimed to be a shady past, may now also be part of history as far as clever tax planning is concerned. As a tax ploy, futures transactions may never recuperate from the Economic Recovery Tax Act of 1981. If you've been put into puts and calls or have, upon careful advice, invested in commodity futures, perhaps you'll be interested to find out just what happened.

Puts and Calls

Puts may be defined simply as options to sell. *Calls* are options to buy. (Don't confuse these options with employee stock options, discussed later.) Traded put or call options are applicable to specific securities for a particular time period at a fixed, or striking, price. Such options are, except in the hands of dealers, capital assets. There is an organized market in puts and calls, with set terms, but the principles apply to unlisted options, too.

Virtually every transaction implies a buyer and a seller. In the option world, they have special designations. A *holder* is the buyer of a put or call option. A *writer* is the seller of a put or a call. The tax effect of option trading varies for holders and writers, depending on the transaction. There may be long- or short-term gain or loss, or even postponement of recognition.

FOR A HOLDER

- *Purchase* has no immediate tax effect. It's like buying anything else—the taxable event hasn't taken place yet, and the expenses involved in buying a put or call are capitalized and added to the cost of the transaction.
- *Exercise of a put* (the enforcement of the holder's right to sell) results in a capital gain or loss, with the cost of the put added to the cost basis of the security sold. *Exercise of a call* (the enforcement of the holder's right to buy) has no immediate tax effect. The cost of the call increases the basis of the acquired security. The holding period of the call option is not tacked to that of the acquired stock for purposes of calculating the holding period, however.
- *Lapse* of a listed option will result in short-term loss to the holder, since the expiration without exercise will necessarily occur, by its terms, before a year passes.

FOR A WRITER

- *Issuing* a put or a call, which involves the taking of a premium from the holder, is not a taxable event. Recognition is postponed.
- *Exercise of a put* by the holder (which obliges the writer to accept, at set terms, delivery of a security) starts the writer's holding period. The premium received is a reduction of his or her cost basis, and the whole matter is deferred. *Exercise of a call* (which obliges the writer to stand and deliver), on the other hand, triggers recognition of gain or loss. The premium taken on issuance is added to the amount received. Gain or loss may be long- or short-term,

depending on the holding period of the underlying security.

- *Lapse* of a listed option closes out the writer's position, and he or she will recognize short-term gain on the premium (even if the option was written more than a year before the lapse).

Sometimes the position of a holder or writer, instead of lapsing, may be offset by a new put or call. The offset will usually cause recognition of short-term gain.

If things aren't complicated yet, now combine these basic rules regarding option trading with the short-sales rules, for the purchase of a put is treated as a short sale, which is covered, or closed out, by exercise or lapse. Thus, we discover tax ploys passing strange, such as "married puts" (a "same-day purchase" of a put and the stock to which it relates, which avoids application of the short-sale rule), "straddles," and "calendar spreads."

A straddle is a graceful positioning of matching puts and calls in the same security, and a calendar spread is the purchase and issuing of either puts or call positions in the same security, but with the option dates or prices at variance. Here's the way it used to work:

EXAMPLE: Fran Tichleigh was in a high bracket in 1979, and she had $1,000 in realized short-term gains. Fran knew that the next year her top tax bracket would be lower, so she entered into an option spread.

Nym and Pistol, Inc., was selling at 140 on November 1, 1979. Fran Tichleigh bought an April 140 call for 12. At the same time, she sold a January 140 call for 8.

If N&P rose to 160 before the end of the year, the April 140 call would have risen from 12 to 28, and the January 140 call would have risen from 8 to 24. The $1,000 short-term gain realized on another transaction could have been deferred to 1980 if Fran repurchased the January 140 call. She would have had a 1979 short-term loss of $1,600 (24 less 8, or 16, times 100 shares). The offsetting gain leg of the spread would not have been recognized until April 1980.

Suppose that N&P dropped to 120. The April 140 call would have shifted to 2 from 12, and the January 140 would have moved to 1, from 8. Fran could have sold the April 140 for a short-term loss of $1,000 (12 less 2, or 10, times 100). In January 1980 she would have recognized income by letting the January option lapse or by offsetting it.

Now all this was very neat and provided some innocent merriment for all the trading expenses. But it should be stressed that supposed tax advantages evaporate if there is no investment rationale for straddles, spreads, or other agile option positions. Options couldn't devise deductions that were otherwise unavailable. When a taxpayer enters into any transaction, there must be some economic purpose and the reasonable expectation of profit—unrelated to tax reduction—if the Service is to accept the return as filed.

The rules changed in 1981 to more severely limit tax advantages of "nonregulated futures contracts straddles." Now recognized losses may be deducted only to the extent that they exceed unrealized gains. The wash-sale rules and the short-sale rules now apply to straddles, too.

Clouded Futures

Commodity futures transactions have gained the esteem of sophisticated investors in recent years. Fundamentally, such transactions involve contracts for the purchase or sale of traded commodities in standard quantities, to be delivered at set times, at specified prices sometime in the future. Futures contracts are traded on exchanges that maintain orderly markets and uniform contract terms.

Futures are traded in a variety of foodstuffs (from beef to wheat), in metals (like gold and silver), currencies (Canadian dollars or Swiss francs), and even intangible obligations (such as Treasury bills).

Cash transactions are made in "spot" markets for real bars of silver bullion or actual bushels of Idaho spuds. The spot market is used by dealers and others whose businesses are closely connected with the traded commodity. For investors, the futures market deals with supposed transfers scheduled to take place later. Though it's possible, one imagines, to have all the pork bellies or frozen orange juice delivered to one's garage or some other convenient depository, virtually all futures contracts are settled by offset. A contract to buy, for example, is settled by an offsetting contract to sell.

Most futures are highly leveraged. Only a small proportion of the contract price must be put up in cash when a position is taken. Thus, with relatively little movement in futures prices, large amounts can be gained or lost on the spread between offsetting contracts.

Those who are involved in business enterprises that deal in commodities traded in the futures market regularly enter into futures contracts to hedge against market fluctuations, rather than for tax reasons. Others, primarily interested in investments rather than commodities, have bought and sold futures contracts by use of short sales, options, and straddles. Until recently, that is.

Before midsummer 1981, trading in commodity futures could, if done just right, defer short-term gains and even convert such gains to long-term. Such transactions escaped the wash-sale and short-sale rules. More interesting, by a drafting error, a loophole was widened in an earlier tax act and the long-term holding period for commodity futures was set at six months, rather than a full year.

The Treasury, long vexed by such heady business, finally obtained changes in the law that eliminated the tax advantages in commodity futures positions entered into after June 23, 1981.

A tax straddle made up solely of futures contracts, rather than being subject to the new loss-deferral rule applicable to other straddles, will be subject to unique rules, which, in effect, put such transactions on an accrual basis—even while the taxpayer is otherwise on the cash basis for tax reporting purposes. A tax will apply even though no taxable event takes place.

The rules now require, for positions entered into after June 23, 1981, that the investor value all outstanding commodity futures contracts at the end of the year. The contracts must be "marked to market." Tax is due on the unrealized net gains on the contracts. The taxpayer must treat 60 percent of the transactions as long-term and 40 percent as short-term. Thus, the maximum tax rate on net unrealized gains will be 32 percent. Don't bother with the math; just note that it's twelve percentage points higher than the maximum rate on normal long-term gains.

If the foregoing has made you wary of dealing in such ephemeral investments, that's just fine. But haven't you always wondered what the tax experts do all day?

6
Americans Overseas and Foreign Taxpayers

Recent decades have witnessed a burgeoning of American investment and presence abroad, and of foreign investment and presence in the United States. This financial internationalization has been accompanied by the increasing sophistication of the IRS Office of International Operations. In 1980, according to IRS estimates, there were more than 2 million U.S. taxpayers residing overseas, and no one is quite sure how much foreign money resides within our borders. Direct foreign investment in U.S. business was estimated by the Commerce Department to be over $65 billion in 1980.

The U.S. has negotiated over two dozen income tax treaties applicable to fifty jurisdictions (and a baker's dozen estate tax treaties), all designed to eliminate the curse of double taxation and, incidentally, facilitate the exchange of information. The taxation of foreign investment in the U.S. and of Americans abroad is a flourishing tax subspecialty.

Americans Abroad

Unlike many countries, the United States asserts that its citizens and residents are subject to taxation by it on all income, no matter where it is derived.

Nevertheless, Americans working abroad may be eligible for significant tax benefits. (Government employees are subject

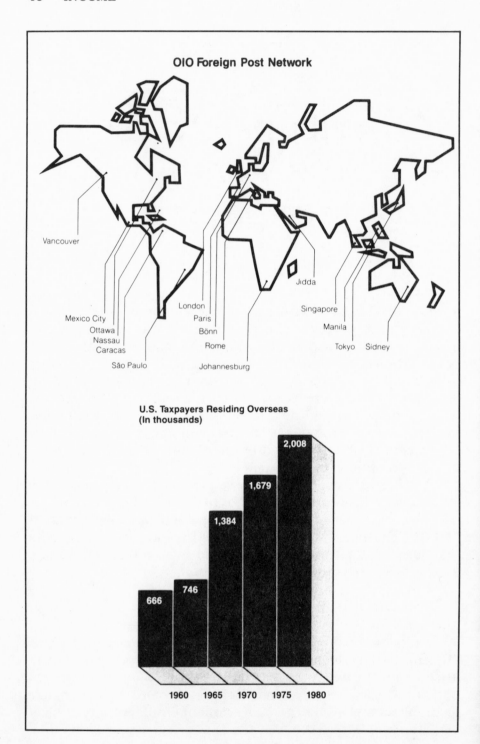

OIO Foreign Post Network

Vancouver

Mexico City
Ottawa
Nassau
Caracas

São Paulo

London
Paris
Bönn
Rome

Johannesburg

Jidda

Singapore
Manila
Tokyo   Sidney

U.S. Taxpayers Residing Overseas
(In thousands)

2,008
1,679
1,384
746
666

1960   1965   1970   1975   1980

to special rules and may not qualify for the general relief provisions.)

From 1978 through 1981, a complex and burdensome system of deductions for U.S. taxpayers posted overseas put U.S. employers at an international disadvantage. At least, that's what was asserted. Something like the older system of flat dollar-amount exclusions replaced the unpopular excess-cost-deduction method of tax relief for expatriates after 1981.

Starting in 1982, the rules provide for the exclusion of foreign earned income in substantial amounts, at the expatriate taxpayer's election. Either a *bona fide residence test* or a *physical presence test* must be met in order to obtain these benefits.

Bona Fide Residence Test. This criterion requires that a U.S. citizen (noncitizen U.S. residents are, by definition, excluded) be an actual resident of a foreign country for an uninterrupted period that covers a whole tax year. That's January 1 through December 31 for calendar-year filers. To qualify, the taxpayer must set up housekeeping in some foreign precinct and not be there for a transient purpose. Thus, while the expression of the hope to return isn't bad tax-wise, a special assignment for a specified time will not allow a transferred worker overseas to meet the test.

> EXAMPLE: Mark Polo, an American citizen, leaves the U.S. and arrives in Singapore in July 1982 for a long-range assignment there. On December 24, 1983, however, he is abruptly ordered home, and he leaves that day. Mark stays overseas for more than a year, but he will not meet the bona fide residence test because his sojourn did not include a full *tax* year. Mark may, nevertheless, satisfy the physical presence test.

Physical Presence Test. Either a citizen or a resident of the U.S. may meet this test. To qualify, the taxpayer must be actually present in a foreign country or countries for at least 330 full days during any twelve-month period. The twelve months must be consecutive, but they don't have to match the tax year. The rules are exact. A day means a twenty-four-hour period, starting at midnight.

An exception to the residence tests is provided for employees who are obliged to leave a country against their wishes. That happens sometimes in the case of civil unrest, war, or similar unpleasantness.

If an individual meets either residence test, he or she may elect to exclude foreign earned income at an annual rate of $75,000 for 1982. The amount excludable increases by $5,000 a year, until it reaches $95,000 in 1986. The exclusions are calculated on a daily basis.

> EXAMPLE: Philip Nolan is a U.S. citizen who resides in London. Nolan first arrives in London on the afternoon of January 22, 1983, and stays there for the rest of the year. Therefore, he meets the physical presence test for 1983, when the limit for foreign earned income is $80,000. In 1983, Nolan has $100,000 of such income. The most he will be able to exclude is $74,958.90 (342/365 times $80,000). "Ah, to be in England..."

For a married couple, the exemption is computed separately for each spouse. "Earned income" means wages, salaries, fees, and similar receipts for personal services. It doesn't include interest, dividends, pensions, annuities, or the like. If a taxpayer is in a trade or business overseas in which both capital and personal services combine to produce the income, no more than 30 percent of the net profits may be treated as foreign earned income.

Income that isn't excluded, however, still carries a tax benefit, since it starts being taxed at the lower brackets.

Beyond the exclusion, a taxpayer may also elect an exclusion for excess "housing costs amounts," which is based on 16 percent of certain government employee salary levels. Currently, that's about $6,000. Meals and lodging received by employees in "camps" (located in picturesque places like Sri Lanka, Algeria, and other designated places) are also excludable.

It's a new feature in the law that these various exclusions are elective. Once they are chosen, they are binding. An election may not be revoked and then reelected, without permission, for five years, even if the foreign stay is interrupted during that time. Why would anyone *not* elect to exclude up to

$95,000 from the ravages of taxation? Well, normal deductions and credits for foreign taxes that are attributable to the excluded income are not available. There might be no saving in the election for a taxpayer residing in a country that taxes him or her highly, and would offer the alternative of a foreign tax credit that would work as well to reduce taxes. It's probable, nevertheless, that the exclusions will be popular with expatriate workers.

Who Are Nonresident Aliens, and What Does the IRS Want from Them?

Simply, nonresident aliens are persons who are neither citizens nor residents of the United States. Those in the trade call them NRAs, an acronym as widespread, in their view, as it was in the days of the New Deal, when it meant something else.

Basically, an NRA is subject to U.S. tax on income generated from sources within the United States. The rate of tax and the method of collecting it depend on whether the NRA conducts business in the United States and whether an income tax treaty applies.

Business Activities. The U.S. trade or business income of an NRA is taxed under normal graduated rates, after allowable deductions and credits. Deductions may be claimed for ordinary and necessary business expenses, casualty and theft losses for business property located in the U.S. (at least until the loss), U.S. charitable contributions, and state and local taxes. The standard, zero bracket amount and medical expenses are not deductible, and one prorated personal exemption (at $2.74 a day) is allowed for the time the NRA conducts business here. But Canadians, Mexicans, and Japanese residents can claim $2.74 per day for other allowable personal exemptions. (Whether or not they are more family-minded than other aliens is not known, but that's the rule.)

If an NRA conducts business here, he or she is obliged to file a tax return (Form 1040NR) and may even have to file estimated tax returns.

Investment Income. Dividends, interest, and other regular investment income from U.S. sources that is not "effectively connected" with a U.S. trade or business activity is subject to tax on the gross amount. The tax is to be withheld by the payer before the taxed income leaves our shores. Normally, the tax is at the rate of a flat 30 percent. This 30 percent rate, however, is subject to reduction or even elimination by treaty. A list of treaties appears below. It shows the applicable rate of U.S. withholding at source on dividends and interest paid to residents of various countries.

The 30 percent withholding tax does not apply to otherwise tax-free investment income. Municipal bond interest is tax-free, but most foreigners would find their rates less attractive than do Americans. Other income is affirmatively excluded from the NRA withholding tax. Leading the list of income that is absolutely free of U.S. tax when paid to NRAs is interest on deposit with U.S. banking institutions.

Capital Gains. If an NRA isn't engaged in a trade or business in the U.S., his or her capital gains are not normally subject to tax. But if the NRA stays in the U.S. for more than 183 days during the year, the net gains are subject to tax at 30 percent or the lower treaty rate. Note that *all* the gain would be subject to the tax, not merely 40 percent of long-term gains.

EXAMPLE: Sheik Yarir is a subject of a land that has no tax treaty with the United States, and he engaged in no business in the United States. He visited America for a two-month vacation in 1982, and during that time he realized some net capital gains. His U.S. investment income for 1982 was:

Dividends	$ 40,000
U.S. corporate bond interest	20,000
Net capital gains	90,000
Interest on Certificates of Deposit in a U.S. bank	50,000
Total U.S. investment income	$200,000

Sheik Yarir's U.S. tax on the $200,000 is $18,000 withheld at the source, and he need not file a return. (The dividends and interest of $60,000 are subject to a tax at the rate of 30 percent. All the rest is tax-free.)

Income from U.S. Realty. An NRA may make an election as to the method of taxation on income from real estate opera-

TAX TREATIES IN EFFECT BETWEEN THE U.S. AND FOREIGN COUNTRIES
Normal Rate of U.S. Withholding Tax at the Source on:

Country	Dividends	Interest
Australia	15%	30%
Austria	15%	0
Belgium	15%	15%
Canada	15%	15%
Denmark	15%	0
Egypt (U.A.R.)	15%	15%
Finland	15%	0
France	15%	10%
Germany, Federal Republic of	15%	0
Greece	30%	0
Hungary	15%	0
Iceland	15%	0
Ireland	15%	0
Italy	15%	30%
Jamaica	15%	12.5%
Japan	15%	10%
Korea, Republic of	15%	12%
Luxembourg	15%	0
Morocco	15%	15%
Netherlands	15%	0
Netherlands Antilles	15%	0
New Zealand	15%	30%
Norway	15%	0
Pakistan	30%	30%
Poland	15%	0
Romania	10%	10%
South Africa, Republic of	30%	30%
Sweden	15%	0
Switzerland	15%	5%
Trinidad and Tobago	30%	30%
U.S.S.R.	30%	30%
United Kingdom	15%	0
U.K. Colonies and Former Colonies	15%	30%

tions in the United States. It may be considered as income that is "effectively connected" with a U.S. trade or business, in which case deductions for related expenses and depreciation become available and regular rates apply to the net income. If the election is disclaimed, gross income from the U.S. realty is taxed, again at 30 percent or treaty rate.

Until recently it was felt that NRAs who invested in U.S. real estate were at an unfair advantage. Because of the special rules regarding the taxation of foreigners' capital gains, as well as other advantages, most foreigners could sell their American realty without suffering any tax at all on the sale. Many U.S. taxpayers were concerned. A Treasury report said it: "a foreign investor with more than a minimal presence in the United States should not bear a lighter tax burden than a comparable domestic investor." So in 1980, a new law was enacted that generally provided that capital gains of NRAs that derive from sales of U.S. realty will be treated as "effectively connected" with a U.S. trade or business, thus subject to tax. This treatment is reserved for sales. Regular real estate income, like rent, is still subject to the election available to NRAs for such income.

PART · II

DEDUCTIONS

7
Interest Expenses

While a taxpayer reaps taxable income, deductible expenses are usually accumulated, too. The IRS itself garners lots of money with comparatively little expense. It spends about 44 cents to collect each $100 in taxes, but theirs is a special business, indeed. They realize that it usually costs a few bucks to make money, and the law is sympathetic. Expenses to earn gross income are, therefore, normally deductible, especially if itemized deductions are claimed.

Deductible Interest

For most of us below the level of a six-figure annual income, interest expense is the largest single itemized deduction. Just about any kind of true interest incurred is deductible. It may be paid or accrued to carry an investment, to operate a trade or business, or for personal reasons. Some common types of deductible interest are

- Mortgage interest
- Finance or installment plan charges
- Credit card interest
- Discounted interest on notes
- Margin account interest
- Business or personal loan interest
- Interest (but not penalties) on late tax payments

It's necessary, in any case of deductible interest, that the obligation to pay it is that of the taxpayer, and that he or she actually does pay it.

> EXAMPLE: Brooke Lynne Bridge pays $2,500 to the Skoveda National Bank on her parents' home mortgage. Mom and Pop Lynne own the old family residence and the mortgage indebtedness isn't Brooke's, so it's not her deduction. Sad to relate, it may not be available to Mom and Pop either, because they didn't make the payment to the Skoveda Bank.
>
> If Brooke had made a gift to her parents rather than paying the bank directly, at least they might have claimed an itemized deduction. Assuming she's in a higher marginal tax bracket than her parents, it would be even better if Brooke became liable on the loan so she could take the deduction.

Mortgage Interest. The most common type of interest expense relates to mortgage indebtedness. It accounts for almost half of the average taxpayer's interest deduction. The expense may be for one's homestead (including co-op or condo), or on business or other property. Each year, most lending institutions report the amount of interest paid to them by taxpayers.

It should be mentioned, though, that sometimes other mortgage expenses assume the role of interest. "Points" paid on a home mortgage by the buyer qualify as true interest, but service charges and appraisal and loan fees do not. To be deductible, payments must be made solely for the use of money. Points paid for services don't meet that test, though they may be added to the cost basis of the mortgaged property. Under the same reasoning, points paid by the seller are usually selling expenses rather than deductible interest.

Credit Cards and Installment Plans. Only the costs of using someone else's money—"pure interest"—is deductible. Normally, such costs are separately stated. Check your American Express or Visa bills. Service charges and fees for check-writing privileges are not interest. If the amount of interest isn't clearly stated, it may have to be calculated at an assumed rate, and the result of the calculation may not be as high as the actual interest charged on the average unpaid balance for the year. Sometimes it may be better to borrow from a bank at fully deductible interest and buy the boat or fridge for cash.

Discounted Notes. Often a debtor will borrow a set amount, only to have interest deducted immediately from the loan proceeds. It may appear to those who don't think like regulation writers that all the interest has been paid and is, therefore, deductible when the loan is made. The interest is, however, deductible each year when it is repaid to the lender.

EXAMPLE: Sammy Conn Schuss borrows $24,000 at 18 percent interest on May 8. He agrees to repay the loan in twelve equal monthly installments starting June 1. The full interest is withheld by the lender up front, and the calculation of the deduction looks like this:

Face amount of note	$24,000
Less: Interest withheld	(4,320)
Net proceeds	19,680
Monthly repayments	2,000
Interest portion of monthly repayment	360
Interest deductible, first year ($360 for seven months)	2,520
Interest deductible, second year	1,800

The general rule is that interest expense on a discounted loan is to be allocated evenly over the life of the obligation. However, there is another method that is used if the installment loan agreement declares that in case of prepayment of the debt the interest is to be calculated using a system entrancingly called the Rule of 78s. It is kissing kin to the old "sum-of-the-digits" method of rapid depreciation. (Seventy-eight is the total of the digits assigned to each month of a year: 12 + 11 + 10 ... + 1 = 78.) The rule provides, for example, that if a discounted loan is to be repaid each month for one year the first month would account for 12/78ths of the total interest. The next month would account for 11/78ths, and so forth. The first month of a two-year loan under the Rule of 78s would cover 24/300ths, and the second 23/300ths.

Use of the Rule of 78s by the lender will yield quicker

interest deductions for the borrower, just as the sum-of-the-digits method yielded quicker depreciation. The math is not often easy for the borrower. The lender should be able to supply the necessary figures on polite request.

Unstated Interest. It often happens that a capital asset is sold or exchanged under an arrangement that provides for deferred payments. The law assumes that there is an unstated interest element in the arrangement if

- it doesn't provide for any interest payments, or they are below a "test rate" (which is currently 9 percent simple interest);
- the payment schedule extends beyond one year; and
- the sales price of the capital asset is over $3,000.

Such imputed interest (now calculated at the rate of 10 percent) reduces the capital gain and increases the ordinary income for the seller. At the same time, it will lower the buyer's cost basis in the asset while presenting a tax deduction for interest he or she may not have expected.

Insurance Interest. Zealous insurance salespeople occasionally refer to interest deductions that may be available in connection with the purchase of a policy. The general rule is that interest incurred to buy or carry most kinds of insurance won't be deductible, but there are, of course, wide exceptions to general rules.

A contract requiring that substantially all premium payments be made within four years, either directly or by advance deposit for future premiums, is designated as a "single premium" contract. If such a policy contemplates regular borrowing against cash value, there will be no interest deductions.

On other policies, however, deductions are available if any of these features are present:

- The interest is not over $100.
- The interest qualifies as a business expense.
- The interest is incurred because of unforeseen financial reverses.
- There are no borrowings in four out of the first seven years the policy is in force.

The last exception is probably the most utilized method of arranging deductible insurance interest.

Interest That Isn't Deductible

Most interest is deductible. However, certain expenses, which look like interest to the casual observer, are not considered so by the IRS, and other costs are affirmatively denied the status of deductible interest.

Carrying Tax-Exempts. It's a fundamental rule that no deduction is available for any expense that can be attributed to tax-exempt income. Thus, no interest is deductible if it is expended to support the purchase of tax-free All Saver's Certificates, tax-exempt municipal bonds, or nontaxable mutual funds. Of course, an owner of municipal or other exempt investments can legitimately claim interest deductions for borrowings unconnected with the tax-free portfolio. But the law says that a deduction is not allowed if loan proceeds are invested directly in tax-exempts or if such securities are pledged as collateral for a loan. A taxpayer who has substantial holdings of municipals while claiming large interest deductions should have copious proof of the absence of connection between the two, backed by the courage of his investments.

Excess Investment Interest. Once upon a time, the law allowed unlimited interest deductions. It helped those in elevated brackets make some snazzy tax-sheltered investments. Now a portion of the deduction for interest paid is disallowed when it becomes "excessive." The excess is disclosed by an objective test: for any year, excessive investment interest is (a) interest expense, related to investments, which is more than $10,000 ($5,000 for a married taxpayer filing separately), *plus* (b) the amount of the year's net investment income (dividends, interest income, and short-term gains). The test does not affect interest that is unrelated to investments, such as auto loan or installment purchase interest, which is deductible without limitation, as is a normal business interest expense. Any excess investment expense disallowed in one year may be carried over to succeeding years, when it will be put to the same test.

EXAMPLE: In 1982, Mr. and Mrs. Sol Vent have a combined salary of $75,000 and dividend income of $12,000. During the year, the Vents paid $23,600 in interest on debts incurred to produce the dividend income. They also paid $1,400 on their car loan. The

Sol Vents paid $25,000 in interest, but the 1982 interest deduction will be limited to $23,400, with $1,600 available as a carry-over to 1983. The math looks like this:

Investment interest paid		$23,600
Less: Annual threshold	$10,000	
Investment income	12,000	
Deduction for investment interest limited to		22,000
Other interest paid		1,400
1982 deduction		23,400
Carry-over to 1983		1,600

If a taxpayer thinks he or she may run afoul of the excess investment interest rule, the realization of short-term gains or a switch to higher-yield investments for the year involved might be advisable. Such moves could generate enough investment income to raise the test level.

Feigned Interest. Schemes and intrigues designed to yield nothing more than interest deductions may never achieve their goal. Some years ago, for example, several taxpayers were persuaded to embark on an intricate plan to obtain interest deductions resulting from borrowing to buy U.S. Treasury notes. They took loans from finance companies that sold the collateralized notes on the day they were purchased. The taxpayers never saw the notes. They expected that their interest income and the value of the deductions for interest (and the promoter's fee) would, after taxes, yield more than the interest paid. The courts didn't see it that way, and uniformly disallowed the deductions on the grounds that the affairs lacked substance.

Transactions involving interest payments between related parties, such as husband and wife, or a shareholder and his or her controlled corporation, are likely to raise the interest of an alert IRS auditor, and steps should be taken to ensure that the bona fides of the deal can be demonstrated.

8
Business and Investors' Expenses, Depreciation, Cost Recovery, and Depletion

What Expenses Are Deductible?

Now we come to the juicy part: expense-account living and all the fabled deductible three-martini lunches. Well, maybe. "All the ordinary and necessary expenses paid or incurred during the taxable year in carrying on any trade or business," declares the Code, are deductible. Included, of course, are interest charges, but there are a host of costs, from accounting fees and advertising to business taxes and uniforms, that are deductible.

What's needed for the deductibility of such expenses is first a clear relationship to legal and taxable income or income-producing property. Second, the expenses have to be "ordinary and necessary" to that relationship. So, the byword is common sense. Let fiscal decorum and restraint hold baser instincts in check because, frankly, there is no simple way to determine what may be "ordinary and necessary." Note, by the way, that the elusive phrase isn't in the disjunctive. It's both ordinary *and* necessary, and lawsuits consistently have been decided against taxpayers when only one aspect was present.

An investor's cab fare downtown to his broker's office for some serious investment palaver is probably deductible. A junket to Gstaad, where there happens to be a sleek adviser with whom to chat, probably isn't. An actress's professional wardrobe is probably deductible; a secretary's work clothes probably are not. The expense of Transcendental Meditation seminars was held, after reflection by the IRS, not to be deductible as a business expense. A cost that is a disguised personal expense won't pass the test. There must be a reasonable link to business or investment that is not only rational but apparent to an IRS agent.

For example, one taxpayer was required by her boss "to be neatly coiffed at all times while at work," so one year she spent $334 at the hairdresser. She deducted the cost as a business expense. It was disallowed. The Tax Court brushed her aside, holding that hairstyling costs "are inherently personal in nature and cannot be considered as business expenses." Moral: don't let the deductions for business expenses go to your head.

Substantiation. It's essential, on audit, to have full substantiation of claimed expenses. George M. Cohan, the famed two-stepper, songster, and playwright, who had a way with an audience, also had a way with deductions. The Yankee Doodle Dandy finally convinced his Uncle Sam that, despite lack of real live substantiation, he had incurred deductible business expenses in connection with his profession. The "Cohan rule," which allowed some deductions if there were expenses that were clearly related to a taxpayer's taxable endeavors, was established a long time ago. It's not really sufficient in these less innocent days.

Travel and entertainment expenses, in particular, require substantiation of the amount, time, place, and business purpose of the disbursement. While agents in certain districts may allow $8 to $12 for meals if they feel the situation is appropriate, others may make arbitrary determinations. In any event, any allowance on less than the fullest substantiation will be hard won and accompanied by a lecture. You surely can't put over a song and dance the way George M. did, so keep detailed records. For business entertainment expenses, for example, this means documentary evidence showing amount, time and place, business purpose, and business relationship of the person entertained. It's worth the effort. Remember the words of tax-wise Senator Russell Long, who is reported to have said, "Entertainment is to the selling business the same as fertilizer is to the farming business—it increases the yield."

"Above-the-Line" Deductions. Certain business expenses

may be taken from gross.income to arrive at a figure known as "adjusted gross income." These are known as "above-the-line" deductions. Tax shelter deductions, as an example, try to rise above the line.

Itemized deductions, on the other hand, which are subtracted from adjusted gross to arrive at taxable income, are taken below-the-line. Deductions may be claimed, below-the-line, for expenditures incurred in the "management, conservation, or maintenance" of income-producing property or for expenses that relate to the determination of taxes. Along with other tax help, the modest cost of this book is deductible.

It's often better to take expenses above-the-line; itemization below-the-line isn't necessary to use the deductions above. Alimony payments, by special provision, are taken above-the-line, and so are portions of some contributions, under a new section of the law. Traditionally, though, above-the-line deductions have been limited to certain expenses that are strictly business. For example:

- Business entertainment by a self-employed worker (or an employee's reimbursed entertainment expenses, so that he or she isn't taxed on the reimbursement)
- Travel expenses (but *not* for commutation between home and work—that's a personal expense)
- Business-related meals and lodging while away from home overnight
- Education expenses (but only to maintain skills in present employment; the cost of tuition, books, and the like to get a promotion or a new job are personal expenses)
- Interest penalties imposed by banks on early withdrawals of Certificates of Deposit
- Other trade, business, or professional expenses, including moving expenses and HR10 (Keogh) or IRA plan contributions

Some deductions may be found on either side of the adjusted gross income line, depending on the facts. Costs of tax preparation and accounting for a small barbershop may go above (as a business expense), while a barber's 1040 preparation fee may have to be an itemized deduction (which relates to the determination of tax). Union dues are usually deductible from adjusted gross income, but if the union member is self-employed, they may be taken from gross income. A safe-deposit box maintained by a lawyer to keep the wills of his clients will be deductible above-the-line. It's a business expense. If the counselor keeps a safe-deposit box to store his own income-producing stocks and bonds, it will be deductible below-the-line. That's to maintain income-producing property. And, of course, if the attorney keeps picnic supplies in a safe-deposit box (so that he can move off to a private cubicle whenever he wants a solitary lunch), or keeps gold coins in it, the expense is personal and not deductible at all.

Home Office Expenses. The home office has been the scene of many a skirmish between a taxpayer and the Service. The government may appear to lose a lot of appealed cases, but on the audit level, the taxpayer undoubtedly doesn't prevail in many home office disputes. While the tax man may concede that a man's home is his castle, he doesn't often believe it's his office.

First, the rules require that, if an employee claims the expenses of a home office, the boss may not furnish him or her with another suitable place to toil. Thus, if you habitually take work home from the company office, you won't find solace in a deduction for the home expenses. Further, such expenses can be claimed only if the home office is used consistently and regularly for business matters. The card table in the living room doesn't rise to the status of a home office. Clipping coupons or entering magazine contests at it won't turn a rolltop desk into a place of business. And even if a home activity rises to the level of regular commerce, remember that the office there must be used exclusively for the business (which includes: meeting clients there consistently, the regular storage of inventory, or, under the rules, a day-care facility).

A recent amendment provides that the home office expense deduction is permitted when the home office is the principal place of a business, even though that business is not the taxpayer's primary work. Now moonlighters, free-lancers and sideliners may claim this tax break. After all, the part-time income is taxable, too.

If a taxpayer who conducts business at home feels entitled to claim the expenses, the total of deductible home office expenses (including interest, taxes, and the like, which are deductible anyway) can't be more than the income from the business. The deduction must represent a fair allocation of all normally nondeductible expenses to operate a home—such as rent, insurance, and utilities. It is generally based on an allocation of floor space.

Auto Expenses. Each year the cost of running an automobile, locally or on the road, may be deducted by either of two methods if the cost represents unreimbursed business expense. Commuting expense remains nondeductible. The actual business-related costs of gas, insurance, depreciation,and such like may be tallied and deducted. Alternatively, these expenses may be claimed by a flat deduction of 20 cents a mile for the first 15,000 miles of business travel and 11 cents a mile beyond that, though substantiation of business use is still necessary. With either method, parking fees and tolls for business purposes are also deductible; interest charges on the purchase of the flivver is generally deductible as interest, also.

The mileage allowance method is simple. The actual-cost method, though, may yield a larger deduction. At the start of the 1980s, it's been estimated, it costs about 40 to 50 cents a mile to operate a car. Twenty cents a mile isn't much, and perhaps the Service can be persuaded to increase the allowance. Keep checking the instructions.

Vacation Homes and Hobby Losses. Why not turn recreation and divertisement into tax deductions? Expenses that are essentially personal in nature certainly can't be claimed as business deductions, but what about the expenses of a gentleman farmer or a landlord who rents out a summer cottage a few weeks a year?

It shouldn't be astonishing to learn that there are rules about such matters.

When a residence or vacation home, or part of one, is rented out for less than fifteen days a year, no deductions related specifically to the rental are allowed. On the other, more heartening, hand, if the place is rented for two weeks or less, the rental income is not includable in income. This rule applies only to deductions for such things as depreciation repairs, utilities and the like. Regular deductions for mortgage interest, taxes, and casualties are allowable, anyway.

If a vacation spot is not used by the owner-taxpayer for

more than two weeks or 10 percent of the time it's available for rental to others, then no special rules apply. General "hobby loss" rules may apply instead.

If the owner rents out the place, but also uses it for more than either a fortnight or a tenth of the available time, the normal deductions (for taxes and interest) attributable to the rental period together with the other expenses (for depreciation, repairs, and the like) can't exceed the gross income from the place.

A "hobby" means, to the tax man, any activity not engaged in for profit—which accounts for a lot of human activity that may result in financial loss. Hobby losses are deductible only to the extent of income from the same activity, except for such normally deductible expenses as taxes, interest, or casualty losses. There are some situations in which it may be hard for the tax collector to determine if an activity is entered into for profit, so there are legal guidelines. Generally, an activity will not be considered to be a hobby, for tax purposes, if it yields profits in two out of five consecutive years. (Most activities involving horses have a more generous test: profit has to be shown in two out of seven years.) The application of this test is available to the taxpayer defensively. Alternatively, the facts of the particular case may be pressed in an onslaught against a proposed disallowance.

One court recently distinguished between a "profit objective" and a "profit expectation" in considering a hobby loss case. It seems that a Mr. Dreicer (who had income from a trust) and his secretary, Brigette, spent years traveling around the world. He stayed at the best places and dined well, for as he said, he was conducting research for a book called *The Perfect Steak*. Expenses for such research ran about $25,000 a year. Mr. Dreicer's activities didn't make a profit at all, but at least Brigette kept excellent records. Mr. Dreicer was a man of parts, it seems, having been active in the early days of television and the author of a published book several years earlier. When no one seemed to want to publish the results of Mr. Dreicer's expensive steak investigations, he abandoned the idea of a book, but not the idea of deducting the expenses. The Tax Court found "strong elements of personal pleasure" and said no, but the Court of Appeals wasn't sure. An expectation of profit may not be necessary, so long as there's an objective of making a profit, it said, and it sent the case back to the Tax Court to see if the steak research was done with the proper, sincere objective. The Tax Court, on review, again said no.

Expenses of Securities Transactions. Some investors' expenses, like accounting fees or "insider" newsletters, are usually deductible. Some others are not, even if they seem like palpable deductions.

Brokerage fees and commissions paid by an investor on the purchase or sale of stocks, bonds, or real estate are *not* deductible. They are, rather, capital expenses, either added to the cost on purchase or subtracted from the proceeds on sale. Because they must be capitalized, on long-term transactions such expenses are worth only 40 percent of comparable itemized deductions.

Transfer taxes may also be treated as a capital expense. But tax experts know that, alternatively, they may be claimed as taxes paid—and deducted as a current expense. On prospective long-term gains, they are fully utilized that way, rather than used to the extent of 40 percent of the expense. Only if the standard (zero bracket amount) deduction is used, therefore, should transfer taxes be capitalized. Special bank handling charges in excess of brokerage commissions may be treated as transfer taxes.

Conventions. It's often nice to go on a trip, and even nicer if Uncle Sam pays part of the way. Attendance at a convention means expenses that are deductible so long as there is a solid and clear relationship to the taxpayer's business or duties as an employee. There are limits to the deductibility of foreign expense conventions, however. If it's mainly a pleasure trip, which agents may suspect it is, only costs directly attributable to business are deductible. Further, only two such foreign trips are allowed each year if deductions are claimed, and Uncle Sam wants you to fly overseas in coach. Higher fares won't be deductible.

On any business trip, by the way, a spouse's expenses won't be allowed unless his or her presence is really necessary. The IRS agent's spouse doesn't get to go along on an audit free of charge, it might be useful to remember.

Business Gifts. Aside from imprinted trinkets, the deductibility of business gifts to customers or clients is limited to $25 in value a year for each recipient. Nevertheless, an employee may be given an award like the proverbial gold watch if it costs no more than $400 under the latest rules.

So long as the donor doesn't accompany the object of his bounty, tickets to the theater or the fights may be considered entertainment expenses that are not subject to the $25 gift ceiling. Considering ticket prices, it may be tax-wise to leave after dinner and wait for the movie.

Job Hunting. An employee seeking a new job in his or her usual trade or business may take an itemized deduction for the expenses of the search. They're deductible even if a new job isn't found. If a new trade or profession is sought, on the other hand, no deduction is available.

Moving Expenses. Normally, moving from one place to another is a personal expense and not deductible. But if a taxpayer moves to a new job or is transferred, many unreimbursed moving expenses become deductible. There are two tests, which involve time and distance.

Generally, to get the deduction, the peripatetic worker must be employed full time in the new locale for at least thirty-nine weeks during the year following arrival. A self-employed worker must, during the two years after arrival, perform services or work full time as an employee for seventy-eight weeks—while also meeting the regular thirty-nine-week–one-year test.

The new job location must be at least thirty-five miles farther from the worker's old home than was the old job location. Thus, changing suburbs of the same city usually won't do the trick.

If the time and distance tests will be met, a moved worker may deduct *all* reasonable direct moving expenses such as trucking, personal transportation, meals, and lodging. For this purpose, auto expenses may be claimed at 9 cents per mile. Indirect expenses may also be deducted up to: (a) $1,500 for house-hunting trips, or (b) $3,000 for temporary living expenses at the new location for no more than thirty days' expenses of selling the old home and buying the new one and (up to $1,500) house-hunting trips.

Form 3903 will help arrange all the arithmetic.

Expenses to Produce Tax-Exempt Income. Patently, amounts expended that are attributable to tax-free income can't be deducted. That's fair. If all of an expense produces fully exempt income, there's clearly no contest, even if the same expense would be fully deductible were it to bring forth fully taxable yield.

But what if an expense is attributable to both taxable and tax-free income? If an investment account throws off both kinds of income, the brokers, bankers, or advisers involved should segregate their fees so that the deductible portion can be determined. After all, some custodian banks have shown that it costs them less to maintain tax-free investment accounts (which tend to be less active). If the fee structure is reasonable, the expense of maintaining a portfolio of municipals need not be as high as that applicable to taxable accounts. Sometimes account managers don't allocate charges, and then expenses must be prorated. If this happens, depending on relative fee structures, it may pay to maintain a separate account for municipals.

When Things Wear Out—Entropy and the Tax Law

Most things wear out or get used up. When some of those things do, a tax deduction may be available.

Depreciation. For tax purposes, depreciation is the allowance, in the form of deductions, for the wear and tear of property used in a trade or business, or for the production of income. It's a way of reclaiming the cost of such property. Even if a taxpayer does not claim depreciation, it may be considered to proceed in its inexorable pace. The Code generally adjusts for depreciation "allowed or *allowable*." The cost basis of an asset is reduced for depreciation deductions.

Not every asset is depreciable. Not only must it be used either in trade or business or, alternatively, as investment property, but it must have a limited, determinable useful life extending beyond a year. (If a business or investment asset lasts less than a year, it isn't depreciable, but a fully deductible expense.)

Under these rules, then, personal property like your body, the family car, or your home aren't depreciable. If it won't ever wear out, it isn't subject to depreciation, either. Land is the prime example, and goodwill is another, of such nondepreciable assets.

Until the law was overhauled in 1981, two methods of

determining depreciable periods were used. The "useful life" system (terminology that, to tax practitioners, has no ethical significance) was based on the periods during which particular depreciable assets might reasonably have been expected to be useful. The appropriate periods depended on the facts, circumstances, and experience with similar assets. The "asset depreciation range," or ADR, system, now also obsolete, was based on useful lives of assets in broad classifications as prescribed by the IRS.

Different methods of depreciating assets over the given useful lives or class lives were devised. Most common were "straight-line," "declining balance," and "sum-of-the-years-digits." The latter two methods provided more depreciation deductions in the early years of an asset's use than simple straight-line, and the art and craft of accountancy had a felicitous time, indeed, in the flood of numbers.

Accelerated Cost Recovery System (ACRS). These time-honored methods of depreciation, and the concept of recovery of capital expenditures over the useful lives of assets that wear out, have been virtually abandoned for property put in service after December 31, 1980. All assets, new or used, purchased in 1981 and thereafter are subject to the new, more generous rules (except for "churned" assets, which are acquired in transactions designed merely to take advantage of the new law). Assets put into service before 1981 are still subject to the old rules.

ACRS provides for recovery of costs over periods ranging from three to fifteen years. Property to be written off, known as "recovery property," is assigned to one of four categories:

- Three-year property—This includes pick-up trucks and cars, for example, and, of course, certain race-horses.
- Five-year property—Machinery, heavy equipment, and most assets fit here.
- Ten-year property—If you have public utility property, a railroad tank car, or a theme park, this is your category.
- Fifteen-year property—Buildings and other real property go into this class.

Instead of the specified, rapid cost recovery allowances, taxpayers may elect to use the old straight-line method over these assigned class lives, or, alternatively, over prescribed class lives, which are longer than the ACRS lives in the four categories.

The new rules are involved and complex, but there is no doubt that they will provide greatly increased deductions. When property is disposed of, however, a portion of the prior cost recovery deducted in earlier years may have to be reported as ordinary income, rather than capital gain. For residential realty, nevertheless, there will be no recapture unless prior recovery amounts exceed straight-line depreciation.

The fun times for accountants haven't ended.

Depletion. What ACRS is to owners of recovery property, depletion is to the owners of oil or gas wells, mineral deposits, or timber forests. Those who have economic interests (including leases) in exhaustible, natural deposits and timber may claim deductions for the depletion of their wonderful assets.

There are two ways to calculate the depletion deduction:

1. *Cost depletion* is the basic method, which is founded on a reasonable guess of the number of units (tons, barrels, cubic feet, or the like) comprising the asset. The allocable cost of the asset is applied to the number of units extracted or sold during the year. The cost basis is reduced accordingly, but not below zero. The guess regarding the number of remaining units may be revised each year, so the depletion rate one year may not match that of another for the same asset.

2. *Percentage depletion* utilizes a legally prescribed percentage of gross income from the depleted asset. The deduction under this method generally can't exceed 50 percent of the taxable income from the asset. But while it also reduces basis, it may continue to be deducted even after the basis for the property has been reduced to zero. Thus, it may permit deductions that surpass the amount originally invested. If cost depletion yields greater deductions, it's to be used. A taxpayer can switch from one method in one year to the other in the next. Want to buy an oil well or a gold mine?

Elective Expensing. New rules permit taxpayers to elect to immediately deduct the cost of recovery property, up to $5,000 of cost in 1982 and 1983, up to $7,500 in 1984 and 1985, and up to $10,000 in 1986 and thereafter. Such amounts, deducted "up front," can't be used for calculating cost recovery or the investment credit, of course, and the election isn't available to estates, trusts, or certain noncorporate lessors. Married taxpayers who file separately must halve the ceiling amounts.

The elective expensing replaces the old notion of "additional first year depreciation," but neither the old rule nor the new one applies to property put in service in 1981.

When property that is expensed under this provision is sold, the installment sale method should not be used. The law requires that amounts expensed be immediately recaptured as ordinary income, and an installment sale could provide proceeds at the time of sale that don't even equal the tax then due.

9
Contributions, Worthless Securities, and Bad Debts

Congress has historically made it especially more blessed to give than to receive. Together with a spiritual brownie point or two, there is a mundane bonus in the form of tax advantage for charitable contributions. The tax quality of one's largesse may even be enhanced by a bit of planning.

Other, perhaps less eleemosynary, contributions in the guise of worthless securities or bad debts that are written off may yield some tax benefits.

Gifts to Charities

Above-the-Line or Itemized Deductions. As we all know, charitable contributions are a nifty type of itemized deduction. Before 1982, though, a taxpayer who did not itemize could not claim any deduction for gifts to qualified charities. After 1981, at least a portion of such gifts offer tax advantage for those who use the "zero bracket," or standard, deduction.

For 1982 and 1983, the special, above-the-line, deduction will be limited to 25 percent of the first $100 contributed. The ceiling is raised in 1984 to 25 percent of the first $300 contributed. In 1985, 50 percent of all contributions will be allowed above-the-line, and 100 percent will be allowed as a deduction in 1986. Then Congress will have to reconsider the matter.

If deductions are itemized, the full amount of charitable contributions is subject to certain ceilings, which depend on several tests. Normally, annual contributions to public chari-

73

ties, private operating foundations, and nonoperating private foundations through which contributions flow are deductible up to one-half of the donor's adjusted gross income.

Gifts of long-term capital gain property (discussed further below), though, which are not reduced by 40 percent of the appreciation, are usually limited to 30 percent, rather than half of adjusted gross income. That rule can be overcome and the ceiling brought back up to 50 percent if the donor elects to reduce the fair market value of the gift by 40 percent of the appreciation. That election may sometimes be worthwhile.

Gifts to certain other organizations, like domestic fraternal organizations, veterans' societies, nonprofit cemeteries, and "non-flow-through private nonoperating foundations," are limited to 20 percent of adjusted gross income.

Thus, we have "50 percent," "30 percent," and "20 percent" charities. If a comparatively large gift is made, this may not be all the arithmetic required. (The cost of a professional arithmetician, though, is deductible, too.) There's a system of carry-over, for use in subsequent years, of charitable deductions in excess of some of the various set limits. Gifts subject to the 50 percent or 30 percent limits may be carried forward for as long as five years; gifts to "20 percent" charities may not be carried forward at all.

Qualifying Contributions. To merit a deduction, itemized or not, a contribution may be made in money or in property.

Mere pledges are not deductible. They must be paid. No deduction is granted for the value of personal services contributed. After all, those services never rose to the status of income. On the other hand, such unreimbursed costs as travel, meals, or lodging away from home incurred on behalf of a charity are valid deductions.

A contribution is not deductible to the extent that the donor receives value for it.

EXAMPLE: Rona de Mille pays $250 for a ticket to the benefit premiere performance of the opera *Semolina Vermicelli*. The net proceeds go to the Bohm-Bastt Opera League, a qualified charity. The regular ticket price is $40. So, even if she abhors opera and doesn't use the ticket, Rona has made a contribution of $210, no more.

Finally, the law requires that deductible gifts be made to qualified domestic exempt organizations. Happily, there are thousands, public and private. The IRS publishes a copious list of most in *Publication No. 78,* or, if there's a question, the organization may be asked to produce a copy of its exemption letter from the IRS.

Canceled checks or similar proof of charitable contributions should be maintained. It has been the practice, however, in many IRS districts not to question modest amounts of unverified cash contributions, and for several years a "modest amount" has informally been held to be about a dollar and a half a week.

Gifts of Property. If it's feasible to donate property rather than cash, it should first be determined if there would be a gain or a loss if the property were sold to someone else instead. When there's a manifest loss (which is not attributable to property used personally, for which, of course, no loss is recognized), the sale should be made. The loss can be recognized and the proceeds then donated instead.

If property has increased in value, special rules apply. Normally, the fair market value is considered to be the amount contributed. (In virtually every tax context, including valuation of contributions, fair market value means the price a willing buyer would give a willing seller under ordinary conditions.)

Sometimes, however, the fair market value may be lowered by a portion, or even all, of the increase in value in order to arrive at a deductible figure, as suggested a few paragraphs ago. The adjustment depends on whether the gift is of "ordinary income property" or of "capital gain property." The former is simply property that, if sold, would *not* produce long-term capital gain. Donations of ordinary income property are deductible to the extent of fair market value *less* the amount that would be treated as short-term gain or as ordinary income.

EXAMPLE: On December 24, 1981, Toby Smollett donated to his church one hundred shares of Perry Greene Pickle Co., with a market value of $1,000. Smollett bought the shares on January 29, 1981, at a cost of $750. A sale of the stock would have resulted in a short-term gain, on December 24, of $250. Therefore, the deductible amount of Smollett's donation is $750 ($1,000 less the putative short-term gain).

Capital gain property is, of course, that which would produce long-term capital gain on a sale. Contributions of such assets are normally deductible at fair market value.

EXAMPLE: Homer Chapman donated to his church one hundred shares of Sheets and Kelly, Inc., with a market value of $5,000. He purchased the shares two years before for $3,000. Since long-term gain would have been realized on a sale, Chapman is able to deduct the full $5,000 without reporting $2,000 as capital gain income.

There are certain times that fair market value is *not* utilized as the measure of the value of a contribution of capital gain property. In both of the following cases, the fair market value must be reduced by 40 percent of the appreciation:

• Contributions to a private nonoperating foundation that doesn't distribute all contributions within two and one-half months after its year ends
• Gifts of tangible personal property, such as works of art, heirlooms, automobiles, machinery, or livestock, but not securities, which the charity does not use for its tax-exempt purposes

Therefore, when property other than securities is the subject of a charitable gift, two things should be done. First, make the gift to an organization that can and will use it to further its charitable purposes, and undertakes to do so in writing. Second, maintain complete records regarding the terms of the gift and the method by which its value was determined. The IRS wants copies of competent appraisals and other pertinent substantiating documents (including date and method of acquisition) attached to a tax return that claims a gift of property worth more than $200.

For a while, it was popular among certain up-scale folks to invest in works of art or books that many a donor never clapped eyes on but held, instead, for disposal to a compliant charity after the requisite year's holding period. The value, often wildly inflated, was determined under the aegis of the promoter of the scheme, who promised large deductions. The Service eventually gets around to scams. In this sort of deal, the obvious weak link is the valuation, which the IRS can easily determine. If need be, for example, the advice of a permanent special panel of art experts is utilized. Furthermore, the Service may assess penalties for underpayment of tax because of "excessive" values placed on property contributed to charity.

Those in the upper brackets know how to obtain the most, tax-wise, for their charitable impulses. They know to contribute capital gain property and hold short-term assets before donating. They know to sell rather than contribute assets bearing paper losses. If less than all of one's position in a security is being donated, the shares with the lowest cost bases would be given, so that the eventual reportable gain on the remaining shares will be reduced. If either capital gain property or cash can be used to redeem a pledge, the property can be delivered while the cash is used to replace it, so that, while the same position is maintained, there's an increased cost basis for it.

Worthless Securities and Bad Debts

Let's be candid. Occasionally, an investment or a loan, formerly in the bloom of fiscal health, withers and perishes. The tax law is at the side of the financially bereaved investor or lender, at the ready with a tax deduction.

The rules require, first, that the actual year in which the loss took place be clearly established. Some identifiable event, like a debtor's bankruptcy, is necessary. The burden of proof is the taxpayer's. Sometimes the year a debt becomes worthless or a security finally hits absolute zero is not easy to determine. In such a melancholy situation, an astute taxpayer should claim a deduction for the first year it may validly be asserted. If that may not be the right year, make the claim again (with full disclosure) for a subsequent year, if necessary, until the IRS can agree on the proper year. The loss shouldn't be lost because the indicated year should really have been an earlier one, even though the statute of limitations on making claims for such losses is extended.

Worthless Securities. Usually, when a security becomes utterly worthless its cost is taken as a capital loss, deemed to be realized on the last day of the tax year. For this purpose, a security must be a capital asset. To meet the definition of "security" it must be a share of corporate stock or a government or corporate bond that is registered or has coupons attached. Uncle Fred's personal IOU isn't a security. Only when a worthless security isn't a capital asset (when owned by a dealer, for example) or is specially treated (like Small Business Investment Companies) will the loss be considered ordinary. That's better, of course.

If there is any kind of market for it at all, the security cannot be said to be worthless. It may pay to sell, however low the price, so that the loss can be recognized.

Business Bad Debts. Debts that go sour in the course of business make the better of a bad thing. Certain business enterprises may establish reserves for predictable bad debts and use the reserve for deductions. But there are two other features of nonreserve business bad debts of value to other taxpayers. First, such a bad debt is deductible against ordinary income, rather than taken as a capital loss. That's a substantial incentive to characterize a debt as business-related. Second, partial worthlessness may be written off. A business bad debt doesn't have to be wholly bad. That's another powerful reason to claim that a debt is business-related.

The facts, however, prevail, and there must be a showing of a relationship of the bad debt's origin to the creditor-taxpayer's business. A loan made to a friend so the friend can join a partnership (that's personal) is not the same as a loan to keep one's own partnership afloat (that's business). A loan to a relative who is out of work is personal. A loan to one's own firm primarily to keep a job secure has been shown to be business-related.

Nonbusiness Bad Debts. Occasionally, the tax law is uncharacteristically simple. Here's an instance: if a debt isn't a business debt, it's a nonbusiness debt. A personal note from cousin Ramon payable on his return from Tahiti or an IOU from niece Shirley so she can finally get her nose fixed is a nonbusiness obligation.

But to rise to the status of debt in the first place, there must be an enforceable, true debt of money. A legal debtor-creditor relationship must exist. Family debts are closely scrutinized when they are claimed to be deductible because they are bad.

We fully believe you expected, without guile, that your daughter in Seattle would repay the $1,000 you sent four years ago, but don't expect the IRS to believe it without a battle. (Assume, however, that a taxpayer's relative gave a note to a third party. If that third party subsequently collected from the taxpayer who signed as guarantor, it may be more clear that a true legally enforceable debt existed.)

Nonbusiness bad debts, however valid, are the worst kind. No matter how long they may have been held, they are considered short-term capital losses. At least that's better than long-term treatment and better financial treatment from the IRS than it was from the debtor.

10
Illness, Taxes, Casualties, and Thefts

When we find ourselves in spells of distress, it's natural to turn to tax deductions as well as to other forms of solace. Medical costs, thefts, taxes, and such misfortunes may be assuaged, to some extent, by tax deductions.

What Is a Medical Expense?

If a doctor prescribes it, it probably qualifies as a medical expense. Neither Dr. J's nor Dr. Kissinger's prescription will do—it takes a medical sort, including physicians, dentists, osteopaths, psychiatrists, surgeons, Christian Science practitioners, optometrists, podiatrists, chiropodists, and chiropractors. Veterinarians don't count for this particular test.

A medical expense must, according to the rules, be for the diagnosis, mitigation, treatment, or prevention of illness, or for effecting some improvement to one's anatomy. Expenditures made to improve one's general sense of well-being are not allowed as deductions very often. Thus, the cost of a nanny for Junior or a guru for Sis is not deductible. The costs of brain surgery or spectacles represent allowable medical expenses. Medicine to reduce blood pressure is deductible; hair tonic is not. Finally, funeral expenses are not the same as medical expenses and aren't deductible as such. It's too late.

Understandably, there are many close decisions regarding the deductibility of medical expenses. The Tax Court has granted a deduction for a hair-transplant operation as surgical treatment "for a specific physical defect, that of baldness." (The majority of the Tax Court judges are not bald.) When prescribed by medicos, birth-control pills and vasectomies have been held to be deductible. Marriage-counseling fees and popular weight-reduction regimens, on the other hand, have been disallowed as expenditures made merely to improve the subject's general vitality. Treatment at a drug addiction or alcoholism rehabilitation center is deductible. The IRS seems to be ambivalent about programs to stop smoking. If a taxpayer is intent on deducting the cost of stopping a bad habit, then doctor's orders, aimed at the specific affliction, seem necessary.

The employment of a registered nurse isn't obligatory for a medical deduction. A practical nurse's salary may also be claimed, but any nursing care is deductible only to the extent that it doesn't cover normal domestic tasks.

The latest tofu-and-kale diet isn't a medical expense. Special foods are deductible only if they are an adjunct to the patient's diet prescribed by a doctor.

Of course, a sojourn in a hospital for medical reasons is deductible. So is the cost of a special-care institution for a physically or mentally handicapped patient. The expense of a home for the aged resorted to only for family convenience may be questioned, and a stay at a spa should be at a real health care facility and at the behest of a doctor if it is to be deductible.

Swimming pools and home elevators have been successfully claimed. Such permanent improvements, though, are deductible only to the extent that they do not increase the value of the property they enhance.

EXAMPLE: Sammy Conn Schuss has a weak heart. On orders from his cardiologist, he installed an elevator in his two-story home. The cost of the installation was $2,500. Sammy's house increased in value by $1,000 because of the elevator. His deductible medical expense was, therefore, $1,500.

Transportation expenses in the pursuit of healthiness are often overlooked as medical expenses. The actual cost of gas and oil (or, alternatively, 9 cents a mile) as well as tolls and parking fees are deductible for an auto trip to the doctor. Plane, train, or bus tickets qualify. The trip need not be local, just medical.

Whose Expenses Are Deductible? Understandably, the medical expenses of the taxpayer, spouse, or dependents are deductible. The definition of "dependent" is expanded for this particular deduction, and expenses of a "medical dependent," who may not otherwise qualify as a dependent, are also deductible. A "medical dependent" is one who fits into the normal familial category of dependent and who might have been claimed as an exemption, except for the fact that he or she filed a joint return with someone else or had gross income of more than $1,000.

How Is the Deduction Calculated? There are currently three segments to the calculation of a medical deduction.

1. For years before 1983, premiums paid for qualified health and accident insurance for the taxpayer and his or her family are fully deductible only to the extent of one-half of the total cost, but never more than $150. The unused portion (the other half of the premiums and any excess over $150) is added to the other medical expenses and is subject to the same percentage reductions as they are. For years after 1982, this separate step is eliminated. The cost of insurance will be treated like any other medical expense.

2. For years before 1984, medicines and legal drugs are considered medical expenses only to the extent that they exceed 1 percent of adjusted gross income. To the extent that they do, they are added to other medical costs. Beginning in 1984, the 1 percent floor will be removed. The full expense for drugs will be treated as medical expenses. The definition of drugs, though, will encompass only prescription drugs and insulin.

3. General medical expenses (bifocals, hospitals, lab fees, doctors, nurses, transportation, and all the rest) and the excess medical insurance and drugs from the first two segments are deductible to the extent that they exceed 3 percent of the taxpayer's adjusted gross income, for years before 1983. After 1983, medical expenses will be deductible to the extent that they exceed 5 percent (rather than 3 percent) of adjusted gross income.

EXAMPLE: In 1982, Faron Hite had adjusted gross income of $24,000. During the year, he paid Blue Cross $160 for medical insurance. Faron also paid $1,200 in doctors' bills, $320 for contact lenses, and $860 for prescription drugs, for which he was not reimbursed. Faron Hite's deduction is calculated below:

Insurance— first half			$ 80
Doctors		$1,200	
Contact lenses		320	
Drugs	$860		
Less: 1 percent of $24,000	(240)		
Insurance—	620		
second half		80	
Subtotal		2,220	
Less: 3 percent of $24,000		(720)	
			1,500
Total 1982 deduction			$1,580

Now suppose Faron Hite had the same adjusted gross income and the same medical expenses in 1983 and again in 1984. Here are the calculations:

1983

Insurance		$ 160
Doctors		1,200
Contact lenses		320
Drugs	$860	
Less: 1 percent of $24,000	(240)	
	620	
Subtotal		2,300
Less: 5 percent of $24,000		(1,200)
Total 1983 deduction		$1,100

1984

Insurance	$ 160
Doctors	1,200
Contact lenses	320
Drugs	860
Subtotal	2,540
Less: 5 percent of $24,000	(1,200)
Total 1984 deduction	$1,340

Of course, medical costs that are reimbursed or compensated for by insurance aren't considered deductible expenses. What if an expense is claimed in one year and reimbursement is received in a subsequent year? The IRS doesn't want the earlier year's return amended. Rather, the reimbursement is treated as income when it's received—but only to the extent that there was a tax benefit attributable to the deduction claimed in the first place. Thus, an insurance reimbursement need not be reported so far as the expense it covers did not reduce taxes, or if the standard, zero bracket, deduction was used.

Taxes

Undoubtedly, what is perceived as the most ubiquitous of predictable misfortunes is the imposition of taxes. Many taxes are deductible. Some are not. Federal income taxes, for example, cannot be claimed on federal income tax returns. To a tax professional, the thought is bizarre.

The taxes that do qualify as itemized deductions for the year of payment include

• *State, local, or foreign income taxes.* This includes state or local taxes withheld from paychecks as well as estimated taxes and additional payments made with last year's state or local return. Foreign income taxes may be claimed, alternatively, as tax credits, and that's normally much better. But the foreign taxes must be true levies against income. (Transnational oil companies used to claim charges for the extraction of petroleum for certain Middle Eastern jurisdictions as taxes, but the IRS stoutly maintains that such charges are merely disguised costs of raw material, deductible as a business expense but not available for full credit.)

- *State, local, or foreign real estate taxes.* All true real estate taxes on personal or business property are deductible. This does not include special assessments that may bear a deceptive label, such as a sewer tax, if the assessment is for a capital improvement. (But any part of such a "tax" attributable to maintenance or interest charges, rather than solely capital improvements, may be allowed.) The deductibility of taxes on realty is one of the true advantages of owning rather than renting, whether it's the old homestead or the latest condo. When realty is sold, it's the rule that real estate taxes must be apportioned between seller and buyer and each is entitled to his, her, or its share.

- *State or local personal property taxes.* Some states levy annual personal property taxes on boats or automobiles, for example, which can be distinguished from the usual, nondeductible, registration fees or license plate costs because they are based on value. Some jurisdictions assert personal property levies on tangible assets, while others tax intangible property, such as stocks and bonds.

- *State or local sales taxes.* You need not keep track of every penny paid as sales taxes, though you may if you're *that* type. The IRS provides sales tax tables that can be utilized to provide unchallengeable figures for income levels in each jurisdiction. Simply follow the instructions (including the minuscule footnotes). Even if the tables are followed, additional deductions may be claimed for sales taxes for certain extraordinary purchases of high-ticket items like home construction materials, cars, or yachts. (The latest tax form just mentions "motor vehicles.") They should be shown separately on the return.

Sales taxes on other purchases, like jewelry, furs, furniture, or household items, are not to be added to the amounts shown in the tables, in the view of the Tax Court. If you had major expenses subject to sales tax, it might pay to do a separate calculation to see which method provides a larger deduction. Use taxes are mirror images of sales taxes and are treated the same way.

• *Other taxes.* Trade or business expenses, such as unemployment taxes imposed on an employer, in the guise of taxes may be claimed, but still only if they are state, local, or foreign.

Certain taxes are simply not deductible. For example:

• *Federal income taxes.* This category includes Social Security taxes paid by an employee or a self-employed worker.
• *Estate, inheritance, or gift taxes.* Such transfer taxes, whether imposed by the U.S. or by a state or local government, are not federal income tax deductions. (The U.S. estate tax law, though, grants a limited credit for state taxes on the same taxable estate.)
• *Other taxes not deductible.* Standard auto license fees, telephone or gasoline taxes, customs duties or stamp taxes, and similar imposts are not deductible as taxes, though they may, under the proper facts, qualify as trade or business expenses. Don't press for the deductibility of dog or marriage license fees.

Casualty and Theft Losses

If, this year, you win more than you lose at the track, you get taxed on the net winnings. Lose more than you win and the IRS isn't interested. When it comes to losses, Uncle Sam is not necessarily willing to become your partner. To be deductible, a loss must (1) be incurred in a trade or business, (2) result from a transaction entered into for profit, or (3) be a casualty or theft loss. We've talked a bit about the first two kinds of losses. Now let's review the third kind.

What Is a Casualty? When the apocalypse comes, it will be deductible for each taxpayer if the damage exceeds $100. (If it comes after 1982, it will also have to exceed 10 percent of the taxpayer's adjusted gross income.) Snow, dust or rain storms, fire, earth slides, and destruction similar to that featured in Irwin Allen movies are deductible casualties—defined by the rules as the complete or partial destruction of property from an identifiable sudden, unexpected, or unusual event.

According to the IRS, the damage wrought by the steady gnawing of termites is not sudden. Dutch elm blight isn't either, but Med flies or gypsy moths may be expected to be claimed, perhaps successfully, as the rascals causing deductible losses because of the suddenness of their sneak attacks.

The loss of an animal by disease is not deductible as a casualty loss because it's not sudden or unexpected. (It may be a business loss.) But if an animal used in business or held as an investment dies as the result of an encounter with a sixteen-wheel trailer rig, rather than from mange, *that's* a casualty.

When Is a Theft Deductible? Being mugged or the victim of any other kind of abrupt theft can easily be assigned, as a kind of casualty, to the proper tax year. Sometimes, though, a rip-off is committed with stealth, as, for example, in an embezzlement. Then it is deductible for the year in which the theft was first discovered or discoverable.

How Is the Deduction Calculated? A total loss of business property is always its adjusted cost basis. The amount of any other casualty loss, business or personal, is (1) the difference in the value of the stricken property before and after the casualty, or (2) the adjusted cost basis of the property, whichever is less.

EXAMPLE: Mona Moore's gazebo had a fair market value of $16,000. It originally cost Ms. Moore $10,000. One dark night in 1982, it suffered heavy storm damage that reduced its fair market value to $12,000. The casualty loss is $4,000, which is the reduction in value because of the storm. (If the storm had reduced the worth of the gazebo down to $1,000, Mona's loss would have been limited to $10,000, her original basis, rather than $15,000, the decline in her gazebo's value.)

Obviously, there is no loss to the extent that there is insurance or other compensation related directly to the property that was damaged or destroyed. The value of food or medical necessities supplied to flood victims doesn't alter the amount of their casualty losses. A check from the insurance company for auto collision repair will diminish the casualty loss, however, and fire insurance proceeds in replacement of a burned building must be tallied as a reduction of the loss.

If the compensation exceeds the basis of covered property, the law calls the event, with winning simplicity, an "involuntary conversion," on which recognition of the gain may be postponed by replacement of the destroyed property.

Normally, though, a casualty results in a loss that is reported as an ordinary loss. But not all the loss may be deducted. For each personal casualty loss (that is, each loss of property not connected with a business or held for the production of income), the deduction is limited to the amount lost in excess of $100 for years before 1983. The $100 floor, below which the rules won't grant a deduction, relates to each casualty as a single sudden event, rather than to each separate loss during the same calamity. If a maple, hit by lightning, falls on a van, damaging it and a three-wheeler inside, the total amount of unreimbursed loss in value (down to bases) in the tree, the truck, and the trike is subject to one $100 floor.

For years after 1982, casualty and theft losses are deductible only to the extent that they total more than 10 percent of the taxpayer's adjusted gross income for the year. This new rule is in addition to the rule which requires that each loss must exceed $100.

Form 4868 may be used to report a loss that isn't connected with a business and doesn't result in an involuntary conversion.

Disaster Losses. In the special situation of a designated disaster loss, a taxpayer may deduct a loss almost as soon as it occurs, without waiting until after the end of the tax year to file a return claiming the loss. In effect, the disaster gives effect to a loss a year ahead of time, if the taxpayer so elects. The loss must be attributable to a disaster that is so designated by the president. The 10 percent and $100 limitations still apply to such losses.

PART·III

COMPUTATIONS AND CREDITS

11
The Tax Return

Now that we've seen how the tax law got that way and have some notion as to what constitutes gross income and how above-the-line and itemized deductions work, perhaps a look at the grim visage of the tax form itself will cause less consternation than it otherwise might have.

Most individual readers will file the celebrated and venerable Form 1040. It may, though, be possible to use the short form, 1040A, if total income is no more than $50,000. Income must not consist of anything other than wages, interest, dividends, or unemployment compensation, and itemized deductions may not be claimed if the short form is used.

The IRS recently introduced a new, even simpler form, called, cutely, the 1040EZ. It may be used by single taxpayers who claim only one personal exemption and whose income consists only of wages, up to $400 of interest, and no dividend income. To use 1040EZ, taxable income must be less than $50,000.

But let's look at the long form, 1040, for if you can understand it, the short forms will be a cinch.

Appendix C contains copies of the generally used forms, and it might be useful to follow the first few pages of Form 1040 in sequence.

Page one first reveals who and where each taxpayer is, his, her, or their filing status, and applicable exemptions (on the 1982 Form 1040 lines 1 through 6e). Don't forget your Social

Security number. This is how you are known to Uncle Sam. Help, beyond that provided by the government's instructions, isn't really required here. Make your own decision whether you want to divert a simoleon to the presidential election campaign fund, please.

Next, the questions start to aggregate gross income (lines 7 through 22). Many of the items in this section will be familiar. Note that totals of various kinds of income are inserted here; generally, the details are found in various designated schedules that must be attached.

Adjustments to gross income are made on the next section of the return to arrive at adjusted gross income (lines 23 through 31). Available deductions, either standard or itemized, from another schedule are inserted into the tax computation section where the basic tax appears (lines 33 through 40, on the second page). The tax is derived from still different schedules or from tax tables. Tax credits are set off against the indicated tax (lines 41 through 50). Other taxes are added (lines 51 through 59). Payments, such as taxes withheld or estimates paid in quarterly installments, are credited (lines 60 through 67), and, before you know it, the bottom line is reached. Simply sign at the end of page two and send your check, or wait for your refund. Easy!

Well, one must admit that there are a few intricate spots. They account for the myriad of schedules and attachments, the complex instructions and computations. Nevertheless, the design of the 1040 becomes clear.

The figures shown on the first two pages of the return are often derived from special schedules or forms, many of which are reproduced in the Appendix. The following list describes the more common current attachments to the basic form:

- Schedule A: itemized deductions
- Schedule B: dividends or interest over $400, and foreign account information
- Schedule C: business or professional income and expenses
- Schedule D: capital gains and losses
- Schedule E: income and losses from a variety of sources, such as pensions, partnerships, rents, royalties, estates, and trusts

- Schedule F: farm income
- Schedule G: income averaging
- Schedule R&RP: credits for retirees
- Schedule SE: paying self-employment Social Security Tax
- Form 1116: foreign tax credit
- Form 2106: employee business expenses
- Form 2119: sale or exchange of principal residence
- Form 2120: for multiple-support agreement
- Form 2210: explaining the underpayment of estimated tax
- Form 2441: child-care credit
- Form 2688: for additional time to file
- Form 3468: investment credit
- Form 3903: moving expenses
- Form 4562: depreciation
- Form 4625: minimum taxes
- Form 4684: casualties and theft
- Form 4797: complex capital gains and losses
- Form 4868: for automatic extension of time to file
- Form 5695: energy credits
- Form 6251: alternative minimum taxes

No wonder the government won't send out postage-paid return envelopes! (See Appendix C for a sampling of tax forms; see Appendix E for a full listing of tax forms.)

Who Must File? It's easy to determine if you must file a return. Even if a return isn't necessary, if tax was withheld or a refund is due for any other reason, one *should* be filed. The chart shows the starting level of gross income at which income tax returns must be filed by taxpayers in each status.

Single	
Under 65	$3,300
65 or over	4,300
Married—filing a joint return	
Both under 65	5,400
One 65 or over	6,400
Both 65 or over	7,400
Married—filing a separate return	1,000
Married—not living with spouse at end of year	1,000

Qualified widow(er) with dependent child

Under 65	4,400
65 or over	5,400
Dependent—claimed on parents' return and had taxable dividends, interest, or other unearned income	1,000

Personal Exemptions. There are four kinds of personal exemptions, and each is worth $1,000. They are

- The regular personal exemption for each taxpayer
- The regular exemption for each dependent (defined below)
- The extra exemption for a taxpayer who is sixty-five or older
- The extra exemption for a taxpayer who is legally blind

Dependents. There are five tests, all of which must be considered in the definition of a dependent.

- *Income.* The dependent's gross income must be less than $1,000. If the dependent is the taxpayer's child, though, and is either a full-time student or under nineteen years of age, the fortunate child may be claimed as a dependent even if the offspring's income may be more than $1,000.
- *Support.* The taxpayer must furnish over half the dependent's support during the year. Remember that "support" includes amounts actually expended for housing (or fair rental value), medical care, education and tuba lessons, as well as food and clothing. It makes no difference how much the dependent has in the bank or receives from investments. The more-than-half test is based on amounts spent.

  Normally, it's easy to assign a dependent's support to one taxpayer, but it sometimes happens that support is a joint effort and no single taxpayer contributes half the dependent's costs. If that's so, one of the contributors may claim the dependency deduction if (were it not for the support test) each of them would be entitled to claim the dependent. The winner of the deduction must contribute more than 10 percent of the dependent's support, and every other contributor of more than 10 percent must sign a written multiple-support agreement (on Form 2120) which is filed with the return of the taxpayer claiming the deduction.

- *Joint return.* A married dependent who pays his or her tax by filing a joint return can't be claimed as a dependent by a parent.
- *Citizenship or residency.* A dependent must normally be a U.S. citizen or resident of the U.S., Canada, or Mexico sometime during the year (or live with and be adopted by an American living overseas).
- *Relationship.* The dependent must be related to the taxpayer in a specified manner, or be a member of the taxpayer's household.

Filing Status and Brackets. The first five numbered boxes on the 1040 determine the taxpayer's tax status. The Congress has provided four different tax rate schedules for folks in five different situations (joint filers and surviving spouses share the same schedules). It might be interesting to compare the relative burdens of taxpayers in each situation. Suppose, for each kind of taxpayer, there is taxable income, after all exemptions and deductions, of $40,000. Suppose, further, that the tax year involved is 1982 (because the rates are lower for subsequent years and higher for prior years. Complete rate tables are provided in Appendix A).

$40,000 TAXABLE INCOME—1982			
Status	Tax	Marginal Bracket	Effective Rate
Married, joint returns	$ 9,195	39%	23%
Surviving spouse	9,195	39%	23%
Head of household	10,571	41%	26%
Single	11,408	44%	29%
Married, filing separately	13,752	49%	34%

In addition to the actual taxes on the same income for different taxpayers, the little chart above shows both marginal tax brackets and effective tax rates. Don't be confounded by the two notions. The marginal bracket is the top rate at which the income is taxed. Most personal tax discourses deal with this concept; when people talk about their high tax brackets, they are really complaining about the marginal tax brackets.

The rates are cumulative, working up from the lowest, so the top bracket doesn't represent the true proportion of each taxable dollar yielded to the Treasury.

A different way of looking at the impact of taxes is the effective tax rate. That demonstrates how many pennies out of each taxable dollar are paid in tax.

In the table above, for example, in which a single taxpayer has. $40,000 of taxable income in 1982, the marginal bracket reaches 44 percent, but only 29 cents are paid from each taxable dollar.

Remember, also, that these comparisons are based on taxable income. That's useful, but the point of understanding taxes is, of course, to plan wisely so that fewer of the dollars received are characterized as taxable.

The Marriage Penalty. The chart above also demonstrates, by the way, that rates for singles are higher than for married taxpayers who file jointly, but not twice as high. Because of the rate differentials and the operation of the standard deduction, under the law through 1981 when both spouses earned about the same amount of income, a higher tax occurred than their combined tax would have been had they been unmarried. The so-called marriage penalty was exacerbated as the joint income rose and as the spread between the incomes of the two spouses narrowed.

To help relieve the marriage penalty (and avoid the taxpayers' "bonus" achieved when people with disparate incomes marry and file joint returns), the law was changed to grant a special deduction equal to a percentage of the earnings of the spouse with lower earnings. The deduction, available even if the standard, zero bracket, amount is used, equals 10 percent (5 percent for 1982) of either $30,000 or the qualified net earned income of the spouse who earned less, whichever is lower. In other words, the special deduction is limited to $1,500 for 1982 and $3,000 thereafter.

Indexing. In the future, to offset the notorious "bracket creep"—by which inflation causes the same buying power to be taxed in ever augmenting tax brackets—a feature previously utilized only in other countries will enter our tax law. Beginning in 1985, the tax rates, the standard zero bracket deduction, and the personal exemptions will all be adjusted for increases in the Consumer Price Index.

Tables and the "Zebra." For the convenience of its patrons, the IRS has contrived four handy tax tables for filers in each of the tax status boxes. These tables, however, are reserved for those with taxable income of no more than $50,000. For those with taxable income above $50,000, the tax will have to be calculated from tax rate schedules. Concealed in the tables is provision for standard deductions.

The old-fashioned standard deduction is now called the "zero bracket amount." Tax professionals, being a frolicsome clique, quickly dubbed it the "zebra" (perhaps thinking wishfully that it wouldn't change its stripes for a while). The zebra is mechanically incorporated into the tables. If deductions are itemized, the amounts over the zebra are used in the tax computation, because everyone gets the use of the zebra automatically.

The zero bracket amounts are

- Joint filers and surviving spouses—$3,400
- Singles and heads of households—$2,300
- Marrieds filing separately—$1,700

If your itemized deductions don't meet these levels, you may put aside that shoe box full of receipts and documentation of deductions and ride the zebra. Only a few taxpayers are obliged by law to itemize, even if deductions are below the zero bracket amounts. A married taxpayer who separately files must itemize if the other spouse does so. Someone who is claimed as a dependent on another's return but who has at least $1,000 of earned income may not use the zebra, nor may a taxpayer who was both a nonresident alien and a U.S. taxpayer during the tax year.

Filing the Return. The IRS likes taxpayers to use the peel-off identification labels and return envelopes they provide because, they say, it eases their paper-handling burden. Suspicious taxpayers see an ulterior motive, supposing that such returns will somehow be identified for audit. There has been no clear demonstration that compliant filers who use them suffer from audit any more than do those who eschew the labels bearing unexplained dots or the envelopes with electronically scanable stripes.

The return for a calendar-year filer, as virtually all individuals are, may be filed any time after December 31, but is due on or before April 15. A popular technique is to file as close to the last day as possible so that the document will be lost in the crowd of returns. It's conjectural whether this technique helps, but it doesn't hurt unless a refund is expected. File at the Internal Revenue Service Center assigned to your region.

If you don't have the money to pay the tax, at least file the return and pay what you can. You'll avoid some part of the penalties and get a bill for what's due. If you can't file the return on time, you may have a four-month automatic extension simply by filing Form 4868 before the due date. It's not an extension of time to pay, just of time to file, so an estimated amount of tax owed is to be paid with the request. Attach a copy of the form to the return when it is finally filed.

When a joint return is filed, both husband and wife are "jointly and severally liable" for the tax. That means, fundamentally, that the tax liability may be asserted against either spouse. (It may even be presumed that, where one spouse signed a joint return alone, a joint return was intended.)

Well, that doesn't seem quite fair, does it? Suppose a dominant spouse incurs significant tax deficiencies together with interest and penalties. The law is not malevolent. There is an "innocent spouse" rule that may relieve the put-upon consort from liability. Certain tests must be met: (1) the amount of income omitted by the guilty spouse must be more than 25 percent of the gross income reported, (2) the omitted income must be attributable to the guilty spouse, (3) the deficiency must relate to omitted income, not overstated deductions, and (4) the innocent spouse must prove lack of knowledge of the omission. If these tests are met, an investigation of the facts and circumstances is then required. The ultimate fairness of the situation is viewed, and the innocent spouse must not significantly benefit from the omission.

12
Mini and Maxi Tax, Averaging, and Installment Sales

The basic computation of tax may be just that: basic. A little tax gavotte might be required to increase the basic tax or be available to ameliorate that doleful figure. Perhaps the computations become a little involved, but they may yield dramatic results.

Minimum Taxes

High-bracket taxpayers may take advantage of certain tax preferences and shelters. Many have, you know. Congress, always eager for equity, felt that such lucky folk should, in all fairness, pay at least some minimum tax. For 1982, the minimum tax is calculated in one of two ways, and whichever yields the most tax is the one which must be used. First, the "add-on" minimum tax is figured and combined with the regular tax, then the "alternative" minimum tax is calculated. The two are compared, and higher tax is paid. The add-on minimum tax will not be applicable after 1982. A modernized version of the alternative minimum tax will then be in operation.

The Pre-1983 Add-On Minimum. "Tax preference items" trigger the add-on tax. Such preferences are, for example:

- Accelerated depreciation on real property and on personal property subject to a lease (that is, the

excess of accelerated depreciation or ACRS over straight-line)
- Percentage depletion to the extent that it exceeds the adjusted tax basis of the property at the end of the tax year (before adjustment for depletion)
- Qualified stock options to the extent that the fair market values of the stock on the exercise date exceed the option prices of qualified employee stock options
- Excess intangible drilling costs from productive wells to the extent they exceed net income from oil, gas, and geothermal properties

The add-on is calculated by first adding up all tax preference items (which, coincidentally, are liable to be integral parts of tax shelters). Then the total is reduced by (a) half the taxpayer's regular income tax for the year, or (b) $10,000 (or, in the case of a married taxpayer filing separately, $5,000)—whichever is more. Then a tax of 15 percent is applied to that figure.

EXAMPLE: Lew Pohl's regular income tax came out to $30,000 for 1981. His tax preference deductions totaled $70,000, consisting of $40,000 in percentage depletion in excess of basis and $30,000 of accelerated depreciation. (He claimed a depreciation deduction of $50,000 when straight-line would have yielded $20,000.) Lew Pohl's add-on minimum tax was $8,250 for 1981. Here's how the figures worked out on his Form 4625, which was used to report the add-on minimum tax:

Tax preference deductions ($40,000 + $30,000)	$70,000
Less: the greater of (a) $10,000, or (b) one-half of regular income tax of $30,000	(15,000)
Amount subject to tax	55,000
At 15 percent	8,250

The Alternative Minimum Before 1983. The alternative minimum tax is calculated, naturally enough, on the taxpayer's "alternative minimum taxable income," or AMTI, which is basically normal taxable income *plus* the total amount of two kinds of preference income:

- *Capital gains deductions*—that is, the untouched part (60 percent) of long-term gains (except for gain on the sale of a principal residence).
- *"Excess adjusted itemized deductions"*—to the extent that itemized deductions are over 60 percent of adjusted gross income. Deductions for medical expenses, casualties and thefts, taxes, and such other unintentional expenses are not included in the calculation.

A special progressive tax rate is applied to the AMTI for years before 1983:

Pre-1983 AMTI Total	Taxed at
$ 0–$ 20,000	0
$ 20,000–$ 60,000	10%
$ 60,000–$100,000 (until 1982)	20%
$100,000 and above (until 1982)	25%
$ 60,000 and above (1982)	20%

A married taxpayer who files separately must multiply the AMTI by two, compute the tax, then divide by two.

Though the applicable Form 6251 may look formidable, the computation of the alternative minimum tax is really rather simple.

EXAMPLE: In 1981, the Sol Vents had taxable income of $40,000. Sol had a long-term capital gain of $90,000, so he was entitled to a deduction for 60 percent, or $54,000, of the gain. He had excess itemized deductions of $12,000, mainly for interest and investment fees. The Vents' alternative minimum taxable income:

Taxable income	$ 40,000
Capital gain deduction	54,000
Excess deductions	12,000
	$106,000

The Vents' alternative minimum tax for 1981:

0 on first	$	20,000	$ 0
10 percent on next		40,000	4,000
20 percent on next		40,000	8,000
25 percent on next		6,000	1,500
		$106,000	$13,500

In 1981, tax at joint rates for $40,000 of taxable income was $10,226 (before the 1¼ percent year-end credit). Since the AMTI of $13,500 was higher, that's the tax liability.

Even though a taxpayer may have no items of tax preference, the AMTI may still apply if the regular income tax is greatly reduced or eliminated by tax credits. A bit of unwelcome intelligence, surely.

The Alternative Minimum Tax after 1982. Starting in 1983, the old add-on minimum tax is repealed and the alternative minimum tax is expanded to cover more than the tax preference items encompassed by both earlier versions of the minimum tax.

The calculation is simple, relatively speaking. The first $30,000 of minimum taxable income—$40,000 in case of joint returns or $20,000 in case of married taxpayers filing separately—is exempt. Minimum taxable income in excess of the exempt amount has a flat rate of 20 percent applied to it. As under the old alternative minimum tax, if the computation yields a higher figure than the regular tax, the minimum tax bill is the one that must be paid.

Generally, in addition to the list of preferences formerly found in the add-on minimum tax catalogue, the new alternative minimum tax preference items include:

- long-term capital gains deductions of 60 percent of the gain;
- bargain element of incentive stock options at the time they are exercised;
- dividend exclusions of $100 or $200;

- interest received tax-free from All Saver's Certificates;
- 15 percent net interest exclusion starting in 1985;
- certain excess development expenses for minerals and magazines, research and development costs to the extent they are not spread over ten years.

The post-1982 minimum tax is calculated by adding the preference items to adjusted gross income, rather than to taxable income. Deductions are allowed, therefore, to reach the AMTI, but not *all* of the usual deductions qualify because some of them may be considered to be preferential. Allowable deductions for this purpose:

- medical and casualty losses in excess of 10 percent of adjusted gross income;
- home mortgage interest;
- charitable contributions;
- investment interest expense up to investment income;
- certain net operating losses and certain expenses for taxes originally incurred by estates.

EXAMPLE: Let's call on Mr. and Mrs. Sol Vent again in 1983. They have salary income of $50,000, another long-term capital gain of $90,000 (again with a deduction of 60 percent of the gain, leaving $36,000), and dividend income of $5,200 (which is entitled to a $200 exclusion, don't forget). Their 1983 adjusted gross income, if you figure it out, is, therefore, $91,000. The Vents have deductions for state and local taxes of $9,000, employee expenses of $6,400, home mortgage expense of $5,000, consumer interest costs of $6,000, a charitable deduction of $1,000, and miscellaneous deductible expenses of $1,000. Their deductions total $28,400. The zero bracket amount of $3,400 reduces itemized deductions to $25,000 and personal exemptions are another reduction of $2,000. Put it all together for taxable income of $64,000. Tax, in 1983, at joint rates is $17,774.

So far, so good. Now let's calculate their alternative minimum tax:

Adjusted gross income		$ 91,000
Preference items:		
Capital gains deduction	$54,000	
Dividend exclusion	200	
		54,200
		145,200
Preference deductions:		
Mortgage interest	5,000	
Charitable contributions	1,000	
		(6,000)
AMTI		139,200
Exempt amount		(40,000)
Amount subject to alternative tax		99,200
		× .20
Alternative minimum tax		$19,840

Because the alternative minimum tax exceeds the regular tax of $17,774, it applies instead.

A Maximum Tax

For tax years before 1982, there was a maximum tax rate of 50 percent generally applicable to personal service income.

The maximum tax on personal service income was repealed as of December 31, 1981. It's now redundant because the highest marginal tax rate on all kinds of income is limited to 50 percent as of 1982.

Income Averaging

Suppose you win a bundle at Atlantic City or Las Vegas, or you realized a substantial capital gain and your taxable income far surpasses that to which you are accustomed. Congratulations! There's a way to avoid the bane of the progression of the tax rates. Income averaging allows much of any real increase in the current year's taxable income over the average taxable income for the prior four years to be taxed at lower brackets. Almost all kinds of income qualify (except for such things as early or excessive distributions from certain retirement plans).

Only individual taxpayers may average and they must pass three tests to do so:

- *Math test.* To meet this test, first the current year's taxable income must be more than 30 percent of the aggregate taxable income for the four preceeding tax years. Next, the excess must be more than $3,000. The excess is the "averageable income." It's taxed essentially as if it were earned ratably over the five-year period.
- *Citizenship or residency test.* For the full five-year period, the taxpayer must have been a U.S. citizen or resident.
- *Support test.* Generally, the taxpayer must have supplied most of his or her own support during each of the preceeding four years. Joint filers must both meet the support test together. (However, the support test isn't applicable if the taxpayer is over twenty-five and has not been a full-time student for four years since reaching twenty-one; the bulk of the current year's income is attributable to work substantially done during two or more of the four years—picture the starving novelist who makes good after being supported by someone else; or the taxpayer files a joint return in which he or she accounts for no more than 25 percent of the total adjusted gross income.)

A taxpayer who takes advantage of income averaging and files Schedule G with the tax return may not exclude income earned outside the United States. A comparison of these methods of tax calculation should be made to see which produces the lowest tax.

Installment Sales

Normally, of course, the full profit realized on a sale must be reported in the year of the sale. An installment sale, though, is a dandy device for deferring part of gain, and the tax on it, to a subsequent year or years. The use of an installment sale is especially nice in a period when future tax rates are scheduled to be lowered, and it's automatic unless you elect otherwise.

For an installment sale, there merely must be provision for later payment or payments. The number and proportion of payments is determined by the taxpayer and the person who is the buyer on the installment plan.

> EXAMPLE: On December 1, 1981, Potash sold Perlmutter all of his Montague Glass Corporation shares for $200,000 (plus interest), payable over five years starting January 2, 1982. Each principal payment is $40,000. The stock cost Potash $20,000 many years ago. In 1982 and the following four years, his reportable long-term gain on the Montague Glass stock will be one-fifth of the full gain of $180,000, or $36,000.

Unlike gains, losses are not reported on the installment basis. The character of an installment gain is unaffected by installments. If a taxpayer had a long-term gain, all future receipts will be reported as long-term. If the original sale yielded a short-term gain, all future collections on the sale are considered short-term, even if they are received more than a year after the sale.

Installment sales treatment may be used only for reporting gain on the sale of real property, or for the "casual" sale of personal property (that is, an irregular sale, not in the course of the taxpayer's business).

The sales contract should provide for appropriate interest payments with future installments. If not, the IRS will consider part of each payment to be imputed interest, taxable as ordinary income, rather than capital gains.

New restrictions were recently added to the law to prevent installment sales to related parties who turn around and resell the assets. If a taxpayer sells marketable securities on the installment basis to a close relative, or to a related trust, who then resells, that taxpayer will be taxed at the time of the resale on any part of the gain scheduled to be received later in installments. For other assets, there is a period of two years during which a resale by a related party will trigger the tax on installments yet to be received. In such cases, then, a tax would be imposed on gain not yet received.

13
Credits, Estimates, and Withholding

Credits

Tax credits are better than just about anything—at least as long as we're talking about taxes. They beat long-term gains. They are more valuable than deductions or exemptions, for credits are, dollar for dollar, direct reductions of the tax otherwise due. That's why they appear near the bottom line of the tax return.

Certain credits, however, may require that they be repaid in the form of additional taxes if the assumptions or facts on which they were earned later turn out to be wrong.

Congress, traditionally wary of benefits that lose the Treasury every penny of a tax dollar, recently has, it appears, become less shy about adding to the list of credits.

The Investment Tax Credit. When fixed assets are purchased for business use, the investment may yield a tax credit. The credit is available to a taxpayer entitled to recover the cost, through depreciation or the ACRS, for qualified property. The property may be new or, to a limited extent, used. The credit is up to 10 percent of the cost of qualified property put in service anytme during the year, even the last day.

Under prior law, the amount of used property eligible was limited to $100,000. For 1981 through 1984, the limit has been raised to $125,000, and after 1984 to $150,000.

For property placed in service after February 18, 1981,

there's an "at-risk" limit to the investment credit. Under the new rule, the taxpayer's basis for purposes of calculating the credit is the amount actually "at risk" at the end of the year.

> EXAMPLE: Anna Graham invests in a big barge costing $1 million in 1982. She buys it for $200,000 cash and a nonrecourse note of $800,000. The barge has a useful life of twelve years. Anna's qualified investment credit basis is $200,000, not $1 million, and her credit in 1982 is $20,000. That's fully used to reduce her 1982 tax.

But if the nonrecourse borrowing is from certain unrelated lenders, like pension funds, insurance companies, or financial institutions, and the amount of the risk is at least 10 percent of the basis, the *full* basis may be used. (Thus, Anna Graham's credit could be $100,000 for the barge bought in 1982 if she didn't borrow from the owner of the barge.) Further, the "at risk" rule doesn't apply to most corporate investors.

Later changes in the amount actually "at risk" could cause a refiguring of the credit.

The calculation of the credit is based on the cost recovery period of property put in service after 1980. For property with a fifteen-, ten-, or five-year recovery period, the full 10 percent credit is allowed. For three-year recovery property, the credit is reduced to 6 percent.

For years after 1982, use of the investment credit will generally require that the cost basis of the qualifying property be adjusted. The basis, which is used in calculating cost recovery through ACRS and in determining gain or loss on eventual disposition, will have to be reduced by one half of the amount of the investment credit. Before 1983, no such reduction is required.

What if, after 1982, the full benefit of the investment credit can't be used? The investment credit, rather than the property's basis, may be reduced at the taxpayer's election. The regular investment credit may be cut back by two percentage points—from 10 percent to 8 percent or from 6 percent to 4 percent—and cost basis will be left intact. The election is on a property-by-property basis.

On early disposition, a markdown, against the amount to

be repaid, of 2 percent is allowed for each year the property was held. Thus, no repayment is required for five-, ten-, or fifteen-year property held at least five years. After 1982, special basis adjustments will be granted for property which suffered basis reductions because of credit.

Qualified property, called "section 38 property" by those who speak tax talk, is, generally

- Tangible personal property, such as railroad cars, machinery, and equipment, including new elevators and escalators
- Other tangible property consisting of inherently permanent structures used in manufacturing, production, or in furnishing transportation, communication, or other public utility services
- Pollution-control facilities acquired after 1976 and having a useful life of at least five years

"Safe-Harbor" Leasing. The 1981 law relaxed the rules on leasing so that corporations became able to transfer their investment tax credits to other corporations. Under the revised law, a company that couldn't profitably utilize its investment credits or depreciation deductions could "sell" them to a company that could. "Safe-Harbor" regulations, under which such transactions were not subject to question, were promptly written and all was well.

Consider how it worked with the following cautionary tale. Ford Motor Company needed nearly $1 billion worth of new equipment. But Ford, operating in a deficit approaching crimson, couldn't utilize the investment tax credits and cost-recovery deductions that went along with such a purchase. Profitable IBM could. So Ford, late in 1981 and not long after the new leasing provisions were enacted, let IBM buy its auto-making contrivances for $400 million cash and a note for $600 million, more or less. Ford actually kept title to the equipment. The IBM purchase was just for tax purposes. IBM's annual payments in satisfaction of its debt to Ford just happened to match the annual rental due them from Ford, so no money changed hands.

Ford got an annual tax deduction for the rental paid to IBM, while the interest income from IBM on its $600 million debt was less (because part of the offsetting payment represents principal repayment). Ford also got $400 million of new working capital. IBM didn't do badly either. It got a massive investment tax credit on the auto-maker's machinery, as well as significant ongoing deductions for depreciation and the interest paid to Ford.

Everybody liked the idea. (Even New York's Metropolitan Transit Authority was able to lease equipment from Metromedia in a similar deal specially designed for certain transportation equipment.) Uncle Sam said doggedly that this was fine.

But when the solons who passed the law realized that such transactions could cost the national fisc about $3 billion in the first full year and it seemed that virtually no alert corporation need ever pay an income tax, the urge to repeal or repair the law was strong indeed. We shall probably never see an enchanting transaction quite like the Ford-IBM bargain again. The Tax Equity and Fiscal Responsibility Act of 1982 contrived to stop the use of such safe-harbor leasing, partially until 1984 and completely thereafter.

Rehab Credit. Buildings don't normally meet the definition of qualified, section 38, property eligible for the investment tax credit. Certain rehabilitation expenditures for nonresidential buildings are, however, qualified. The 1981 rules revise the credit for property put in service after 1980.

A three-tier system is now operating that provides a credit of 15 percent for structures at least thirty years old, 20 percent for buildings at least forty years old, and 25 percent for certified historic structures.

After 1982, use of the rehab credit will, like use of the regular investment credit, require a reduction of cost basis by half the credit. The election to reduce the credit instead is not available for rehab property, though.

Foreign Tax Credit. To prevent double taxation of U.S. firms, citizens, or residents who pay taxes to foreign jurisdictions or to U.S. possessions, the law provides a credit in lieu of the deduction for such taxes, if the taxpayer so elects. Of course, the credit, as an offset against tax rather than against adjusted gross income, is normally to be preferred.

An individual's foreign tax credit can't be more than the actual amount of foreign tax paid or accrued, and it can't exceed what the U.S. tax would have been on the foreign income, even if the foreign tax is higher.

EXAMPLE: Upton O. Gude has taxable income of $18,300 in 1981. His U.S. income tax for the year comes out to $3,600, and his foreign tax is $2,000 on net income from foreign sources of $6,100. His credit calculation:

$$\frac{\$\ 6,100}{18,300} \times \$3,600 = \$1,200 \text{ maximum}$$
$$\text{foreign tax credit}$$

Upton will pay a net U.S. income tax of $2,400 ($3,600 less the foreign tax credit).

There are provisions for carry-back or carry-over of unused foreign tax credits (such as Upton O. Gude's $800). Form 1116 shows an individual's foreign tax credit.

Child- and Dependent-Care Credit. A tax credit is allowed for child- or dependent-care expenses necessary in order to allow a taxpayer to work. The care must be for a dependent under fifteen or a spouse or dependent incapable of caring for himself or herself.

The credit is a full 30 percent of qualified expenditures for taxpayers with household incomes no higher than $10,000. The credit is lowered 1 percent for each $2,000 of income over $10,000. Taxpayers with income of $20,000, for example, are entitled to a credit of 25 percent of qualified child-care expenses. Those with income over $28,000 are entitled to a 20 percent credit. The maximum expenditures to which the credit applies after 1981 are increased to $2,400 per dependent for the first two dependents.

If a taxpayer is married, a joint return must be filed in order to claim the credit. Expenses paid to a dependent don't qualify, but if the taxpayer isn't entitled to a dependency exemption for a parent, for example, that parent may care for a grandchild for pay without impairing the credit.

Form 2441 is the one to use for the child-care credit.

Other Credits. The list of credits is long. For instance:

- *Residential Energy Credit.* This credit is for investment in energy-saving property at the taxpayer's principal residence (even if it's rented) for "energy-saving components" (weather stripping, storm windows, or the like). The credit is limited to 15 percent of the first $2,000 spent. There's also a 40 percent credit for the first $10,000 invested in "renewable source property" (like solar panels or windmills).

- *Political Contribution Credit.* This credit is for individuals who contribute to (a) a candidate for federal, state, or local office in a primary, general, or special election; (b) an organization set up solely to support one or more such candidates; or (c) a national party. The credit, separate from the campaign fund check-off, is allowed for one-half the amount contributed and is limited to $50 for a single taxpayer and $100 on a joint return. By the way, though there ought to be *some* proof of the political contribution, it is not necessary to specify, in the tax return, the names of candidates or parties. That's the American way. This credit has nothing to do with the $1 or $2 check-off for the Presidential Election Campaign Fund.
- *Credit for the Elderly.* The unfortunate nomenclature has no relation to senescence; it's available to taxpayers sixty-five or older who live on limited incomes. As income increases, the maximum credit ($562.50 for joint-return filers) is reduced, so that if a married couple, both over sixty-five, have gross income of $17,500 or more, exclusive of Social Security, no credit is available.
- *Targeted Jobs, Work Incentive, Earned Income, and Other Credits.* These are also available in special cases. The first is for those who hire members of certain disadvantaged groups, the second is for those who employ participants in certain federal programs, and the third is available to married couples who have dependent children and who have earned income below $10,000. Credit is also available for federal tax on special fuel oils.

Estimates

Our tax system is supposed to work on a general pay-as-you-go system. That's the rationale of wage withholding and withholding on dividends and interest, but obviously not all taxable income is subject to withholding. Individuals as well as corporations may be required, therefore, to make payments of estimated tax. Self-employed taxpayers know this well.

Individual taxpayers are required to make quarterly estimated tax payments, using Form 1040ES, if their tax liability is expected to exceed any taxes withheld, or otherwise credited by a given amount. After 1982, the filing of declarations of estimated tax will not be required—but the payment of estimated tax, be assured, may still be obligatory. It's just the form alone that isn't necessary. (The IRS is planning to use banks to receive estimated tax payments, rather than receiving them directly.) Penalties are assessed against those who underestimate. In 1981, the law was revised to raise, in stages, the threshold above which estimated payments are required, as follows:

1981	$100
1982	$200
1983	$300
1984	$400
1985 and thereafter	$500

An individual who has a tax liability, beyond withholding, that does not exceed the threshold amount isn't required to pay an estimated tax, and no penalty will apply for underestimation.

There are other shields against the penalty imposed for underestimation. There's no penalty for failure to file an estimate—just for failure to pay enough. No penalty applies if total estimates and taxes withheld equal either

- the tax shown on the previous year's return;
- a tax calculated on the prior year's facts, using the current year's rates;
- 80 percent (66⅔ percent for farmers and fishermen) of the actual tax, calculated on a quarterly basis; or
- 90 percent of the actual tax, calculated on a quarterly basis, which is determined on the basis of actual taxable income as of the ending of each quarter.

Estimated payments, if necessary, are normally due on April 15, June 15, and September 15 of the affected year, and the following January 15. If the final tax return is filed before January 15, the last installment is unnecessary.

Withholding

As 1943 began, *Time* magazine named Joseph Stalin "Man of the Year," and three weeks later Henry Morganthau, Jr., secretary of the treasury, was its cover boy. The sale of war bonds was insufficient to finance a staggering burden of wartime federal expenses. Early in 1943, over a presidential veto, Congress passed the first wage withholding program since 1913. The American taxpayer, depicted by cartoonists in his ample barrel, began paying as he earned. The lag in tax collections, which could run over a year, was eliminated, and a sea change overtook the taxpayer that is still with him and will be for a long time to come.

Employers are required to withhold taxes on wages, which implies that the wages are paid to persons who have the status of "employees." It's natural, therefore, for workers to claim that they are not employees, but free and independent contractors instead and not subject to wage withholding. Real estate agents and direct sellers are classified as independent contractors under the tax law passed in 1982. For our purposes, it's enough to know that an employee, no matter how designated, is one who performs services under the discretion and control of someone else. The latitude permitted the employee may be wide indeed, but if the boss has the legal right to control the result of the services and the methodology, there's an employer-employee relationship.

Few wages are exempt. Reimbursements of expenses aren't wages, and payment for agricultural labor or for a clergyman's labor in the vineyards of the Lord is exempt. Domestic services in a private home are not subject to withholding. But even if a category of wages is exempt from wage withholding, Social Security taxes may still have to be withheld if the wages are high enough.

Deferred compensation, after 1982, is subject to withholding, but the recipient may notify the payer that he or she doesn't want withholding to apply.

The government now is obliged to provide a mechanism for upward or downward adjustment of wage withholding to make it more closely correspond with the expected tax liability. That may sound fine, but the law now also provides new weapons in the IRS campaign against schemes to avoid withholding. For some time it has had the capability of comparing, by computer, the number of exemptions claimed on the return with the number reported to the employer so that wage withholding can be reduced. Now the civil penalty for such activity, if willful, has been increased to $500 and the civil penalty (in addition to a possible one-year sojourn in the calaboose) raised to $1,000.

You may ask an employer to increase taxes withheld from wages so that you need not file estimates and still avoid penalties for underpayments.

And, on the other hand, if your employer withholds more taxes from your wages than necessary to meet your tax obligation, you can do something more effective than threaten the payroll clerk. Allowances are available for personal and dependency exemptions, of course. In addition, other special allowances are provided for certain known reductions in the current year's tax. A nonworking spouse or alimony payments, various tax credits, business expenses, and excess itemized deductions, all may serve to reduce wages withholding. It's all done by filing Form W-4 with the employer, who is obliged to withhold at the highest rates without it. A timely W-4 can even be used each year to claim exemption from withholding if the worker had no tax liability the year before and expects none for the current year.

If more than fourteen allowances, worth $1,000 each, are claimed by a worker making more than $200 a week, the boss is required to forward the W-4 to the IRS for a look-see.

After June 30, 1983, withholding at the flat rate of 10 percent applies to payments of dividends and interest. (See Chapter 2.)

Another Credit Reminder

In a real sense, estimated tax payments and wage withholdings are tax credits, as are amounts withheld on dividends or interest. There's another that may be overlooked.

For an employee, half of the Social Security payments on his or her account are the obligation of the employer. The other half is withheld from the wages of the employee until the maximum annual contribution is made. It sometimes happens that during the year an employee has more than one employer, each of whom starts Social Security withholding from the worker all over again. They are required to do that. Therefore, excess withholding for Social Security may occur. This excess withholding is available to the worker as a tax credit. Simply aggregate the amounts shown on all W-2 forms and subtract the maximum for the year to arrive at the proper credit.

This credit may be available only if there are two or more employers. If a single employer withholds too much, the employer, not the IRS, should reimburse the aggrieved worker.

PART · IV

TAX CREATURES

14
Partnerships

Individuals are not the only ones subject to the tax law. Some beings, such as corporations, are required to pay taxes like more conventional, human creatures. Others, such as partnerships, may be obliged merely to file annual tax returns.

Former tax law, in the Internal Revenue Code of 1939, dealt with the entire subject of partnerships in nine sections. When the Code was completely overhauled in 1954, the Ways and Means Committee said that the old treatment of partners and partnerships was "among the most confused in the entire income tax field." Now there are three times as many Code sections dealing specifically with partnerships; the appropriate multiplier for the confusion is unknown.

It's certainly not simple. Gone are the days when partnerships were formed by two cowpokes on horseback grasping each other's leathery hand and intoning the sacred word "pardner." Now partnerships may be vast enterprises, in some cases with a thousand partners who have never met one another. And yet, there still remain the small groups of entrepreneurial partnerships.

What Is a Partnership and Who Is a Partner?

A partnership under the Uniform Partnership Act, which applies virtually nationwide, is defined as "an association of two or more persons to carry on as co-owners a business for profit." The IRS, for its purposes, expands the definition to include joint ventures, pools, syndicates, groups, and certain other unincorporated assemblages organized for business.

A profit making and sharing motive is necessary, but there are no rules that require that each partner contribute capital or be responsible for partnership debts.

Corporations pay taxes, but partnerships merely report income or losses of its members, so the IRS likes to be certain that an organization is really a partnership, rather than "an association taxable as a corporation." There are several litmus tests provided by the regulations to detect the presence of a corporation, and the IRS will treat a business involving more than one person as a corporation for tax purposes if it has a majority of these important characteristics:

- Continuity of life of the enterprise
- Centralized management
- Free transferability of interests in the business
- Limited personal liability of the owners

Other attributes of a corporation are associates and the objective of carrying on a business and dividing the profits, but those attributes are common to partnerships as well. If a business organization has one or two of the four main attributes, it will be viewed as a partnership. More, and it will be taxed as a corporation.

A partner may be defined, simply, as a member of an organization recognized as a partnership. A partner becomes one because of the contribution of capital or services to the partnership. Many former partners will agree with the IRS that a partner doesn't have to be human. A corporation, trust, estate, or even another partnership may qualify.

Types of Partnerships

General Partnerships. One of the two distinctive classes of partnerships is the general partnership, which embraces a family partnership, a professional enterprise, or an everyday business venture.

Family partnerships may be organized for business or for

the splitting of income. The notion behind income splitting, of course, is to reduce the high marginal tax bracket of one member of the family by spreading the income among several family members.

> EXAMPLE: Mr. Domby, a merchant, has taxable income of $60,000 from the business in 1982, and his tax is $21,318. He files as a single taxpayer in the 50 percent marginal tax bracket. If Mr. Domby made his son Paul a partner and paid him $25,000 in 1982 while he took home the other $35,000, Paul would have been in the 35 percent marginal bracket, and Mr. Domby would have been in the 44 percent marginal bracket. Their combined tax would have been $14,570. Net saving: $6,748.

That may sound nifty, but be assured that the IRS subjects such partnerships to close scrutiny. If a person is a partner in an enterprise in which his or her capital investment accounts for much of the earnings, he or she will be recognized as a partner. The partnership interest need not be purchased if there is a real gift of the capital ownership interest to the partner. But if capital *isn't* a material income-producing factor, the recipient of a gift of a partnership interest had better contribute ongoing and worthwhile services to the enterprise. The IRS, therefore, is especially dubious about partnership interests owned by minor children.

Partnerships of those in learned professions, such as doctors and lawyers, are traditional. Now, if professionals choose, they may also practice together in corporate form, which offers attractions in the form of retirement and other benefits. Though the professional services are the same sort provided by their brethren still operating as partnerships, professional corporations are taxed differently.

Limited Partnerships. A limited partnership is a unique creature, sometimes resembling a corporation, but still not taxed as one. A limited partnership, by statute, has one or more *general partners* with virtually unbounded liability. It also has one or more *limited partners* who have fixed frontiers to their liability. Often the details of the arrangement must be published upon the formation of the limited partnership. Proportionately more cash is usually invested by limited partners, while the general partners contribute more effort.

Limited partners have no right to run the partnership. That is the job of the general partners. Limited partners are silent. Their money is required, not their talent or time. If they attempt to exercise control of the day-to-day affairs of the enterprise, they may be held to be general partners and lose the valuable shield of limited liability.

Limited partners are normally liable for debts of the partnership only to the extent of their interest, or capital, in the business. Normally, when the partnership winds up and the creditors are satisfied, the limited partners are entitled, according to agreement, to share in the remaining capital and profits before the general partners.

Because tax characteristics, notably deductions, are passed through to investors, limited partnerships are favored configurations for tax shelters. The IRS looks closely at such partnerships to see if they can be treated instead as associations taxable as corporations. (There are guidelines the IRS applies, if anyone asks for a ruling on the matter, regarding the general partner. A corporate general partner should meet math tests regarding its net worth, for example.)

The Service is fond of auditing the returns of investor-limited partners, especially those in partnerships reporting net losses of $25,000 or more during a tax year. Even if such a limited partnership is absolutely legitimate, the Service may require the partners to waive, or extend, the period of time during which an additional assessment of tax may be made. (Without the agreement to extend, instant and larger assessment follows.) It's possible to restrict the length and extent of the waiver while the audit progresses. The government wants to make the same kind of proposed tax adjustment for all members of a tax shelter limited partnership, and that takes time. Audits now are to be conducted on the partnership level rather than directly with the partners separately. The general partner must exert significant effort on behalf of the investor-limited partners during that time.

Partnership Income and Deductions, Contributions, and Distributions

No matter how much, or how little, a partnership earns, it does not pay federal income taxes. Tax folk call it a "conduit." That means it passes income and deductions through without altering the tax character of such income and deductions. The partnership simply reports information on Form 1065 each year, so the partners can be taxed on, or deduct, their distributive shares of the partnership's annual income or loss.

As a conduit, a partnership doesn't get any personal exemptions, charitable contribution deductions, capital loss carry-overs, or long-term capital gains deductions. They go to the partners, reported on Schedule K-1, on a detailed, unaggregated basis. Each item of partnership income or deduction is added to similar items on each partner's personal income tax return.

A partner's cost basis, or current investment, in the firm is increased by the amount of income not actually distributed to him or her, but upon which he or she is taxed under the conduit theory. Similarly, basis is reduced when the same income is paid out of the partnership in a later year when the conduit rule doesn't require tax.

Losses are deductible by partners only to the extent of their basis, or investment, at the end of the year. Further, as a restriction on certain tax shelters, losses may be limited to amounts actually "at risk." In any event, once basis hits zero, no further loss deductions are available. If losses exceed basis, they may be carried over to a time when basis again rises sufficiently to cover the losses. Thus, if an excess loss is available to be used, it might be worthwhile to invest a little more in the partnership, to lend money to it, or to have it borrow enough to raise the partner's basis (because the partner is personally liable on the debt).

Guaranteed Payments. It is sometimes important to agree that a partner will be guaranteed a fixed draw from the partnership, whether it thrives or languishes. Such guaranteed payments are ordinary income to the partner, who is not regarded as any different from anyone else paid by the partnership, for purposes of partnership accounting. Nevertheless, there is no withholding for taxes, Social Security, or the like on guaranteed payments.

Contributions. A partnership contribution has no charitable connotation. Rather, it means the money or property a partner contributed to acquire an interest in the partnership. There is no tax effect when such a contribution is made, to either a new partnership or an old one.

Since there is no tax event on the contribution of property, a partner's basis in the enterprise is taken from the adjusted cost basis of any property contributed to the firm.

> EXAMPLE: Smyth and Dail decide to form a medical partnership. Smyth contributed $30,000 in cash, medical supplies with an adjusted cost basis of $6,000, and waiting-room furniture with an adjusted cost basis of $4,000. Dail contributes $35,000 in cash and equipment with an adjusted cost basis of $5,000. The partnership starts with a capitalization of $80,000, and each partner's cost basis in it is $40,000. Good luck, boys!

If mortgaged property is contributed, an adjustment is made for any part of the mortgage debt assumed by other parties.

Distributions. The distribution of property or money does not necessarily cause a tax. It's the distributive partnership income that's taxed, whether or not it's actually distributed.

When income is distributed to partners as it is earned, there is no adjustment to partners' bases necessary. A partner's basis increases to the extent that his or her distributive share of current income isn't received.

When a distribution exceeds a partner's basis in the partnership, there's a recognized capital gain to the extent of the excess. It's as if the partner sold some of his or her interest in the business.

When a partnership goes out of business and makes a final distribution in liquidation that is less than a partner's basis, there's a recognized capital loss, as if a sale had been made.

Suppose there's a distribution during a partnership's tax year that is disproportionate to a partner's interest? That's normally considered a taxable event, yielding a capital gain to the recipient partner. (A loss is recognized only on liquidation of the partnership.) A distribution may be disproportionate because it's too much in one category (for example, ordinary income) and too little in another (say, capital assets). The arithmetic starts to get a bit thick in such cases, because an adjustment for the partnership's basis is necessary.

EXAMPLE: Burke and Hare each have a current $10,000 basis in their partnership. This year, Burke takes a distribution of $4,000 in cash and $11,000 in capital assets (which have a cost basis, for the partnership, of $5,000). Burke's distribution is $15,000. Hare simply takes $15,000 in cash. Thus, there's a disproportionate distribution. Burke has no gain or loss yet, while Hare has a taxable capital gain of $5,000. The math:

	Burke	Hare
Cash distributed	$ 4,000	$15,000
Property, at partnership basis, distributed	5,000	0
Total distribution	9,000	15,000
Less: Partner's basis	10,000	10,000
Capital gain	$ 0	$ 5,000

Burke has postponed his capital gain, not avoided it. You'll recall he took property that has a built-in gain, on which he will be subject to tax when he sells it.

Not all distributions or transfers of partnership property involve capital assets. When unrealized receivables, appreciated inventory items, or recaptures of deductions are involved, the normal result is ordinary income (or loss) to someone, since such distributions are essentially the passing out of ordinary income that was retained in one form or another in the partnership. Here, of course, the accounting is complex indeed.

Dealing with Partnership Interests

Partner's Transactions. Like guaranteed payments, sales or loans between a partner and a partnership are considered, for tax purposes, to be between unrelated parties. Therefore, when a partner sells to his or her partnership, there's no escaping the tax on the grounds that there was really a transaction, at least proportionately, with oneself. And when a partnership sells to its partner, that partner can't exclude the proportionate gain realized by the partnership, on the grounds that it should be attributed to a severable interest in the property.

Generally, when dealing with his or her partnership, a partner must assume two roles. But if the partner has more than a 50 percent interest in the firm's capital or profits, losses will not be allowed on a sale between a partner and the partnership. Moreover, if the partner has more than an 80 percent interest, capital gain treatment will be unavailable for certain transfers between the partner and the partnership. Thus, if it were not for this rule, such a controlling partner might be tempted to sell depreciable assets to the partnership, which could step up partnership depreciation or cost recovery while personally posting a capital gain.

Disposing of Partnership Interests. An interest in a partnership qualifies as a capital asset, yielding capital gain or loss on sale or exchange. But some of the interest may represent ordinary income property. To the extent that the taxable disposition of a partnership interest transfers unrealized receivables or substantially appreciated inventory, there will be ordinary, rather than capital, gains.

Unrealized receivables are really amounts due from customers or clients for goods or services. Inclusion as ordinary income applies only to sales or dispositions of interests in partnerships on the cash-basis accounting system. Accrual-basis partnerships will have already accounted for receivables.

Inventory items, for purposes of inclusion as ordinary income, are considered "substantially appreciated" under mechanical tests. They must have a fair market value greater than 120 percent of basis and greater than 10 percent of the value of all noncash partnership property.

The Leaving of a Partner. For tax purposes (which may not always conform to local law), upon the death of a partner a partnership's year may not close until the normal year-end if the deceased partner's interest is not sold or liquidated. Often, though, the terms of the partnership agreement provide that the death of a partner is to be considered as a sale or exchange of his or her interest. In that case, for the deceased partner only, the tax year for the partnership, like everything else mundane, ends with death. Partnership agreements ought to, and generally do, provide machinery for paying for a deceased partner's interest by the surviving partners. Insurance can be helpful.

When a partner retires, his or her interest may be disposed of in two ways. The interest may be sold to the partnership itself or, alternatively, to the remaining or new partners. There are important tax differences, which explain the need for understandings in partnership agreements in the form of buy-sell arrangements.

- *A sale to the partnership* gives the tax advantage to the partnership rather than the retiring partner. The retiring partner's distributions are treated like guaranteed payments. They are subject to ordinary tax rates to the extent they exceed basis, and the remaining partners' taxable income, through reduced partnership income, will be reduced.
- *A sale to partners or others* places the tax advantage in the hands of the retiring partner. The partnership itself doesn't get a deduction for payments it's not obliged to make. The departing partner gets capital gains (except for unrealized receivables or substantially appreciated inventory, of course) on payments received above his or her basis in the partnership.

Termination of a Partnership. The IRS considers a partnership ended if it stops doing business completely or if, within a period of a year, half or more of its capital and profit interest changes hands by sale or exchange. A change of ownership by gift or inheritance is not subject to this test.

A sale or exchange that terminates the partnership may be to new partners or to existing partners. If some partners remain, they are considered to have contributed their liquidating distributions to a new partnership.

When partnerships merge, the fruit of the merger is treated as a continuance of one partnership and the termination of the other, and the continuing firm's old tax year is utilized. The surviving firm is normally the one whose old members have most of the interest in the new one.

Sometimes partnerships divide or clone themselves. In such cases of division, the firm with partners who had the most interest in the old one is the continuing partnership. If no new partnership has partners who owned more than half of the progenitor, then the old partnerships are declared dead for tax purposes.

15
Corporations

A corporation is legally a person—not human, we all agree, but a "creature of statute." It is given life not by a wild-eyed scientist, but by state law. Whether it's a small family affair or a transnational megaconglomerate, the same fundamental rules of federal taxation apply to each corporation. A corporation is a distinct person, required like the rest of us to file returns and pay taxes (unless it can take advantage of certain special rules). Corporate earnings are, therefore, said to be taxed twice—once when the corporation pays its tax and again when the shareholders receive dividends.

Buoyant hope attends the birth of a corporation. Mergers, offspring, redemptions, and reorganizations are part of their lives, and eventually corporations pass away. As with people, there are passages that mark corporate existence, and each step may have special tax significance.

Corporate taxation is a complex matter. Many professional careers on both sides of the tax return are devoted to the subject. Here we will simply survey the terrrain.

Corporate Birth

Aside from state law, all corporations have, according to the regulations, six characteristics. They have (1) associates, (2) an objective of carrying on a business and dividing the profits, (3) continuity of corporate life beyond that of the proprietor-

131

owners, (4) centralization of management, (5) free transferability of interests in the business, and (6) limited liability. As we learned in the previous chapter, if three out of the last four of these attributes are present, the Service will usually recognize a corporation. But if the corporation is established merely to avoid taxes, for example, even the presence of all the corporate earmarks will not make the tax collector agree to its existence for tax purposes.

Normally, gain or loss is not recognized on corporate formation if the incorporators transfer property to the new corporation solely in exchange for its stock or securities. Those who make the exchange must together own at least 80 percent of the new corporation's stock immediately afterward, so that they are in control. The rules regarding such a nonrecognized transfer are a bit complex, but commonly applied.

Nonrecognition is not based on an election. It is automatic, so a purported "sale" of assets to a new corporation, in an attempt to "step up" the basis of the assets, will be looked upon unhappily by the Service and not recognized if the seller, together with others, is in control.

The cost basis of the assets used to establish a corporation without tax effect is the same in the hands of the corporation as it was in the hands of the incorporator (with an increase for any gain recognized). The cost basis of the corporate stock interest in the hands of the new owner is the same as that of the assets transferred.

Thin Incorporation. As with fashion mannequins and most of the up-scale set, so it is with corporations. Thin is beautiful.

Upon incorporation, a part of the initial capitalization of a business is designated as stock, or equity, and another part is represented by loans to the business. Such a loan may be made "outside," by a bank, for example, or "inside," by shareholders. The higher the ratio of debt to equity, the thinner the corporation.

The advantages are obvious. Debt, of course, means interest payments, which are deductible for the payer corporation. The same amounts, paid as dividends, are not deductible. Repayment of the principal of a loan is tax-free to the lender. On liquidation, creditors stand in preferred positions.

The use of thin capitalization is apparently Paleozoic and

well known to tax practitioners and the IRS. Recently, regulations have been proposed to provide guidelines for the acceptability to the IRS of thin incorporation. Too much debt may be treated as preferred stock. There are, however, several safe harbors based on various ratio tests. The proposals are complex, certainly, but once within the safe harbors, thin incorporation may still be of real advantage and a consideration not to be ignored when explaining the new business enterprise to the lawyer.

"1244 Stock." Another useful provision for a small business corporation should not be overlooked. Under section 1244—sorry to have to mention a Code section, but it is known as "Section 1244 Stock"—a *loss* on the eventual sale, exchange, or worthlessness of such qualified stock is considered an ordinary loss to the hapless original shareholder. But *gain* on the sale or exchange of the same shares would result in capital gain to the same original shareholder.

The unique tax insurance is not available to those who are not original shareholders, and the amount of ordinary loss allowed annually on 1244 stock issued after November 6, 1978, is $50,000 for single filers and $100,000 for joint returns. (The limits for 1244 stock issued before November 7, 1978, are half the current limits.) Losses in excess of the limitations are treated as capital losses, as usual.

The 1244 stock can't be convertible. It must be common stock issued initially by a small business corporation. A small business corporation, you may be relieved to learn, is one capitalized at no more than $1 million.

There are some tests regarding the gross income of a losing corporation with section 1244 stock, but the whole scheme isn't very complicated and is well worth considering when incorporating.

Controlled Corporations. The tax collector is quite interested in transactions between corporations and those who control them because, alas, some dealings are motivated by little more than tax considerations.

On the one hand, a taxpayer may argue that his or her corporate alter ego really shouldn't be taxed—that, for example, it's used merely to hold title to the owner's property. If it looks like a corporation, it's probably going to be taxed independently.

On the other hand (the one lawyers always seem to favor), a series of corporations may be established simply so that corporate income can be spread among several lower tax brackets. In that case, the IRS will aggregate the income and treat the several corporations as one business. The Code empowers the IRS to reallocate income, deductions, and credits until it looks right to them.

Shareholders may certainly deal with their corporations, but here, too, the tax man has the authority to reallocate more to his liking. Deductions claimed by a corporation may not be allowed if they represent no more than the transfer of income to shareholders. This may affect what, on audit, turns out to be unusually high rent, salary, or interest paid to a controlling shareholder. Occasionally, corporate officer-shareholders will agree with their corporate employers to refund amounts determined on audit to be excessive. Such agreements should long precede audits, if they are to be effective.

Corporate Tax Life

The basic tax return, on which a U.S. corporation reports its worldwide income, is Form 1120. The organization follows the scheme of the personal Form 1040. Gross income is first disclosed. Then there are ordinary deductions and special corporate deductions. Taxable income is shown next, against which the corporate rates are applied. Then credits and add-backs are entered, and the bottom line appears.

Income and Deductions. All corporate income not specifically exempted (such as municipal bond interest) is reportable. Gross income includes receipts from sales or services, rents or royalties, interest, or any other income. Capital gains are included, subject to special rules. Dividends received by corporations from other corporations bear special tax deductions.

Net capital gains are taxable as ordinary income, and there is no 60 percent deduction applicable to a corporate long-term gain. Instead, there is a special 28 percent alternative capital gains tax if that produces a lower tax.

Net capital losses are not simply deductible, but must be carried backward or forward and applied against gains as if they were short-term.

Deductions related to carrying on corporate business must,

of course, be ordinary and necessary, as all business expenses must be. The regular deductions include

- employee compensation, such as salaries, wages, bonuses, and normal fringe benefits;
- retirement plans, such as contributions to pension and profit-sharing trusts;
- repairs to keep up corporate assets;
- bad debts, which are business bad debts by definition;
- rents allocable to the current year;
- taxes (not including federal income taxes, of course);
- cost recovery, as well as depletion and depreciation (important as corporate deductions);
- interest, including a large allowance for interest expended in corporate take-overs;
- advertising, to the extent it's not political;
- contributions to charities, up to 10 percent of taxable income (5 percent for years before 1982);
- net operating losses for the year, which may reduce prior or subsequent years' taxes; and
- other ordinary deductions, such as casualty or embezzlement losses, that, incurred in the pursuit of profit, may be claimed by corporations as well as individuals.

There are certain deductions that may be claimed only by corporate taxpayers. For example, a part of organization expenses may be claimed each year during a period of at least sixty months from the inception of the business.

The major special deduction available to corporations relates to dividends received. Basically, corporate taxpayers may deduct 85 percent of the dividend received from qualifying domestic corporations.

EXAMPLE: If Billy Rubin/Sarah Tonin Associates, Inc., P.A., a professional corporation, receives $1,000 in dividends from Coagulated Oil Co., only $150 is taxable. The other $850 is deducted. If Billy and Sarah had received the same $1,000 as personal dividend income, the special corporate deduction would not have been available; it's only for corporations.

Even better than that is the ability to deduct the full amount of dividends received. That's possible in two cases. The first is for small business investment companies, which are specially regulated. The other is for a constituent corporation in an affiliated group that may deduct all of the dividends received from another corporation in the group. Thus, if Coagulated Oil Co. pays a $1,000 dividend to its parent, Cosmological Holdings, Ltd., with which it files a consolidated return, Cosmological will pay no tax at all on the dividend.

Dividends paid, of course, normally yield no deduction to the paying corporation (though there are certain exceptions for a few public utility dividends on preferred stock issued before October 1, 1942).

Tax Rates. Corporations are subject to regular tax brackets graduated in five income increments. Capital gains may be taxed at special alternative rates. In addition to the regular tax, corporations may be liable for minimum taxes on preference income or penalty taxes on undistributed accumulated earnings or personal holding company income.

The highest marginal basic tax rate is 46 percent, but the law was recently changed to reduce, in two steps, the lower brackets. The rate schedule:

REGULAR CORPORATE TAX RATES			
Taxable Income	Before 1982	1982	After 1982
Up to $25,000	17%	16%	15%
$25,000 to $50,000	20%	19%	18%
$50,000 to $75,000	30%	30%	30%
$75,000 to $100,000	40%	40%	40%
Over $100,000	46%	46%	46%

Thus, if a corporation earned $100,000 in 1981, its tax bill was $26,750. If it earned another $100,000 in 1983, the tax would be $25,750 because of the drop in the first two brackets.

The additional accumulated earnings tax is designed to prevent the utilization of a corporate piggy bank in which earnings and profits of controlled corporations are sequestered while shareholders avoid taxation on unpaid dividends. Except for personal holding companies (which may be subject to other tax retribution) and tax-exempt organizations, all corporations are subject to the rules regarding accumulated earnings. The penalty tax, which quickly reaches 38½ percent, is imposed on unneeded undistributed earnings that exceed $250,000 for most corporations after 1981. For corporations dealing in personal services, like architectural, medical, legal, or performing arts, the ceiling is still $150,000, as it was for all corporations before 1982. Despite the threshold amounts, if it can be shown that accumulations are necessary for the reasonable needs of the business, the tax will not apply. Because the penalty applies only to unreasonable accumulations—a factual determination—there are, of course, heavy negotiations and extensive litigation regarding the accumulated earnings tax.

Credits. Corporations, like others, may claim credits against the tax reckoning. The new law provides a freshly minted goody for research and development.

Expenses for research and development ("R&D," in tax talk) may be amortized and deducted over a few years or deducted currently. The law now permits, in addition, a credit of 25 percent for qualified R&D costs that exceed normal expenses. The normal R&D expenses are found by calculating "base period expenses." The credit is available for wages paid in conducting research and for 65 percent of amounts paid for contract research services. Qualifying R&D expenses after June 30, 1981, and before January 1, 1986, are eligible.

The investment tax credit, available to all kinds of taxpayers, is often used by corporations, and the foreign tax credit is certainly important to multinational corporate taxpayers. In addition, there are credits for transfers of employer securities to qualified employee stock ownership plans (or ESOPs), targeted-jobs credits, credits for investment in energy property, and others.

Reorganizations

Corporations take part in reorganizations all the time. It doesn't necessarily signify financial trouble. A "reorg" may be a merger or a divestment, an acquisition or a recapitalization. If it's done just right, it can be a tax-free reorg, and substantial amounts of taxes may be deferred for the participating corporations or their shareholders.

Substantial sums of money may be involved, and this is an area that provides lots of fun and profit for crowds of tax lawyers in three-piece suits. They have to ensure, for example, that there is an evident business purpose to their reorgs, that the prior shareholders continue to have continuity of interest and control in the resulting entity, that the proper parties take the necessary steps, and that a formal plan is followed.

After all this, the IRS may act as dance master, inspecting all the components of the reorganization to see if it is what is termed a "step transaction." That can be defined as a transaction that will fail if a step is omitted, and therefore is worth watching. While the IRS doesn't like step transactions, it may decide, on the other hand, that if each step *isn't* followed exactly according to instructions, the reorganization will not be tax-free. See your tax lawyer for dance lessons; this gets very complicated.

In a reorganization, if cash or other taxable assets are paid even if the reorganization otherwise qualifies as tax-free, that's called "boot," and boot is always taxable. Boot may be ordinary income or a capital gain, depending on the character of the property that was exchanged for it in the course of the reorganization.

There are seven statutory kinds of tax-free reorgs, each one more complex than the other. Additionally, there are tax-free corporate separations, described as spin-offs, split-ups, or split-offs.

It gets intricate and a bit mucilaginous, but the tax rewards of properly constructed corporate reorganizations can be substantial. There's the possibility of carrying over from the old corporations their valuable corporate tax attributes, such as net operating losses, foreign tax credits, capital losses, and a myriad of other tax accounts for use by the reorganized taxpayers. That's in addition to nonrecognition of the event for purposes of current taxes. Just leave it up to the pros.

Corporate Liquidation

Though corporations may be entitled, theoretically, to perpetual life, sooner or later last rites must be performed for each of them. When corporations are liquidated, the liquidating distributions are considered payment for the stockholders' interest. A liquidation may be complete, or it may be partial if it is encompassed within a plan of corporate contraction or a larger scheme of complete liquidation. In either case, as full or partial payment for a shareholder's ownership, a liquidating dividend or distribution is normally a capital transaction.

So far, this is familiar. Liquidations become more complicated, though, because under simple tax theory there may be double taxation when a corporation expires. The shareholders are taxable on the liquidating distributions, and the corporation itself is taxable before that on the sale of its assets. Naturally, there are ways to eschew such double taxation and, naturally, most liquidations are arranged to do that.

One-Month Liquidations. Under this method, the corporation need not sell assets. Full distribution in redemption of all corporate stock must be accomplished within one calendar month. Shareholders must elect to utilize this plan. If enough of them do, the rules allow them to receive certain property in liquidation without immediate tax recognition. Gain on such property is postponed for the shareholders until they sell the assets.

To prevent ordinary income from being taxed as capital gain later, certain rules are applied to distributions under the one-month liquidation method. For noncorporate shareholders, those liquidating dividends that represent undistributed earnings and profits are considered normal dividends. The distribution above that amount that represents the worth of stock or securities acquired by the company since 1953 (when this provision entered the law) is recognized as capital gain on receipt. All other property distributed, however, is subject to deferral of tax, with an adjustment in the basis of the redeemed shares. (The basis of such property is that of the redeemed stock, increased by the ordinary income recognized, the capital gain recognized, and liabilities assumed, and decreased by any cash received.)

Because of these complicated rules, the one-month liquidation is suitable only for certain kinds of corporations, notably those that are not holding companies.

Twelve-Month Liquidations. This technique, which requires a complete liquidation within twelve calendar months, will eliminate tax at the corporate level rather than the shareholder level. During the year, the corporation must distribute all of its assets, except for those needed to meet claims, to its shareholders. Certain corporations, like "collapsible" corporations, may not use this method, and cerain assets, like inventory, do not come within the rule.

During the twelve-month period, the corporation must dispose of its assets and liquidate, and only the shareholders will individually recognize gain or loss, based on the difference between the value of the assets received and the cost bases for their shares.

Reincorporation. Since these arrangements are possible, shareholders sometimes think of liquidating a corporation and reincorporating their business. It would be simple then to produce capital gains out of what might otherwise be ordinary dividend income and to write up the basis of the investment in the company. It probably won't work. The Service looks upon liquidation-reincorporation of the same enterprise as bad business. It may consider the transaction as a reorganization that doesn't technically rise to the status of tax freedom. The amounts distributed to shareholders could then be treated as dividend income.

Special Corporate Breeds

So far as Uncle Sam is concerned, some kinds of corporations are naughty and some others are nice. The naughty ones are punished if they don't behave properly, and the nice ones may receive some agreeable tax cookies. Let's name names. The wayward corporate types include collapsible corporations and personal holding companies. Those favored include Subchapter S corporations, DISCs, and certain qualified investment companies.

Collapsible Corporations. If a corporation is "formed or availed of" primarily to hold assets that will increase in value, "with a view" to disposition of the corporate stock before the corporation has recognized a major part of its income, it may be considered a collapsible corporation. That's bad, because if the shareholders' gain on liquidation is attributable to assets that would have been treated as ordinary income to the corporation, their gain will be ordinary, not capital. There's a list of ordinary income type property that, if appreciated sufficiently, will be dangerous if the business is liquidated within three years after the acquisition. If it were not for constraints against collapsible corporations, it would be easy to form a corporation to earn lots of ordinary income quickly (as, for example, the production of a movie or the construction of a residential subdivision), and liquidate promptly at capital gains rates.

But the collapsible corporation rules work mechanically. The rules are—you guessed it—very complex, and there are tricky escape hatches. The longest single sentence in the Code (and probably the longest anywhere since the heyday of James Joyce) is found in an important subsection providing relief from the provision. It is over 450 words long. And those 450 aren't easy.

Personal Holding Companies. Some corporations, closely held, are little more than incorporated personal exchequers. They receive considerable investment income and try to retain it, rather than distribute dividends to shareholders in high brackets. Some personal holding companies start life that way. Others fall into that mold after operating assets are sold and the profits remain in the hands of the corporation.

Either way, the law does not smile upon such lickpenny corporate cupidity. A punitive tax of 50 percent in addition to the regular tax is imposed on "undistributed personal holding company income." (The penalty tax before 1982 was 70 percent.) The threat of such a tax compels remarkable corporate liberality. To avoid the 50 percent tax, a corporation need only pay out the requisite income as a "deficiency dividend."

To be sure, there are technical definitions as to which closely held companies may be ensnared and the kind of income that may be considered personal holding income. Operating income is generally all right; it's "passive" income the law wants distributed. It's interesting to remember, though, that one kind of passive income—municipal bond interest—does not enter into the computation at all.

Subchapter S Corporations. Called "small business corporations" because they may have, after 1982, no more than thirty-five qualified electing shareholders, Subchapter S corporations are, to put it plainly, not subject to corporate taxation at all. The conduit theory operates, much as it does in case of partnerships. The happy band of shareholders pay tax on the corporation's income, recognize its gains, and deduct its losses proportionately on their own returns.

Not all corporations can qualify, of course. But under the latest rules enacted on October 19, 1982, Subchapter S is more prepossessing than ever and should be considered whenever a new firm is created.

Making the election to be such a small business corporation can be especially attractive for new businesses in which initial losses are expected. Shareholders can use the losses, and consideration can be given to revoking the election once operations become profitable.

Other Favored Corporations. The list of corporations that may receive special tax dispensation is varied. There are, for example, *Small Business Investment Companies* (SBICs), which are privately owned investment companies licensed by the Small Business Administration. Because of their service to the economy, they receive a variety of tax benefits. *Regulated Investment Companies,* such as mutual funds or certain venture capital firms, are not taxed on amounts distributed to investors if they distribute at least 90 percent of their dividend and interest income currently. *Real Estate Investment Trusts* (REITs) resemble, in many aspects, mutual funds (though technically not corporations). *Domestic International Sales Corporations* (DISCs) derive virtually all their income from export sales and rentals, and, for most practical purposes, pay no corporate tax. The shareholders pay on part of the DISC's income when it is distributed and on part of the DISC's undistributed income. They may even claim a credit for foreign taxes that the DISC paid.

No one ever said the subject of corporate taxation is simple or orderly. It's real, it's earnest, like life, like . . . taxes.

16
Tax-Exempt Organizations

Certainly the tax law is used to scrape together some revenue. It has also frequently been pressed into the service of national policy. So, traditionally, the policy of fostering good works has exempted charitable enterprises from taxation. Assuming that an altruistic organization meets certain qualifications, contributions to it will be deductible. They are gifts and not taxable to the charity. Moreover, the organization's earnings will normally escape taxation.

Some years ago, however, Congress had the uneasy feeling that certain private charitable foundations had not only helped people in general, but also might have specifically helped their sponsors avoid some taxes. To uncover and curtail abuses, detailed restrictions and restraints have been imposed on charitable organizations.

Public Charities

If a charity is exempt under the law, receipts, including dues, contributions, and earnings on investments, will not be taxed. There are myriad such exempt organizations, such as

- Charitable, religious, scientific, literary, or educational institutions
- Organizations to foster amateur sports, to test for public safety, to prevent cruelty to children and animals

- Civic leagues and labor, agricultural, and horticultural organizations
- Business leagues, chambers of commerce, and fraternal societies
- Cemetery companies and mutual insurance companies
- Employee trusts

To qualify, no portion of the net earnings or the assets of such an enterprise may benefit any particular person. Most charitable organizations may not engage in political discourse, either. Political organizations are usually exempt from tax under other rules (except for subversive outfits, of course).

To obtain exemption, a charity must initially demonstrate its eleemosynary character and then file annual tax reports. You can, as a citizen, inspect such reports, as well as others that may be required by local law.

Despite the general rule of nontaxability, all charities may be taxed on business income that is not really connected with the charitable, educational, or similar purposes that are the basis for the organization's exemption. Separate businesses, called "feeder organizations," are taxable on their earnings, even if all the stock is owned by an exempt organization. The dividends paid to the charitable owner, however, may be tax-free. An entity organized merely to hold property for a charity is not considered a feeder, since it's not an operating business.

EXAMPLE: The College of Musical Knowledge is a tax-exempt organization. It owns all of the stock of the John Harrington Plumbing Corporation and receives dividends from the plumbing company without paying a tax on them. The John Harrington Plumbing Corporation, however, must pay taxes on its business operations under the usual corporate tax rules. It's a feeder organization.

The College of Musical Knowledge also owns an auditorium and dormitories, though title to the real estate is in the name of Musical Knowledge Holding Corporation, which is wholly owned by the college. Since the holding company is merely a title-holding entity, it is not subject to tax.

Some Ecclesiastical Words

Churches are not obliged to seek affirmative exemption from tax, nor to file any reports. Religious organizations have always been exempt from tax. The Code declares that there shall be "no examination of the books of account of a church" (unless there is a suspected unrelated trade or business). "No examination of the religious activities of such an organization shall be made," it says, "except to the extent necessary to determine whether such organization is a church...."

A sign of the times—one worldly divine posed a simple rhetorical question in a recent advertisement. "Why not let everybody participate in these blessings?" asked the founder of the Universal Life Church. Many newly found religions said, to hell with charity, let's operate for the benefit of ourselves and not pay taxes anymore—an attitude increasingly troublesome to the Internal Revenue Service. With the number of tax-evasion schemes cloaked in sanctimonious vestments increasing, the wall separating Church and State begins to develop a chink here and there. Now the Treasury feels obliged to consider the kind of organization that claims exemption as a religion, its purpose, and its actual operation.

To help determine whether or not a church is truly a church, the commissioner has listed some divine attributes:

1. A distinct legal existence
2. A recognized creed and form of worship
3. A definite and distinct ecclesiastical government
4. A formal code of doctrine and discipline
5. A distinct religious history
6. A membership not associated with any other church or denomination
7. A complete organization of ordained ministers ministering to their congregations
8. Ordained ministers selected after completing prescribed courses of study
9. A literature of its own
10. Established places of worship
11. Regular religious services
12. A regular congregation
13. Sunday [sic] schools for religious instruction
14. Schools to prepare ministers

The Service confesses that these aren't very solid tests. Lots of legitimate religions don't have all the characteristics. They merely provide guidelines, and the courts may not necessarily be inclined to apply them mechanically. Judges are more likely to look to the true purpose of an organization claiming a divine right not to be taxed, or look to its actual operations.

The law is still developing, but huge donations to unusual and hitherto unheard of denominations may someday be questioned, and certainly a "church" that is founded merely to avoid taxation of income properly attributable to its proprietor will be weighed in the balance. The handwriting is on the wall between Church and State.

Private Foundations

You may recall 1969 as the year we put a man on the moon. Some tax practitioners are more likely to remember it as the year of the Tax Reform Act. It created the concept of the private foundation as a kind of tax-exempt organization that bears close watching.

The tax law says that any charitable organization is considered a private foundation unless it is in a specifically excluded category. (Those excluded are normally those with broad public financial support, those that actively support such publicly financed charities, employee trusts, and as you surely suspected, organizations that test for public safety.) It's simpler to say that private foundations are established, operated, and supported by a few people. Don't think that they must be small. The Ford Foundation, because it is not supported by the general populace, is a private foundation. And they need not be incorporated: charitable trusts must meet the tax rules applicable to private foundations.

Excise Tax. In 1969, Congress imposed an excise tax on the net investment income of private foundations. The tax was set at 4 percent to cover the cost of policing the operations of the foundations. Unexpectedly, the excise tax brought in more money than was needed, and, astoundingly, the rate of tax was reduced promptly to 2 percent. Perhaps someday it will even be abolished. The 2 percent tax is imposed on gross taxable investment income, including net capital gains, less allocable expenses.

Required Distributions. Before 1982, private foundations annually had to distribute amounts equal to (a) their adjusted net income, or (b) a minimum investment return, whichever was greater. Now the distribution requirement has been eased so that foundations are obliged to pay out only their minimum investment return, which is generally equivalent to 5 percent of the fair market value of their assets. There are, of course, various mathematical tests to determine what constitutes fair market value and special rules to determine what the minimum investment return should be. (It sometimes happened under the old law that a foundation was required to distribute more than it earned in a particular year, and had to pay out some of its capital or some of the next year's earnings.)

One year is allowed to meet the distribution requirements. Otherwise a penalty, ranging from 15 percent to 100 percent, may be assessed on the undistributed income for each year income remains undistributed.

Private *operating* foundations, which must spend most of their income under other rules, are excused from the distribution requirements. Nonoperating private foundations may obtain dispensation from the rules if they can show the need to set aside funds to accomplish a particular charitable project. Five years is about as long as such dispensation will last.

Restraints and Retributions. There are certain dealings that are prohibited to private foundations:

- *Self-dealing.* A private foundation is forbidden, under the tax law, to take part in a variety of transactions with "disqualified persons." Such tainted folk are, in general, those in control of the foundation, such as its managers, those who are considered substantial contributors (as determined by mathematical tests), and other related parties. There's a solid catalogue of acts, direct or indirect, that are considered to be self-dealing. Even if it's for fair market value, a sale, exchange, or leasing of property between a disqualified person and a private foundation is self-dealing, for example. So is payment of compensation or expenses for unnecessary services or in unreasonable amounts to disqualified persons.The list includes an agreement by a foundation to make payment to a government functionary, other than an employment agreement to take effect no sooner than ninety days after the official leaves government service. It's possible to become a disqualified person inadvertently, and it's therefore wise to check into a private foundation's operations before contributing more than $5,000. Penalties for self-dealing may be imposed on the disqualified person and the foundation manager. They start at 5 percent, but if not corrected, rise to 200 percent, up to a maximum of $10,000.

- *Excess business holdings.* There are several mechanical tests to determine if the combined ownership of a business enterprise by a private foundation and related disqualified persons is excessive. The foundation's tax on its excess business holdings starts at 5 percent of the value of the discommended securities and may rise to another 200 percent if the problem isn't cured.

- *Speculation.* An investment that financially endangers a private foundation's exempt purposes is cause for the imposition of a penalty. The investments of the foundation must be sensible and prudent, but no absolute guidelines are provided. Dealing in puts and calls, commodity straddles, or the like might well be called into question, however. Despite the prohibition against speculative investments, charitable program-related investments are permitted. Such investments might include high-risk involvement in nonprofit, low-income housing or low-interest loans to small businesses owned by members of disadvantaged groups when other loans aren't available, for example. The penalty for speculative investment starts at 5 percent and may rise to $10,000 or more if not corrected. A manager may be excused for his or her dereliction if the participation in the transaction wasn't willful and resulted from reasonable cause. Reliance on legal advice may be a reasonable cause.

- *Taxable expenditures.* Now and then, the individual force that drives a private foundation may think it appropriate to have the foundation send a deserving young person to college, even if the particular youth is closely related. That is a taxable expenditure, and won't do. Taxable expenditures include grants to an individual for study or travel, lobbying, or expenditures for any purpose that doesn't further the foundation's exempt purpose. Generally, scholarship-grant-making procedures must receive the tax man's prior blessing, and the foundation must monitor the recipient's progress if grants are not to be considered taxable expenditures. "Expenditure responsibility," which means procedures to follow, and report on, uses of funds, is required when grants are made to other nonoperating private foundations. There are penalty taxes starting at 2½ percent on unexcused taxable expenditures, assessable against the foundation and its management, rising to a possible $10,000 if no corrective action is taken.

- *Termination.* Not only are there punitive taxes on the various prohibited transactions, the IRS may terminate a private foundation's tax standing for flagrant and repeated misbehavior. To add more sting to Uncle Sam's asperity, a termination tax is also applicable. That tax is the lower of either (a) the value of the foundation's net assets, or (b) all the tax benefits received by the foundation and any of its substantial contributors since 1913—plus interest.

Like aristocratic families that adapt somehow to the overthrow of the regimes under which they once thrived, the great old private foundations of the country have adapted and survived since the Tax Reform Act of 1969. On the whole, they keep their books scrupulously and make their reports just as required. It is probable that the abuses of the past, committed primarily by the more plebeian foundations of the charitable world, have been significantly curtailed. Meanwhile, the big business of philanthropy evolves in its uniquely American style.

17
Estates, Gifts, and Basic Estate Planning

We won't be discussing income taxes in this chapter. The subject now is another kind of tax. It's the tax on the transfer of property, rather than the receipt of income. Estate and gift taxation is the source from which the estate planning industry springs.

The Economic Recovery Tax Act of 1981 made some significant changes in the income tax law. But the changes wrought in the taxation of estates and gifts were, in their way, momentous. Invariably, when a new tax law is enacted its inherent complexities earn it a sobriquet something like "The Lawyers' and Accountants' Relief Act of 19—." When the 1981 law was first enacted, though, many professional estate planners thought their occupation might have been dealt a mortal blow. Their fears were premature, but the need for extensive planning is manifestly less widespread than it once was.

So far as estate and gift taxation goes, now the rich are discernibly different from the rest of society, as Scott Fitzgerald always suspected; the rich will have to be concerned with such matters and the multitudes won't. The only problem is that, even if no one else thinks so, inflation may soon cause Uncle Sam to consider you rich. Review your expectations and assets, including real estate, investments, insurance, and employment benefits, and you may find that the dollar value will dictate some estate planning. After all, if you can't take it with you, your property will eventually pass to someone else. You can probably think of someone just as deserving as the federal Treasury.

Talking Like a Fiduciary

The tax specialty of estate planning concerns the impact of taxes upon entities that have roots centuries old. Modern trusts, for example, greatly affected by the Code, trace their lineage directly to the Statute of Uses passed by Parliament in 1534. Naturally, special parlance has developed and been incorporated into the Code.

An *estate* or *trust* is a legal entity that holds title to property for the benefit of another or others. The entity is a separate taxpayer. The entity's manager, human or corporate, is named a *fiduciary*, who has exceptional duties of faithfulness and bears substantial responsibility. There may be more than one fiduciary at a time for an estate or trust—they are *cofiduciaries*. One who follows another is a *successor fiduciary*.

The income taxes, dealt with in the next chapter, are, naturally, *fiduciary taxes*. When a gift is made, either directly or in trust during the life of the one who establishes it, there may be *gift taxes* due. When an estate is created upon someone's death, there may be *estate taxes* payable by the estate to the U.S. Treasury. There may also be estate taxes or *inheritance taxes* payable to local jurisdictions by those who inherit the property before they may take their inheritances.

The fiduciary manages the trust or estate in accordance with the mandate of the will or trust agreement and of local law, not for himself or herself, but for *beneficiaries*.

A trust may be established by a *grantor*, or *settlor* (or even *trustor*) during lifetime. The trust assets, the *corpus* (or *principal*), are managed by a fiduciary called a *trustee*. If a trust is set up during the grantor's lifetime, it's an *inter vivos* trust. If it is established by last will and testament, it's a *testamentary* trust.

Trusts may last for a long time, but there are ancient legal impediments as well as modern tax restrictions against trusts lasting in perpetuity or skipping generations. Trusts, nevertheless, may occasionally outlive a healthy tropical alligator.

Those who make wills may survive a named fiduciary. It's common practice, therefore, to name alternate and successor fiduciaries.

An estate is born at the death of the owner of property, who is called the *decedent*, post-mortem. The decedent's last will directs the management and disposition of the estate. One who makes a will is a *testator* or *testatrix*. (The law still distinguishes gender.) The named estate fiduciary is the *executor* or *executrix*. On the death of the testator, the will is offered in court for *probate*, which formally establishes its authority. The probate bar tends to believe that dying without a will is conclusive proof of churlishness, but if that happens, the appointed fiduciary is known as the *administrator* or *administratrix* of the decedent's assets.

The life of an estate is limited. An executor is obliged to marshal the assets of the decedent, pay debts, pay taxes, and distribute the remaining assets as required by the will and the applicable law.

Estate and Gift Taxes Now

The tax transfiguration of estate planning caused by the Economic Recovery Tax Act of 1981 has several parts worth review. There's an increase in what is known as the "unified credit," a reduction in the top estate and gift tax rates, an unlimited marital deduction, an increase in the annual gift tax exclusion, and other helpful provisions.

Increase in Unified Credit. Estate and gift taxes have never been significant sources of our national revenue. In 1980, such taxes accounted for 1¼ percent of all taxes collected. Less than 3 percent of U.S. estates were subject to tax. But estate taxes have been known to severely damage some individual estates.

Before 1976, the amount of property that could pass free of tax at death was $60,000. That year, the rules changed to provide a unified transfer tax to replace that exemption figure and the lifetime exemption for gifts up to $30,000. The amount of property that could pass by gift or through an estate free of tax was increased in stages. That was accomplished by a tax credit, reaching $47,000, that completely exempted from tax all reportable transfers up to $175,625. The credit applies to gifts and estates on a cumulative basis. Because it applies to both lifetime gifts and estates, it's said to be "unified," as is the tax on transfers by gift and by death.

The recent change increases the unified credit over six years. In 1987, the credit will be $192,800. That will be the unified tax on $600,000. When the credit is taken, the tax on that amount is eliminated altogether. It is estimated that by the time the new credit reaches its maximum in 1987, less than .5 percent of all estates will be subject to tax.

The table below shows the schedule of the unified credit and the taxable transfer exemption equivalent as the new credits are phased in.

Year of Transfer	Unified Credit	Exemption Equivalent
1982	$ 62,800	$225,000
1983	79,300	275,000
1984	96,300	325,000
1985	121,800	400,000
1986	155,800	500,000
1987 and after	192,800	600,000

Rate Reductions. Under the law before 1982, the unified gift and estate tax rates ranged from 18 percent on taxable transfers under $10,000 to a top rate of 70 percent on transfers of $5 million or more. Starting in 1982, the top rates are reduced by five percentage points a year to a maximum of 50 percent. That top rate will apply to transfers of $2,500,000 or more. Brackets below 50 percent are not affected.

Year of Transfer	Top Rate	On Transfers Over
1981	70%	$5,000,000
1982	65%	4,000,000
1983	60%	3,500,000
1984	55%	3,000,000
1985 and after	50%	2,500,000

Marital Deduction. It is traditional for estate tax purposes that a deduction is granted for property passing to a surviving spouse. That deduction used to be limited to half the adjusted gross estate, which is the whole estate less all other deductions. In 1976, a minimum marital deduction was set at $250,000, or half the estate, whichever was more.

After 1981, though, the marital deduction is simply unlimited. If the entire estate passes to a spouse, there is no taxable estate at all.

There used to be a formula for similar marital deductions for lifetime gifts, but after 1981 the law provides for a full marital deduction for lifetime gifts to spouses.

Gift Tax Exclusion. The gift tax rates used to be three-quarters of the estate tax rates, before the two kinds of transfer taxes were unified. There still are other tax encouragements to lifetime generosity. Donors are permitted to give specific amounts free of gift tax to each lucky donee each year. (That way, a benefaction to a panhandler doesn't require a gift tax return.) And if a gift is made by one spouse to a third party, the other spouse may consent to treat such a gift as being made by both, thus doubling the annual exclusion.

The only problem was that, until 1982, the amount that could be given to each donee was only $3,000 ($6,000 with marital consent). That figure was forty years old. Congress agreed that it was time to give the annual exclusion a raise. After 1981, it's $10,000 for each donee in any single year.

Further, after 1981 any amounts paid directly to an educational or medical facility as school tuition or medical expense for anyone will not be considered a gift. Grandpa can send the kids to college or Mr. Korn can pay for Pop Korn's medical expenses without being concerned with a gift tax after the $10,000 exclusion is exhausted. There's no time limit. The kids can go to school as long as they like, either full- or part-time. And there's no requirement that those who benefit from the tuition or medical payments be related in any way to their benefactors. The rule doesn't cover books or dormitory fees or medical expenses reimbursed by insurance, however.

The Gift Tax Mechanics

For tax purposes, a gift is the free transfer of property of any kind. It entails delivery, relinquishment of control by the donor, and some kind of acceptance by the donee. A "bargain sale," in which there is some consideration received for the transfer of more valuable property, may be a gift to the extent of the difference between the fair market value of the property transferred and the bargain sale price. Gifts may be made to adults or to minors, who often are given cash or securities through the good offices of custodians. The custodians hold the gifts for the children under the simple terms of state-legislated Uniform Gifts to Minors Acts.

The value of a gift for tax purposes is its fair market value when the gift is made. For a security, the fair market value is the average of the high and low prices on the day the donor relinquishes control of the security.

The annual exclusion, $10,000 for years after 1981, does not apply to gifts of future interests. Such an interest is one in which the donee does not receive an unrestricted right to use or enjoy the gift immediately. Typically, a gift of a future interest involves a transfer in trust, rather than outright. (There are, however, special rules that will allow gifts to wait until a minor reaches the age of twenty-one, while still qualifying for the annual exclusion when it is made.)

Gifts to qualified charities above the annual exclusion are still not subject to gift tax. They are deductible for gift tax purposes as well as income tax purposes.

The computation of the annual gift tax, on Form 709, is cumulative. All prior taxable gifts are added to the current gifts so that the current gifts are taxed in the appropriate bracket, and each year's gifts are prevented from starting again at the bottom of the rate schedule. A credit for all prior taxable gifts is allowed so that they aren't taxed more than once.

Once the tentative gift tax is calculated, the unified credit must be applied to it. Any part of the credit used reduces the amount of the credit available later, but its use is mandated.

EXAMPLE: Suppose Marshall Ayres gives his son stock valued at $7,500 and gives his daughter stock valued at $12,500 in 1982. The gift to his son is below the annual exclusion. Forget it. The gift to Marshall's daughter, after the annual exclusion is applied, results in a gift subject to tax of $2,500. If Marshall Ayres never made any prior taxable gifts, the tentative tax is $450, at the lowest bracket of 18 percent. No tax is due, because $450 of Marshall's lifetime unified credit is used as a credit.

Suppose, however, that Marshall also made $22,500 worth of taxable gifts in 1981. The computation gets more involved:

1981 taxable gift	$22,500
1982 taxable gift	2,500
Total	$25,000
Tentative tax on all taxable gifts (now at the 22 percent bracket)	$ 4,900
Less: Tentative tax on 1981 taxable gifts (at current rates)	(4,350)
Tentative 1982 gift tax	$ 550

Still there would be no gift tax due, but the unified credit used up would be $550 for 1982 and $4,350 for 1981, a reduction of $4,900 in the unified credit against future gifts and Marshall Ayres's eventual estate.

The Operation of the Estate Tax

A decedent's gross estate, for tax purposes, includes everything in which the late owner had an interest. Even assets not disposed of by will, such as life insurance or jointly owned property that passes by operation of law to a survivor, are included in the gross estate. Virtually every material asset accumulated during life and retained at death is included in the gross estate.

The adjusted gross estate is the gross estate less (1) funeral expenses, (2) expenses of administering the estate, including fiduciary fees, (3) debts of the decedent, and (4) casualty and theft losses. For estates before 1982, the most compelling need for computing the adjusted gross estate was the determination of the base for calculating the formerly limited marital deduction. It is still useful for that, especially if the full marital deduction is not used. The amount of the adjusted gross estate is also needed to figure the amount of credit for state or foreign taxes.

The taxable estate is the adjusted gross estate less the marital deduction, and if anything is left after that, the charitable deduction is claimed before arriving at the taxable estate.

The tax is calculated on that figure, and then the available unified credit is taken.

> EXAMPLE: Rich widow Vesta Buhl breathes her last in 1982, leaving many friends and a gross estate of $6 million. Administration expenses, funeral costs, and other expenses equal $600,000. (Executors' fees and lawyers' costs can add up.)There was no marital deduction, of course, but Vesta left $400,000 to charity. The rest was left to her children and grandchildren. Vesta Buhl never made any taxable gifts during her lifetime. The computation of the estate tax:

Gross estate	$6,000,000
Expenses	600,000
Adjusted gross estate	5,400,000
Charitable deduction	400,000
Taxable estate	5,000,000
Tentative estate tax	2,530,800
Unified credit	(62,800)
Tax due	2,468,000
Available for heirs	$2,532,000

Now suppose we can extend Vesta's life until 1987. If her estate were the same, there would then be over a third of a million more available for distribution to her heirs. That's because the rates are lowering and the credit is rising.

Taxable estate	$5,000,000
Tentative estate tax	2,275,800
Unified credit	(192,800)
Tax due	2,083,000
Available for heirs	$2,917,000

Clearly, the best estate plan is to stay alive and well. (Macabre tales are being devised by waggish estate planners about keeping moribund wealthy folk on life-support systems past a new year, to take advantage of the rate and credit changes. As you may imagine, estate planners are not noted primarily for their comicality.)

The Gross Estate

Valuation. In determining the size of an estate in the first place, it is necessary to properly value the decedent's assets. For assets other than listed securities, this can be a difficult task indeed, and the most common point of debate between the decedent's fiduciary and an estate tax auditor. The rules require that fair market value be reported, but what is that?

For securities listed on an exchange or over-the-counter, the value is the midpoint between the high and low quoted selling prices on the valuation date.

Generally, real estate must be valued at its "highest and best use." If special requirements are met, however, certain family farms and real property used in small businesses may be valued at "current use" value rather than "highest and best use," if an election is made to do so. The amount of the reduction from the highest to current use is limited. The 1981 law increased the limit on the use of the special valuation from $500,000 to $600,000 in 1981, $700,000 in 1982, and $750,000 after 1982. These rules were designed to prevent property from being lost to a family along with the owner of the property. If the family relinquishes control of the property within a decade, therefore, the tax benefit may have to be repaid. There are several technical rules that apply to the special valuation election, but they are easier to deal with than they were under prior law.

That still leaves the problem of proving the value of assets that are not traded regularly and publicly. Closely held stock, realty, patents, copyrights, unincorporated business interests, tax shelters, and works of art must all be valued appropriately, and the formal appraisals of experts are frequently required.

Valuation Date. The valuation of a decedent's assets for estate tax purposes is generally made on the date of death. But the executor may elect to use an alternate valuation date instead. The alternate valuation date is six months after date of death. It's effective only if an estate tax return is filed on time, so if there is no reportable estate for tax purposes, there is no election.

If the election is made to use values six months after the date of death, all the estate's assets must be valued at that time.

There's no choosing which date would be better for which assets—it's all valued on one day or the other. If it's the alternate valuation date, any assets distributed, sold, or otherwise disposed of during the half year after the date of death are valued on the date of disposition.

Joint Property. William Shakespeare obviously realized that owning property in joint names is no substitute for estate planning. After all, he left his "second best bed" to Mrs. Shakespeare under the terms of his will, which indicates that the furniture wasn't owned "jointly with right of survivorship." If it were, the Bard's widow would have owned it automatically.

Under the law relating to decedents dying before 1982, it was the general rule that the full value of jointly held property was taxed in the estate of the first spouse to die. That general rule could be overcome by proof that the surviving spouse contributed to the cost of the property. That proof could often become a bit sticky, especially as more marriages were composed of two income earners. The 1976 law tried to help a bit, but the rules were often difficult to satisfy.

Now the law provides that, for a qualified joint interest, one-half of the interest will be included in the estate of the first spouse to die, regardless of who paid for the property. The other half will not be included in the estate. This becomes important in determining basis in the hands of the survivor. Remember that for determining capital gain or loss, inherited property receives a stepped-up basis—one that is equal to the date of death value or the alternate valuation. Under the new rule, only half of jointly held property will receive a step-up in basis when the first joint owner dies, and in a small estate that may not be of long-range advantage for the survivor who later sells the property.

Other Assets. Most payments from retirement plans may be excluded from the gross estate if they meet certain requirements. If a beneficiary other than the decedent's estate is designated as the payee, the part of the death-related payments attributable to the employer's contribution must meet two tests. To be excluded, the payments must (1) be received for a tax-qualified employee benefit plan, and (2) not be in the form of a lump sum distribution. HR-10 (Keogh) plan payments and IRA (Individual Retirement Account) annuities can also be excluded under such rules. Rules regarding special ten-year averaging and capital gain treatment (described in Chapter 18) may also be applicable.

There is a kind of asset called "income in respect of a decedent" that is includable in the gross estate. Income owed to a decedent but due to be received after death—like salary, dividends, commissions, interest, gains—is not included in the decedent's final income tax return. Rather, such income in respect of a decedent is reportable by the living recipient. Since such income probably would have augmented the decedent's estate had it been received before the owner's quietus, it must be included in the estate for tax purposes. To avoid double taxation, the one who pays income tax on it is granted an itemized deduction for estate taxes attributable to the income in respect of a decedent.

Gifts in Contemplation. Before 1982, gifts made within three years of the donor's death were considered to be made "in contemplation of death." They were, therefore, automatically included in the donor's gross estate, and after 1976 the donor's state of mind at the time of the gift didn't make a difference. There was an irrebuttable presumption of intimations of mortality.

Gifts made within three years of death are no longer considered part of the donor's estate. (Of course, the basic rule of the unified tax, which requires that date-of-gift values of reportable gifts be used to calculàte the tax, is unaffected.)

Gifts of life insurance are still subject to the old rules, however, if they are made within three years of death. The proceeds will continue to be considered part of the gross estate.

Moreover, any gifts made within three years of death, though generally excluded from the gross estate, may affect provisions regarding special valuations, deferred payment plans, and redemptions of corporate stock to pay estate taxes. There may also have to be adjustments to account for gift taxes on such transfers.

It's possible to make a gift of appreciated property to someone who is moribund and about to leave this life. That's done sometimes to increase the basis of the property before it promptly passes back to the donor on the donee's death. The appreciation would simply escape taxation. The law now obviates such gifts in contemplation of another's death. Starting in 1982, the step-up in basis on the new owner's death does not apply to appreciated property acquired by a decedent by gift after August 13, 1981, and within a year of death if the property passes right back to the donor or the donor's spouse.

Estate Tax Deductions

The decedent's outstanding debts, the estate's casualty and theft losses, funeral expenses, and administration expenses are deducted from the gross estate to arrive at the adjusted gross estate. Then certain special deductions are available.

Marital Deduction. The new unlimited marital deduction, available for all property left to a surviving spouse, is a good thing, certainly, but the maximum marital deduction may not always be the most beneficial from a tax point of view. If a husband and wife have combined assets above the unified credit equivalent—$600,000 in 1987—some planning may be worthwhile.

EXAMPLE: Ed U. Caton has assets worth $1,200,000 in 1987. His wife, Cindy, has no property of her own. Ed decides to leave everything to Cindy. He dies in 1987; Cindy dies in 1995. (Estate planners generally give the *coup de grâce* to the husband first. They traditionally assume, for their illustrations, that he's got the money.) The tax picture for the two estates:

	Ed—1987	Cindy—1995
Gross estate	$1,200,000	$1,200,000
Marital deduction	1,200,000	0
Taxable estate	0	1,200,000
Tentative estate tax	0	427,800
Unified credit	0	(192,800)
Tax due	0	$ 235,000

Suppose, on the other hand, Ed U. Caton does not leave all his assets outright to Cindy. Instead, he leaves her $600,000—the traditional half—and leaves the other $600,000 in a nonqualified trust for her benefit, with the principal going to others when she dies. The trust, as a "terminable interest," need not be qualified for the marital deduction. The full tax of $235,000 could be avoided:

	Ed—1987	Cindy—1995
Gross estate	$1,200,000	$600,000
Marital deduction	600,000	0
Taxable estate	600,000	600,000
Tentative estate tax	192,800	192,800
Unified credit	(192,800)	(192,800)
Tax due	$ 0	$ 0

Estate planners use the marital deduction in such ways in attempts to equalize projected estates. Other estates may adopt the same routine. For different sized individual and combined estates, the technique must be adjusted in various ways. If, for example, Ed U. Caton's supposed estate was $1 million, he might still leave the full $600,000 to a trust, to use up the credit. If his estate were $2 million, he could leave the same $600,000 amount to the trust, to use up the credit, or he could leave $1 million to the trust, to equalize the expected estates. That would save $14,000 while requiring that a tax on Ed's estate be paid well ahead of the tax on Cindy's estate. Would that be worthwhile, or would it pay to postpone the tax, even if it is higher, for a few years? Perhaps that depends on life expectancies and assumed investment yields.

What if Cindy dies first, after all? Estate planning, whether or not the marital deduction is involved, isn't a science. It's educated speculation, based on known facts and assumptions. When they change, so do the estate plans.

If an estate plan was based on the tax law before 1982, it should be reviewed. Wills or trusts created before September 13, 1981, that involve a formula for a maximum marital deduction—which was then limited—will generally *not* qualify for the new marital deduction (unless amended or a state law provides otherwise).

A trust for a spouse, over which the spouse has a general

power of appointment (the right to say who gets the principal on his or her demise), is one way to obtain the marital deduction.

The new law, unlike the old, provides that an election may be made by an executor to qualify bequests of certain "terminable interests" for the marital deduction. The qualifying property is known as "qualifying terminable interest property," or "Q-tip." To meet the Q-tip test, the surviving spouse must be entitled to all the income from the interest for life. The income must be paid at least annually, and no one may have the ability to allocate any of the interest or the income from it to anyone other than the surviving spouse. Income interests for a stated period of time, or that stop when a bereaved spouse remarries, won't qualify. If the election is made, the surviving spouse or his or her estate will be subject to tax either on disposal of the interest or on death, whichever happens first.

Charitable Deduction. There is no limit to the amount of the deduction available for property included in the gross estate that passes to a qualified charity. The charitable bequest may be made in trust or given outright. If a trust arrangement is involved, however, the requirements are strict, especially if the trust operates for both charitable and personal purposes. The formation and operation of such trusts are stringently restricted if an estate tax deduction is to be available.

Orphan's Deduction. A partial deduction was available before 1982 for property, included in the gross estate, that passed to a minor child of the decedent if the child became an orphan. The 1981 law repealed this special deduction.

Credit Against the Estate Tax

The fundamental credit is, of course, the unified estate and gift tax credit, but certain other credits are available.

Other Jurisdictions' Death Taxes. A limited credit against the federal estate tax is available for estate, inheritance, or similar duties imposed by a state, territory, or the District of Columbia on property also found in the decedent's tax return. Some states impose a tax equal to the federal credit. That's called a "sop tax." Others impose taxes well in excess of the credit, while others may impose little or no such taxes. The credit, of course, can't be more than the actual tax, though it may be less. Taxes imposed by foreign jurisdictions may also yield limited credits. There are also estate tax treaties that not only alleviate double taxes but provide "situs" rules that decide which jurisdiction gets first crack at an asset owned by a decedent whose property is subject to tax by a foreign country as well as the United States.

Prior Transfers. So that there will be no untoward doubling of estate taxes, another limited credit is allowed for estate taxes paid on property transferred to the decedent from someone who died within ten years before and up to two years after the decedent's death. The credit is based on a sliding scale and gets smaller the longer the decedent holds the inherited property.

Paying the Estate Tax

The estate tax return, Form 706, is due, if necessary, nine months after the decedent's death. The tax is generally due then. Extensions for reasonable cause are available, with interest running, of course.

The Form 706 is copiously detailed, but for decedents dying after 1981, most of the schedules need not be filed if the total gross estate is $500,000 or less. For larger estates all the schedules must be filed.

Special Extensions. There are special extensions available for estates involving closely held businesses. Under the 1981 law, payment of estate taxes may be extended over a fifteen-year period if the estate's interest in a closely held business (including a farming business) exceeds 35 percent of the adjusted gross estate.

Stock Redemptions. A related portion of the income tax law provides that stock in closely held corporations may generally be redeemed at capital gains rates, rather than as dividends, to the extent the redemption equals estate taxes, funeral expenses, and administration expenses. The decedent's interest in the closely held corporation must be at least 35 percent of the decedent's adjusted gross estate.

Flower Bonds. A "flower bond" is one of a specially designated series of Treasury bonds that may be redeemed at par to pay estate taxes. To be used this way, a flower bond must have been owned by the decedent. Flower bonds sell well below par because their yield is not great, but they may be useful estate planning tools. The apparent savings by the use of flower bonds should be accurately calculated, taking into account the low rate of interest, the supposed holding period, and the cost of money borrowed to purchase them.

"O, but they say the tongues of dying men enforce attention like deep harmony," sighed John of Gaunt in Shakespeare's *Richard II*, "more are men's ends mark'd than their lives before." Death, one of the two eternal certainties, coincides directly with taxes—the other. Now the tax collector's attention may be particularly enforced to a decedent's testamentary wishes.

18

The Income Taxation of Estates and Trusts

Estates and trusts are separate entities for purposes of income taxation. While estates are not commonly established intentionally, trusts are very often specially created, frequently with a view to valuable tax considerations.

The Conduit

An estate or trust is a separate taxpayer, distinct from the one whose funds are its foundation, from its fiduciary, and from its beneficiaries. The estate or trust is the repository of income and disburser of expenses; the beneficiary is not the primary recipient of income or payer of expenses while the estate or trust exists.

The estate or trust is, quintessentially, a conduit or pipeline for distributions to beneficiaries. Double taxation is averted through application of a deduction allowable to an estate or trust for distributions made or required to be made under the terms of the governing will or trust agreement. An estate or trust, therefore, is granted a deduction that is equivalent to the amount of taxable income reportable by its respective beneficiaries.

Income that streams through the conduit to the beneficiaries retains its tax character. Dividends coming in remain dividends going out, foreign dividends stay foreign dividends through the pipeline, municipal bond interest continues to be exempt, and capital gains retain their unique benefits. The fiduciary reports all the appropriate information to beneficiaries and to the IRS, on Schedule K-1 of Form 1041. The beneficiaries include the appropriate amounts on their own 1040 forms.

When income is not paid, or considered paid, the pipeline doesn't work. That may happen when the terms of a trust entitle it to accumulate income. In that case, the trust is the taxpayer to the extent that income is retained. When it's paid out later, adjustments will be required. (As a general rule, though, the complex arithmetic, under the "throwback rule," does not apply to distributions of income accumulated before the beneficiary reaches the age of twenty-one.)

The Tax

Estates and trusts are taxed like individuals, though they have their own graduated tax tables. The U.S. Fiduciary Income Tax Return, Form 1041, is organized like a personal return, but certain deductions and credits aren't suitable for it. For example, medical expenses, dependency exemptions, the zero bracket standard deduction, child-care expenses, income averaging, and similar provisions designed for human taxpayers are not available on fiduciary returns. On the other hand, special deductions and exemptions are granted.

Distribution Deduction. An estate or trust takes a deduction for income distributed to beneficiaries. The computation depends on the distributable net income as well as the amount actually distributed. Unless the trust is one that is required to pay out all its income, the arithmetic can seem quite arcane sometimes. Since a taxpayer (in this case, a fiduciary) is not entitled to a deduction that relates to tax-free income, however, the distribution deduction can never be more than the income that would have been includable in the fiduciary return were it not for the conduit rule. Capital gains, being related to principal, not income, are normally taxable to the estate or trust.

Charitable Deduction. The amount of the charitable deduction is virtually unlimited for a fiduciary, unlike the rules relating to personal returns. But here the deduction is limited to taxable income received by the estate or trust. (There may also be deductions for amounts set aside for later payments to charities, under certain restricted circumstances.)

The distribution of income-producing property does not result in a charitable fiduciary income tax deduction. Rather, such a distribution of principal or corpus yields an estate tax deduction or an income tax deduction to the trust grantor on the creation of the trust.

Personal Exemption. An estate or trust may have one personal exemption, though it's not a human person. An estate may take an exemption of $600. A trust required to pay out all income currently (a "simple trust") gets an exemption of $300, and any other trust (a "complex trust") is allowed $100.

Tax Year. The fiduciary may select either a calendar year or a different fiscal year for a newborn estate or trust, without IRS approval. The initial income tax return is simply filed on the basis of the year selected. If a trust is considered to be a "grantor trust" (described below), it must be on the same tax year as its owner-grantor, however.

An adroit fiduciary may choose an advantageous tax year. The fiduciary might, for example, balance first-year income with that expected in future years. The beneficiaries report income in their own returns as if all the distributions were made on the last day of the estate's or trust's tax year, and it may be possible to coordinate the fiduciary tax year with the particular requirements of the beneficiaries.

EXAMPLE: The Tree Trust chooses a fiscal year that ends on June 30. During its first year it distributed to beneficiary Ephron Tree the following amounts:

On December 15, 1981 $10,000
On June 29, 1982 $10,000

Ephron Tree doesn't have to pay a tax on the $20,000 distributed to him until April 15, 1983.

When a final return is filed and the trust or estate ceases to exist, any unused carry-overs or deductions are allocated to those beneficiaries who receive the final distribution.

Calculating the distributable net income of a trust or estate each year may be formidable indeed. Happily, there are specialists, known as fiduciary accountants, who look upon such a vocation with equanimity.

Some Types of Trusts

Ancient as they are, trusts are remarkably flexible devices. Some are created by will and spring into life when the grantor dies. They are known as "testamentary trusts." Trusts are often established during the grantors' lives, and they are called "*inter vivos* trusts." Whether testamentary or *inter vivos*, trusts may be established to accomplish almost any legal end. They may be for small amounts or may hold fortunes. They do tend to fall into categories, however, especially when tax rules must be applied.

Lifetime Trusts. In the usual *inter vivos* trust, the grantor commonly relinquishes all rights to the assets placed in the trust. The income from those assets becomes taxable to the trust or, under the conduit theory, to the beneficiary on distribution. Thus, such an arrangement can effectively shift income to someone else, as well as capital gains realized on any future sales of trust property. It's even possible to have the trustee "sprinkle" or "spray" income among the designated members of a group. And property placed in trust does not become part of the grantor's estate, so long as the grantor relinquishes all rights to, and over, the trust property.

EXAMPLE: Rhoda Train created an irrevocable *inter vivos* trust for the benefit of her two grandchildren. She funded the trust with stock that had appreciated in value from $100,000 to $150,000, and Rhoda expected it to continue to rise. The gift was not taxable because Rhoda still had enough annual exclusions and unified credit to cover it. The designated trustee, Skoveda National Bank, is to distribute the trust's total income between the grandchildren as necessary for their college and postgraduate educations. The dividends, less the bank's fees, are taxable to the children, not Rhoda. Even if the principal value of the trust assets is $350,000 when Rhoda Train dies, the appreciation is not subject to gift or estate tax. The stock is no longer Rhoda's. The tax on the appreciation (of $250,000 if the stock is sold then) is the responsibility of the new owner at the time it is realized.

Grantor Trusts and the Two-Year Rule. If the use of a trust sounds like a tax shelter to you (and they are often advertised as just that), it's time to consider some additional rules. A trust will be bereft of tax benefits and the grantor treated as owner of all or part of the trust if he or she may

- personally use the trust's income,
- control the beneficial enjoyment of the trust or its income,
- reclaim the corpus, or
- simply control the trust too much.

Such trusts are called "grantor trusts" because the grantors are treated, in whole or in part, as the trusts' owners. Under the grantor trust rules, the income of the trust will be taxable to the grantor, and at the grantor's death the principal generally will be subject to estate tax. Nevertheless, sometimes such trusts are established to avoid publicity, formal probate, and court supervision of assets on the owner's death. During the grantor's life, there may be advantage in the management of the trust by professional trustees.

There's a unique, special rule regarding the sale of assets within two years of transfer to a trust. If appreciated property transferred to a regular, nongrantor trust is sold by the trust within two years of the transfer date, a special tax is imposed on the gain. The gain is taxed to the trust, not at its rate, but at the transferor's rate. The gain so taxed is limited to the appreciation at the time of transfer. It's a singular instance of one taxpayer being taxed at rates that apply to another, designed to deter the transfer of capital gains from a taxpayer in the top gains bracket (the transferor-grantor) to one in a lower bracket (the trust).

Ten-Year Trusts. The rules of the Code regarding grantor trusts emanate from the *Clifford* decision by the Supreme Court in 1940. Now there are special kinds of grantor trusts, known as "short-term trusts," or "Clifford trusts," that may still have income taxed to a beneficiary, rather than to the grantor. Such a trust must last either

- at least ten years and a day,
- for the beneficiary's lifetime (regardless of whether

it's expected, according to actuarial tables, to be long or short), or

- until the happening of some event that can't reasonably be expected to take place within a decade from the time the trust is created.

Because such a trust must be fabricated to endure for ten anniversaries (except for the loophole of the beneficiary's death, which is not presumed to be within the grantor's control), it's often called a "ten-year trust." Thus, a trust that is created to benefit someone just for the lifetime of the grantor might not qualify. It is not for the *beneficiary's* lifetime, and will be considered a grantor trust if the grantor's life expectancy is less than ten years.

Applicable local law often requires capital gains of a Clifford trust to be considered principal. If principal is to be distributed to the grantor on the trust's termination, the gains realized during the existence of the trust are taxed to the grantor. Similarly, capital losses are also attributed to the grantor each year.

Short-term trusts are more useful in effecting income tax savings than in sheltering assets from estate or gift taxes. With such a trust, a parent may divert investment income to a child for a stint at Harvard Law School, or allocate income from a particular property to support venerable parents in a California condominium. Of course, the trust property must not be subject to control or beneficial enjoyment by the grantor during the term of the trust. When it ends, however, the grantor may regain the principal of the trust.

Apocalypse and Reciprocal Trusts. Stay away from a trust with such an ominous appellation as "apocalypse." Sometimes, it may use the pseudonym of "family estate trust" or, innocently, "educational trust," but under any name, it simply does not work. The scheme is to persuade a family to establish a trust to which all it possesses—home, investment realty, stocks, bonds, and even lifetime services—is transferred. In exchange, members of the family are given proportionate beneficial interests in the trust. It is anticipated that not all the income will be distributed, and to the extent that it is not distributed, it will be taxed to the trust rather than to those who really earned it.

The IRS readily concluded that the grantor trust rules are violated by apocalypse trusts, which are controlled by those who establish them. Family member grantors are taxable on income they claim is earned by their trust.

Suppose you say, I don't involve a family unit. Why don't I set up a trust for *you* if you establish an equivalent trust for *me?* Same problem. Reciprocal, identical trust agreements, under which grantors designate each other as beneficiary, won't avoid income taxes because of the grantor trust rules.

Foreign Trusts. Establishing a trust in a foreign tax haven used to be almost as good as living there in person. Income and capital could accumulate and appreciate, in the right climate, with no interference from U.S. taxes. When the accumulations were finally brought home from the benevolent foreign jurisdiction and taxed to the beneficiary, the earlier accumulation and reinvestment, tax-free, proved to be a wonderful thing.

That's history. For some years now, trusts planted in foreign soil have been subject to stringent tax rules. Special grantor tax rules operate to trigger a tax, payable by the grantor, as soon as a U.S. beneficiary makes an appearance. Detailed rules and irrebuttable presumptions make foreign trusts considerably less appealing than they were in the old days.

Life Insurance Trusts. A life insurance policy may become a thing of worth indeed, but not to the insured who is expected to die before the thing is turned to value. If the insured doesn't get to enjoy the proceeds, they ought, in fairness, to be removed from his or her estate. That can be done easily enough by having the policy payable to someone other than the estate or its executor (acting not as a beneficiary but as a fiduciary) or for the benefit of the estate. The insured decedent must also have parted with all "incidents of ownership," such as the right to change the beneficiary or borrow against the policy.

Sometimes additional advantages may be achieved with the use of an irrevocable life insurance trust. Such a trust becomes fully funded upon the death of an insured grantor. Skilled management, of the grantor's choice, may then operate. The trust may provide necessary liquidity for an estate by being allowed to lend to the estate or buy assets from it.

There are certain complex gift tax aspects involved in the funding of an insurance trust. (There is a rule that requires the inclusion of transfers by a decedent within three years of death, including the payment of premiums, to be added to the estate.) Your friendly insurance agent no doubt will be delighted to work with you and your attorney. Just ask.

Totten Trusts. A Totten trust isn't a trust at all. When a bank passbook account is established in the name of the depositor "in trust for" someone else, it's called a "Totten trust." That's what Totten did generations ago, and sentimental lawyers don't give up nomenclature easily. Called a "poor man's will," a Totten trust indicates to whom the account is to go if the depositor dies without closing the account or changing the name of the beneficiary.

Such a tentative trust, revocable at the whim of the depositor, is an inconstant thing. It's automatically revoked, of course, if the designated beneficiary dies before the depositor. It is subject to claims by the depositor's creditors, and there are no income tax, estate tax, or gift tax advantages at all.

Generation Skipping. Trusts that are famous for their age as well as their size have historically lasted for several generations. Recently, a special transfer tax has been written into the law to discourage the establishment of trusts that spread their largesse over successive generations. The generation-skipping transfer tax does not apply to amounts, up to $250,000 per parent of grandchildren, ultimately given to grandchildren after an intervening generation. A grandparent may also leave property directly to grandchildren in trust, leaving out the intervening generation. All that isn't easy to put into a law, and the generation-skipping tax is replete with some of the most complex provisions in the Code. Forms have just been designed, though the inventive provision first appeared as part of the Tax Reform Act of 1976. It is still being studied by estate planners amid reports that it may be repealed soon. Some ideas just aren't popular. *De gustibus non est disputandum.*

PART · V

TAX
PLANNING

19
Tax Shelters

"Gimme shelter!" is an antediluvian cry. Today, for the afflu-ent, it means "construct some refuge from the onslaught of taxation." Naturally, the IRS doesn't care to see such construc-tion. Like many old-fashioned Southerners who must add to "Yankee" the prefix "damn," successive commissioners of in-ternal revenue must, perforce, growl "abusive" before saying "tax shelter." It's expected. The IRS, with helpful changes in the Code, has had some success in curbing abusive tax shelters in the recent past. Investing in a commodity futures straddle no longer is a shelter, and further changes may come about in the course of time. Some shelters will fade in popularity, while others become more attractive.

What Is a Tax Shelter?

What I may perceive as your shifty use of an egregious loophole becomes, when I employ it, merely the tax-wise use of a shelter, availed of with congressional blessing, thank you. "These activities," grumbled former Commissioner Jerome Kurtz, "come about largely as a by-product of provisions put into the tax law to achieve nontax goals." Special benefits are awarded to foster national objectives, like the discovery of oil or the rehabilitation of real property.

Under this general notion, there are certainly a variety of widely used provisions that might be called shelters—municipal bond tax-exempt interest, for example, or pension plans—but the real tax shelters involve investments that often are specially designed in whole or in part to protect income from the ravages of taxation by use of one or more of these techniques:

- Providing substantial current deductions
- Deferring the realization of income until a future year
- Deferring income, through present deductions against ordinary income, which will be taxed later at long-term capital gains·rates

These classic goals of shelter investments have spawned all kinds of shelters, from coal mines to catfish farms, from professional sports franchises to computer leases, from oil drilling to Scotch whisky aging. There's cattle feeding and cattle breeding. There have been African gold mine shelters and Mexican vegetable shelters. The glory days of swinging shelters have been subdued lately by changes in the tax law, court decisions, and administrative fiat. But that's not to say that there are no more good shelters as well as shelter rip-offs. There will always be dreadful ways to lose money in the name of tax savings.

It used to be said that tax shelters were recommended only for taxpayers who were in federal marginal tax brackets above 50 percent. Now, of course, there aren't any brackets above 50 percent, but no one seriously supposes that shelter activity will disappear. The primal urge is too potent. The new capital cost recovery system, with rapid write-offs in lieu of the old depreciation rules, will provide renewed attraction to real estate shelters; enhanced leasing and other shelter activity will evolve, based on the 1981 law. Even taxpayers below the top 50 percent bracket will want to accelerate deductions and defer income. It's only natural.

There are certain principles that any prospective player must carry next to his or her anxious heart:

- *Your suitability for shelters must be clear.* Your disposition must be right. Can you afford to lose the

entire investment, and perhaps take some tax pun-
ishment, with a reasonable display of equanimity?
It's commonly said in the industry that the real oil
and gas deals never go beyond Dallas, Oklahoma
City, or wherever they originate. Ask yourself (not the
promoter, certainly) how and why such a wonderful
deal reached you. Your investment sophistication (or
that of your trusted adviser) should be as substantial
as your free assets.

- *The shelter must be appropriate for you.* The widow
living on regular, though ample, trust income may
not be right for investment in a glitzy, quick Broad-
way show deal. A long-term real estate shelter may
not be suitable for this month's rock star. Each kind
of shelter offers unique features. But clearly, even
though you are temperamentally suited to shelter
investing, if you don't honestly understand how a
deal works, it's not the one for you. What do *you*
know about South African diamond mining, anyway?
- *The shelter must be valid as an investment.* This
canon of shelter investing has often been piously
repeated by shelter promoters, but it's still true and
fundamental. Anyone can offer you tax deductions
simply by taking your money. That's no shelter.
That's foolishness. The deal should first make sense
as a business proposition. Tax considerations come
after that. If it would not be a good proposition,
except for the advertised tax benefits, it's probably no
good at all. A convoluted, tricky or fun shelter will
lose its attraction when Uncle Sam starts to unravel
it. If it does not make fundamental business sense to
you, it won't look too good to the IRS either.

Why, then, do people enter into shelters that
don't make too much sense or which offer dubious
tax benefits? Former Commissioner Kurtz blames it
on the "audit lottery." He thinks "there is little or no
risk or cost in playing and losing." He may be too
modest about the power of the audit process. The
taxpayer may be simply beguiled. The result of a bad

shelter investment sometimes resembles the Ancient Mariner's albatross. Untying it from your neck is difficult indeed once the IRS enters the scene.

How They Work

After all that, if you now have the idea that tax shelters simply don't work for anyone, think again. They can be real tax savers, and legitimately so, if all the homework is done. There are myriad shelter configurations. Let's look at two basic kinds of shelters to get the feel of the thing.

Real Estate. The most fundamental kinds of shelter may be founded on the single resource that can't fluctuate in supply: a physical piece of the planet—land. Of course, a sole taxpayer may take advantage of real estate tax benefits without going into a partnership, but most real estate shelter programs, whether offered to the public generally or kept within a private circle, are syndicated as limited partnerships.

A limited partnership doesn't pay taxes. It's a conduit. Such a partnership offers the developer substantial capitalization and spreads the risk, all to the investor's advantage. A limited partner-investor can lose no more than his or her investment. (For more on such partnerships, see Chapter 14.)

The shelter garners (and distributes to investors) deductions for interest on its debt, real estate taxes, cost recovery allowances, and operating expenses while it is in business. There may be some rental income, but after offsetting current expenses, the amount of income passed through to the investors probably won't be significant in the beginning. When the property is sold or otherwise disposed of, gain on the investment (and gain is certainly the expectation) will be at low long-term capital gains rates (after adjustment for excess depreciation or cost recovery recapture).

EXAMPLE: Major Hoople is in the 50 percent marginal tax bracket and expects to stay there forever. He invests in an apartment building through a limited partnership. His share of the partnership's figures are:

Investment	$100,000	
Mortgage	400,000	
Total purchase price		$500,000
Price allocated to land		25,000
Price allocated to building		475,000
Annual rental income		$60,000
Annual cash expense (for taxes, mortgage interest, maintenance)		60,000
Cash flow		$ 0

So far, no gain or loss—the major's income is offset by deductions. There may even be enough, if rental income is higher, to pay for reduction of the mortgage. But don't forget about depreciation or cost recovery (discussed in Chapter 8).

An investor is able to depreciate the full cost of a building, even though most of its cost was paid for with borrowed funds. Using the straight-line recovery method over fifteen years, there would be an annual deduction for depreciation of $31,667. (The partnership's accountants will do all the arithmetic, never fear.) In Hoople's bracket, that's putting $15,833 into his pocket every year, an *after-tax* cash return of 15.8 percent.

There's more. Now assume that the property is sold after ten years. Though everyone expects a profit through appreciation, suppose, conservatively, that it's sold at the same price for which it was purchased, $500,000.

Hoople will have reduced his cost basis, through cost recovery over the decade, by $316,670, producing a long-term gain of the same amount. The long-term capital gains tax on that is $63,334. That's almost $437,000 left after federal taxes, in addition to the $158,330 received after taxes during the ten years. Don't forget that the mortgage still has to be paid off. If it remains the same $400,000 after ten years, there's still a bit of cash left over for Major Hoople (about $36,666). But, of course, the major had the use of the tax savings each year, which should have been invested profitably. All this is based on the assumption that the property is sold for cost. Most investors feel that inflation makes that a silly assumption. If the property is eventually sold at a whopping profit, tax mirth in the form of long-term gain ensues. (Naturally, it's the investor's job, not the adviser's, to pick a property that is bound to appreciate.)

Note the areas of conjecture: the expected tax brackets, the actual value of the property, the expected eventual sales price, the operating costs, and a whole host of imponderables that must be understood reasonably well on entrance into the shelter.

One provision of the law casts a severe shadow over the cheery aspect of most tax shelter investments. The "at-risk" rule (discussed below) allows an investor to take deductions only up to the amount he or she is personally liable to repay—the amount actually at risk, and no more. There's one significant exception to the at-risk rule. It does not apply to real estate, since most real estate purchases are "leveraged." The purchase price is met in large measure through borrowing in the form of a mortgage. When other shelters are leveraged, the at-risk rule comes into play, but not for leveraged realty. Good for real estate!

There are, of course, other general rules regarding tax shelters that do apply to real estate. Deductions for prepaid interest are limited so that cash-basis taxpayers may claim deductions only in and for the period to which the interest payments relate. Likewise, construction-period expenses may not be deducted "up front." Further, there may be tax preferences for quick cost recovery that might trigger a minimum tax. Cost recovery or depreciation deductions may be subject to recapture.

There's more value now to investing in old buildings, because of the increased credits for rehabilitation provided by the 1981 law.

It can be said, in general, that a real estate shelter is most useful for those with high ordinary income that is going to remain high. The tax consequences are probably more predictable than in other kinds of shelters.

Oil and Gas. The chance to be affiliated with the national search for hydrocarbons may come in various guises. You may send your money either to seek new oil or gas through a "wildcat" program, or to exploit known fields through "development" drilling. There are also "balanced" programs, combining wildcat and development drilling. Programs may be in diverse forms, but here, too, limited partnerships are popular.

The primary feature of most oil and gas investments is the opportunity to deduct the costs of labor, supplies, and the like for punching those deep holes in the earth's surface. These "intangible drilling and development costs" (IDCs to those in the business) are deductible in the year incurred. There may be other deductions for equipment depreciation or investment credits for equipment purchased. It doesn't matter whether the wells are productive. If there is income produced by the drilling, the depletion allowance (described in Chapter 8) may offer further tax benefits. On the other hand, the IDC may have to be counted as a tax preference item (see Chapter 12).

> EXAMPLE: Anson Pansky, on January 1, 1982, invested $20,000 in the "Beaufort-Skayle Wildcat Drilling Program 1982-A." He is in the 50 percent marginal tax bracket. In 1982, there was a $16,000 intangible drilling cost deduction, worth $8,000 to Anson. In 1983, the rest of the investment, $4,000, is expended and, therefore, is available as an IDC.
>
> The wildcat drilling succeeds in 1984. (Accept this on the faith that's applicable to such transactions.) During 1984, Mr. Pansky receives gross revenues of $14,000 with drilling deductions of $3,000 from the Beaufort-Skayle Program. Net income in 1984 is thus

$11,000. He takes a depletion deduction of $2,100 (or 15 percent of $14,000), too. Total deductions are $5,100.

Just for the first three years, Anson gets gross revenues of $14,000 on an investment of $20,000. In addition, he gets $25,100 in deductions, as follows:

Year 1: IDC	$16,000
Year 2: IDC	4,000
Year 3: Drilling Costs	3,000
Depletion	2,100
	$25,100

The example, you realize, is optimistic. It's just as likely that drilling will produce a dry hole. How many people do you know who've hit a gusher? But there's the downside protection of the current deductions for the IDC write-off, as well as the possible depletion allowance once the hydrocarbons start to flow. That's sufficient to make the investment attractive to high-bracket taxpayers.

Gain on the disposition of oil and gas holdings held over one year qualifies as long-term capital gain, but there may be ordinary income recognized because of the recapture of certain intangible drilling costs.

In the old days, before the at-risk rules, some oil and gas investments were leveraged to such an extent that they produced prodigious deductions, if nothing else. The deductions ranged from twice to ten times the amount of cash invested. That's gone.

The risk in oil and gas drilling is normally high, but there's often an attractive "risk-reward ratio," as the dealers like to say, if an investor can afford to take the chance.

Other Shelters. Each kind of shelter has its own characteristic way of reaching for the salient tax advantages peculiar to an industry. There are special tax benefits to certain agricultural enterprises, for example. Christmas trees, crossbred "beeffalo" bulls, and Black Angus breeding and feeding are old-time shelters.

Special accounting conventions that apply to the publishing of periodicals, sports franchises, or the production of motion pictures and television programs have been made the keystones of many shelter offerings. Tax shelters have been drawn from lithographs and master recordings. Don't discount the ingenuity of the tax shelter inventors.

Some Pertinent Restraints

Several sections of the Code, enacted as tax reforms, have particular application to tax shelter investments.

At-Risk Rules. Except for real estate (and certain leasing arrangements), tax losses generated by shelters are precisely limited to the amount at the investor's risk. It used to be commonplace for nonrecourse loans to finance shelter investments. The loans were "nonrecourse" because the collateral was the investment property, and there was no recourse, in case of default, against the borrower personally. Investors could obtain tax deductions for depreciation expenses on the whole value of the property bought largely with borrowed funds by the shelter enterprise. With immediate tax deductions reaching two or three times the amount of cash invested, tax savings could easily exceed the cash required to enter the game. What the happy investors didn't realize, and what was never stressed sufficiently by promoters, was that when and if the loans were repaid, the investors would have to recognize taxable income on the relief of their debt. The recognized income often far exceeded cash flow. The days of highly leveraged shelter deals, save for real estate and some specialized leasing transactions, are gone.

With those exceptions, the at-risk rules now apply to all nonrecourse borrowings made by the taxpayer either directly or through a conduit corporation or partnership. The at-risk limitation is calculated annually to prevent a taxpayer from reducing amounts at risk after deductions are claimed. A barred loss may become available in a later year if the risk is increased. An amount won't be considered to be at risk if protective devices, like guarantees, or stop-losses, are employed in an effort to skirt the at-risk rules.

Overvaluation Penalty. An additional penalty was written into the Code in 1981 that gives the Service another weapon against beleaguered shelters, though it will probably also be the subject of lots of litigation. If property is valued by the taxpayer at more than 150 percent of the "correct value" and an underpayment of tax is attributable to the overstated value, a penalty of 10 percent to 30 percent of the underpayment may be asserted. Thus, if there's a substantial valuation overstatement in a partnership return, in order to increase cost recovery deductions, for example, a partner's underpayment of tax could be the trigger for the penalty. (If you think overstating the value of property contributed to charity constitutes a kind of shelter, be advised that the rule operates in this area, too.) The penalty, though, is only applicable to underpayments of $1,000 or more and to valuation of property acquired within the previous five years. The penalty may be waived by the tax collector on a showing by the taxpayer that the overstatement had a reasonable basis and was made in good faith. It would be a good idea, therefore, to document fully the basis of the valuation (and contributors of property to charities should support their deductions with appropriate appraisals).

Promotion of Abusive Shelters. The 1982 law provides new civil retribution against promoters of abusive tax shelters or tax-avoidance schemes, and against those who help preserve specious returns. The basic penalty assessable is $1,000 or 10 percent of the gross income derived from promoting or selling the offending shelter if that is more (which is likely, of course). The nasty activity can also be the subject of an injunction.

Other Restrictions. In the good old shelter days, it was traditional for all shelter partnership activity to take place at year-end, when high-bracket taxpayers suddenly discovered the need to protect the year's impressive income. The shelter would, in those bygone days, present a full year's losses. Such special or retroactive allocations are no longer allowed. Deductions may be allocated to partners only for the part of the year they were actually partners.

Immediate deductions for construction-period interest payments or taxes that are prepaid are now curtailed. Such expenses are subject to special accounting rules that require them to be charged to a capital account and deducted over periods as long as a decade.

Other tax restrictions, discussed in other chapters, should not be forgotten when a shelter investment is contemplated. Remember the ceiling on excess investment interest deductions, the minimum tax on tax preference income, and the alternative minimum tax.

Leaving a Shelter

It's often desirable to back out of a shelter before its business is concluded. That may be difficult for an investor who wants to avoid an awkward tax posture.

Sometime during its life, a shelter may "burn out." That normally happens when it starts to produce taxable income instead of tax deductions—the "crossover point."

Different modes of shelters generally reach their crossover points fairly consistently. The IRS has provided this representative schedule.

Real estate	10–15 years
Print tax shelters	9–13 years
Low income housing	5 years
Research and development	5 years
Coal	3–4 years
Cattle feeding	1 year
Commodity spreads	1 year

Partnership agreements, in accord with the idea that interests in partnerships ought not to be freely transferable, limit the ability to sell one's interest. Even if a partner's interest can be sold, if he or she has a low basis or capital account, complications set in. When nonrecourse borrowing characterizes the shelter, these complications can be serious. If a partner is able to claim losses because a mortgage supports the deduction, when that partner is relieved of the obligation there will be a taxable gain. There will be no cash received in connection with this phantom gain, except for prior (and probably forgotten) tax savings.

EXAMPLE: Andrew Gump invested $20,000 in a limited partnership seven years ago. The partnership owns mortgaged real estate. Andy's share of the losses over the years totals $40,000. Now the deductions are no longer meaningful, because the interest on the mortgage is decreasing. Mr. Gump sells his partnership interest for $4,000. That's all he can get because the early tax shelter features have been used already. Though Mr. Gump gets only $4,000 in cash, he's got a taxable gain of $24,000, figured this way:

Cash received	$ 4,000
Plus share of losses	40,000
Less: Basis	(20,000)
Taxable gain on sale	$24,000

If Andy Gump is in the top bracket, his normal tax on the gain is at least $4,800 (20 percent of the gain), or $800 more than the cash received.

Well, how about just giving the partnership interest to a receptive charity if one can be found? Not so simple, because that phantom gain can't be given away. That part of the gift will be treated as a sale, rather than a contribution. The same tax problem encountered in a straight sale is met when the shelter is given to charity.

One method to divest oneself of a shelter is to give it to a poor relation. Subsequent income can be reported by the new owner, who doesn't need the shelter the investment used to give. Let the donee worry about any future recapture problems.

It's also possible to exchange a partnership interest for a "like kind" interest in a different partnership without recognition of gain, but that doesn't do much more than postpone taxes while another, perhaps worse, investment is made.

From a tax point of view, the best way to handle an out-moded shelter is to die with it. That way, a new basis for the property goes to whoever may inherit the thing.

A Word About the Offering Material

The flattering invitation to play the tax shelter game is normally accompanied by voluminous written material. You or someone on your side had better study the package before you decide to invest. Don't be bewitched by the supposed magical tax savings. The offering material will probably bear all sorts of dire warnings, simply because such offerings to the public are required by law to do so. "This private offering memorandum," it may say, "does not contain an untrue statement of a material fact or omit to state a material fact necessary to make the statements made, in light of the circumstances under which they were made, not misleading." No kidding—you may be faced with several prefatory pages of that sort of singing prose.

Buried in the offering memorandum, though, should be a full description of the transactions contemplated, the proposed uses of your money, the promoters' track records and what they propose to set aside for themselves, a summary of the expected tax effect of the deal, and, most important, a full recapitulation of the risk factors. If all of it isn't intelligible, it's time to ask questions, including "What am I doing?" Remember, some notorious shelters, including those selling nonexistent cattle or water instead of oil, gulled well-advised bank presidents and famous show folk, and they were sold with attractive and seemingly blameless offering memoranda.

20
Retirement Plans and Deferred Compensation

The flourishing American predisposition to provide for pensions, profit sharing, or postponement of earned income received added encouragement in the Tax Act of 1981. Individual as well as corporate interest in reasonably comfortable retirement has been regularly fostered by the tax law, to be sure, and the time-honored device of a nest egg is nurtured in a number of new tax ways. The Tax Act of 1982 attempted to achieve more parity between corporate and noncorporate plans. For those who are eligible, and that includes most of us, there may be some real shelter, easily established.

IRAs

Individual Retirement Accounts, or IRAs, were originally designed to benefit individuals who were not active participants in qualified or government pension plans, but for tax years after 1981, coverage has been expanded to include taxpayers in those categories as well as self-employed taxpayers. They are good for virtually all workers. The contributions to an IRA are deductible against income. The deductible amount that an individual may contribute is increased to either $2,000 ($2,250 for a "spousal IRA"), or 100 percent of the covered compensation, whichever is less. (Before 1981, the limit was 15 percent of compensation, up to $1,500, or $1,750 for a "spousal IRA.")

Spousal IRAs apply to married couples, filing jointly, with only one wage earner. In effect, the spouse who works for money contributes to the other spouse's IRA. Under the new rules, the amounts set aside on behalf of both spouses cannot be more than $2,250 (or 100 percent of earnings), but the amount may be allocated in any way, up to $2,000 for either. When both husband and wife have earned income, the $2,000 or full compensation limit applies separately to each. The maximum deduction may therefore reach $4,000 on a joint return. (A new special rule may allow a divorced taxpayer to continue a spousal IRA if it was established at least five years before the divorce and if the former spouse has made contributions to a spousal IRA for at least three out of the five years. In that case, the deduction is limited to the lesser of $1,125, or the total of the divorced spouse's earnings and includable alimony.)

The expansion of deductible amounts will probably increase the number of IRAs established for part-time workers.

> EXAMPLE: Jerry Mander is a well-paid corporate executive who is provided with corporate pension benefits. Jerry adds another $2,000 to his own retirement plan through a deductible IRA contribution. His wife, Sally Mander, is a homemaker, who recently took a part-time job selling real estate. Sally earns $1,800 this year, which she doesn't need now. She can establish her own IRA, contribute her full earnings to it, and pay no taxes on her earnings. Under the old rules, Sally could have deducted only $270. She would not have bothered with an IRA for that amount. (And under the former rules Jerry couldn't have set aside another $2,000 for his old age, either.)

Now that workers who are also covered by corporate or governmental pension plans may contribute deductible amounts to IRAs, they may make voluntary contributions on their own behalf directly to their employer's plan, if the plan permits it and is qualified.

Under the old rules, if a taxpayer was a participant in an employer's qualified plan at any time during the year, an IRA contribution was not allowed for that year. Thus, if a worker left a corporate plan in January there was no IRA for the rest of that year. That rule no longer applies. Contributions to an IRA may be made for any year up through the due date (including extensions) for the year's tax return. Contributions to an employer plan must be made, if the plan permits, by April 15 of the following year. Nevertheless, IRA contributions should be made as early as possible so that they may be invested for maximum earnings.

Contributions to IRAs, up to the allowable ceilings, are tax-deductible and, in addition, they accrue earnings tax-free. Upon the contributor's retirement, funds distributed from IRA accounts are taxable as ordinary income. The distributions are not eligible for capital gains treatment or the special ten-year averaging provision for certain lump-sum distributions from other qualified pension plans. IRA distributions, though, do meet the normal, five-year income-averaging rules. If an IRA distribution is in the form of an annuity contract, the full value is not immediately taxable; each annuity payment will be includable in full when received. The decision as to form of payment can be deferred until retirement if the options are built into the IRA.

Many retirement plans provide that the contributor-taxpayer may direct investments. IRAs, by their nature, admit of such direction. It was a nice notion, therefore, to contribute to one's IRA the Queen Anne tea service in the cupboard or the Brueghel the Elder painting on the wall and claim a deduction. After 1981, alas, amounts invested in collectibles (works of art, rugs, antiques, metals, gems, stamps, coins, or similar valuables, including collectible booze) are treated as distributions to the hapless taxpayer and taxed, with additional penalties. That still leaves stocks, bonds, mutual funds, and lots of other investments, of course, which may be directed. Financial institutions offer a variety of IRA packages.

Except in a case of death or disability, if a distribution is made from an IRA before the taxpayer reaches age 59½, not only is the distribution subject to regular tax, but there is a penalty, for the premature payment, of 10 percent of the total distribution. IRA rules require, on the other hand, that distributions start no later than the year in which the taxpayer reaches 70½. (The IRS seems to be as interested in half-year birthdays as are first-graders or insurance actuaries.) Contributions to qualified employer or government plans may be retained after that time, unless "rolled over" to a regular IRA.

To attract investment in the new IRAs, many banks have advertised aggressively, demonstrating the ease with which one could eventually become a millionaire. For example, a working couple, investing $4,000 each year in an IRA, could have over $1 million in thirty years. And a stripling of twenty-four, by investing $2,000 every year, could have $2 million at age sixty-five.

These projections are certainly accurate, but they are founded on an assumption that, for the life of the IRA, it will consistently earn 12 percent, compounded daily to yield 12.94 percent each year. *That* presupposes an annual inflation rate approaching 10 percent. If the economy continues to behave in such a zany fashion, what will a million buy for our twenty-four-year-old when he retires at sixty-five? It will buy just about what $25,000 bought when his IRA was first established.

All this is not to say that an Individual Retirement Account is a bad idea. Just be skeptical. Clearly a million dollars won't support very many Rolls-Royces, mink coats, H. Upmann stogies or world cruises if the banks' projections do prove accurate.

HR-10, or Keogh, Plans

HR-10 plans (also known as "Keogh plans") are pension or profit-sharing plans created by self-employed individuals for themselves and their employees, if they have any. Since the deductible contributions are substantially more than may be made to IRAs, HR-10 plans can provide bountiful benefits indeed. Financial institutions are happy to handle them, too, but that is not a requirement under the latest rules.

After 1981 and before 1984, the maximum annual deductible amount is, in the case of "defined contribution" plans, the lesser of $15,000 or 15 percent of the individual's net earnings from self-employment for the year. (Before 1982, the limit was $7,500.) For 1984 and after, for defined contribution plans, the limits are increased to 20 percent of earned income or $30,000—with cost of living increases starting in 1986. Regulations provide scales of deductible limitations under "defined benefit" plans (which have, in essence, also been increased).

Defined *contribution* plans are generally based on a percentage of earnings contributed annually to a plan. Defined *benefit* plans, on the other hand, involve annual contributions in amounts, actuarially determined, required to attain a specific benefit amount upon retirement. For many, defined benefit contributions may considerably exceed amounts deductible under defined contribution plans.

A self-employed taxpayer who wants to establish an HR-10 plan is obliged by law to make appropriate contributions for employees, too. Plans which are "top-heavy" in favor of key employees or owner-employees are not countenanced. There are not many ways to discriminate against lower-paid employees. The requirements are similar to those for qualified corporate pension plans relating to vesting of benefits, minimum funding, or employee participation in the plan. One technique to decrease the proportionate contribution for employees is integration of the plan with Social Security, since the maximum Social Security contribution accounts for a smaller proportion of the retirement income of the high-income folk. Other tests involve years of service, or a minimum age for admission into the plan.

Funds in HR-10 plans, as in IRAs, may be invested, free of taxes, to compound and grow. If withdrawals are made before the taxpayer reaches age 59½, or becomes disabled, they will be subject to normal tax and a 10 percent penalty as well. Unless an early distribution is a result of a plan termination, it will operate to prevent the owner-employee from making contributions to another HR-10 plan for five years. A loan from an HR-10 plan to an owner-employee, or the use of plan assets as security for such a loan, is generally treated as a taxable distribution.

Contributions on behalf of an owner-employer that exceed the allowable ceiling by design or miscalculation are subject to a penalty of 6 percent on the excess, but the penalty may now be avoided if no deduction for the excess is claimed, and the excess, together with its earnings, is pulled out before the taxpayer's return is filed.

Payments made upon retirement from HR-10 plans are taxed like payments from any qualified corporate pension plan.

Lump-sum distributions may be subject to special ten-year averaging rules (and special capital gain treatment for the pre-1974 portion of the lump-sum distribution).

After 1981, there is no impediment to a participant in an HR-10 plan who wishes to contribute to an IRA, too, subject to the rules applicable to IRAs. If a taxpayer's HR-10 plan investments are self-directed, care should be taken regarding "collectibles." The rules that apply to IRAs also apply to self-directed accounts in other qualified plans.

SEPs

The tax law recently produced SEPs, or Simplified Employee Pension plans, which are amalgams of HR-10s, IRAs, and corporate pension plans, all in tax harmony. In essence, a SEP is an employer-financed IRA. The employer may make a contribution, up to 15 percent, of an employee's compensation (limited to $15,000) and claim a deduction for it. The employee includes such amounts in income, but takes a deduction for the included amount of compensation. If the employer contributes less than the amount normally deductible by an employee under the IRA rules, the employee may make up the difference and claim a full IRA deduction. Even better, the employee may also contribute, subject to the regular IRA rules, to his own independent IRA.

Roll-overs

A "roll-over" is merely the method of transferring assets from one tax-exempt retirement fund to another—tax-free. An IRA is the normal vehicle for a roll-over. It's more than the simple change of trustee or custodian of an IRA account, which is simply a switch of fiduciary. A roll-over is a means of deferring tax on a lump-sum or plan-termination distribution by reinvesting it in another qualified plan or IRA. As in any tax-free transaction, there are certain requirements, such as:

- Cash or securities (or proceeds from the sale of the securities) taken from one plan must be rolled over into the recipient plan within sixty days.
- Employee contributions under a qualified plan,

which are recovered tax-free, can't be rolled over into an IRA.
- Only the covered employee (or surviving spouse) may roll over.
- Only one roll-over a year is allowed between IRAs.

A distribution isn't subject to tax when rolled over. There will be a tax only when amounts are actually distributed, and the tax consequences of a roll-over should be considered carefully. The employee may relinquish the chance of getting certain tax benefits of a lump-sum distribution when an amount from a qualified plan is rolled over to an IRA. Neither capital gain treatment nor the special ten-year averaging is available on a payout from an IRA.

Corporate Employee Benefit Plans

Of course, it's not always necessary for workers to prepare for their own retirement by way of IRAs and HR-10 plans. Benevolent employers, if they want to stay competitive, provide substantial packages of retirement benefits. Qualified employee plans may be fashioned into pensions, profit sharing, stock bonuses, annuities, bond purchases, or similar arrangements. To qualify, a plan must meet the criteria of the regulations regarding such matters as the proportion of employees covered in the plan, the distribution of benefits, amounts to be contributed for employees, the vesting of benefits, and how the plan is funded. Normally, employers, or the administrators of their plan, will obtain an advance ruling on the plan's qualification from the Service.

An employer receives current deductions for its contribution to a qualified plan, but there is no concurrent inclusion of income for employees. That is postponed until distribution is made. Income earned by the plan's fund may accumulate and grow tax-free until the amount earmarked for the employee is distributed. An employee may be able to augment the growing fund by making contributions also.

Any distribution from a qualified plan is taxable only to the extent that it is in excess of the employee's own unrecovered contributions. The employee, after all, was taxed on that amount before. The rest of the distribution (which consists of the employer's contribution and the accumulated earnings of the contributions of both worker and employer) is normally taxed to the employee as ordinary income on distribution.

But there may be special treatment for "lump-sum distributions." If a distribution is fully paid out within one tax year because of the worker's retirement, death, disability, or reaching age 59½ (whichever first occurs, one must believe), it is considered a lump-sum distribution. Such a distribution may be eligible for favored tax benefits, notably the use of a special ten-year averaging provision that allows the taxpayer to avoid bunching all that taxable income into one year. The tax rates under the ten-year averaging provisions are those for unmarried taxpayers applicable to a tenth of the distribution. The resultant tax is then multiplied by ten, all of which produces the benefit of nice low marginal tax brackets for the full amount taxable. To use this kind of averaging the employee must have been a participant in the plan for at least five years before the distribution.

The ten-year averaging provision is applicable to ordinary income received in a lump sum. An alternative capital gains treatment may be elected for the taxable amount of a distribution attributable to pre-1974 active plan participation. (It's hard to present a general rule as to the value of this election. If it's available, two sets of computations should be made. That's what the professionals do in such cases.)

There may be a variety of options available to an employee under the terms of any qualified plan. Some plans may not offer the option of receiving a lump sum, or may provide only for joint and survivor annuities. It's obviously necessary, therefore, to consult with the administrator of any qualified plan before a strategy for receiving payment is decided upon. "Understand and review the options" applies here particularly as well as to taxes generally. The retiring worker's world view and financial outlook have much to do with it. An optimist may select a long-term annuity, for example, while another pensioner may take the lump-sum money and run.

Stock Options

Traditionally, corporate bigwigs love employee stock options. Such privileges to purchase shares of a corporate employer's stock at set prices for specific periods of time have been dandy ways of compensating key personnel—generally, the bigwigs themselves. If the value of the option stock doesn't rise, the option can be forgotten. If it does rise the stock can be bought at the option price and there is an assured profit with no cash investment. There's also the benefit of deferral and long-term gain treatment for what might otherwise have been taxed as earned income.

Over thirty years ago, "restricted" stock options were given special tax treatment by the Revenue Act of 1950. The Revenue Act of 1964 did away with "restricted" options and replaced them with "qualified" options. The Revenue Act of 1976 phased out the "qualified " options by May 21, 1981, but the pendulum has swung back again with the Economic Recovery Tax Act of 1981. Now we have "incentive" stock options, not much different from the "restricted" or "qualified" options of blessed memory.

An incentive stock option, under the latest rules, has no tax effect when granted or when the option is exercised by purchase of stock. The recipient employee is entitled to long-term capital gain treatment when he or she sells the option stock if (1) the stock is not disposed of within two years after the option was granted or a year after exercise, and (2) the holder-employee works for the company that granted the option (or an affiliated firm) continuously from the date of the grant until three months before it's exercised (or a year if the employee is disabled).

If these two requirements are not met, when the stock is sold, the employee will recognize ordinary income. The amount recognized will be the lesser of (1) the gain realized, or (2) the difference between the option price and the fair market value on the exercise date. Any further gain would be subject to regular rules regarding capital gains.

Unless the employee recognizes ordinary income, the employer gets no deduction on the granting of an incentive stock option.

EXAMPLE: Percy Flage receives an incentive stock option on January 1, 1982, to purchase 10,000 shares of common stock in McKenn-Brennan, Inc., for which he works. The option will allow Mr. Flage to buy the stock at $1 per share, which is the fair market value at the time of granting. On July 1, 1983, Percy exercises the option. (At that time, McKenn-Brennan common is selling at $2.50 a share, but the exercise isn't a taxable event.) On January 2, 1985, he sells the stock for $4 a share. For 1985, Percy Flage recognizes a long-term capital gain of $30,000 ($4 sales price less $1 cost price times 10,000 shares).

To be considered an incentive stock option, entitled to all the rights and privileges appurtenant thereto, an option must meet certain tests:

- The issuer's shareholders must approve, within a year before or after, the adoption of a formal plan that states the number of shares involved and those employees (either by name or class) who are to receive them.
- Within a decade of the plan's adoption (or approval by the shareholders, if that's first), the option must actually be *granted* to the eligible employees.
- The options must be *exercised* within a decade of granting. (But if the grant is made to an employee who owned at least 10 percent of the company, the period is reduced to five years.)
- The option to purchase stock can't be transferred (except by death) and may be exercised only by the employee (unless he or she is dead, in which case the holding-period rules don't apply).
- An honest effort must be made to have the option price at least equal to the stock's fair market value on the date of the grant. (If the grant is made to an employee who owned more than 10 percent of the company, the option price must be at least 110 percent of fair market value.)
- An option can't be exercised while a previously granted incentive option is outstanding (and, for this purpose, an outstanding option can't be canceled; it has to lapse or be exercised—a good reason for keeping option periods reasonably short).
- The fair market value of options granted to any employee in a single calendar year must be limited to $100,000. (In case that's a hardship, there's also a

carry-over amount that may be added to the $100,000. Half of any prior year's excess can be carried over for three years. In one year, it's possible, therefore, for an employee to be granted options of $250,000.)

The new incentive stock option rules generally apply to options granted after 1975 and exercised or outstanding after 1980. Thus, they may be applicable to options already exercised.

Other Plans

There's a long list of ingenious methods of deferring compensation in an effort to defer taxes until the taxpayer settles into lower tax brackets.

ESOPs. Employee stock ownership plans (ESOPs) are tax-qualified retirement plans that must be made available to all employees and not restricted to the top execs or favored employees. They are used by relatively few companies.

Ordinarily, ESOPs acquire, for later distribution, the common stock of the employer by either employer contribution or employer loan to the plan. (That may provide a sanctioned method for the employer to leverage its stock with the help of the tax-protected retirement fund. Perhaps that's why some employers have promoted the idea. Most employers who have ESOPs declare that the best interests of their workers are served because the employees at least get a piece of the action by owning some of the company. Who knows?)

An ESOP generally has the same tax advantages as other qualified plans, including postponement of recognition and the possibility of capital gains when shares distributed are disposed of by an employee.

The employer, of course, gets a tax deduction for contributions to the plan. Corporate employers may also receive an extra tax credit for contributions. In an effort to increase the number of ESOPs, in 1981 a new enriched credit, based on payroll, replaced the old one, effective after 1982 and running through 1987.

Deferred Compensation. Deferring compensation makes the boss happy because the employee is encouraged to wear the corporate yoke faithfully awhile longer. The employee likes it because it may increase compensation, to be brought home at some time in the future when lower tax brackets will, presumably, be applicable. The standard scheme credits salary increments or bonuses to accumulate for later periodic payment. The employee's rights to the amounts credited are usually contingent on staying with the firm a given number of years or until retirement, death, or disability.

The general rules of constructive receipt, which require that earnings are taxed when earned, are suspended if certain rules are met. First, the employee must agree to the plan before the deferred compensation is earned. Then there must be a "naked promise," or contractual obligation, unsupported by any special security by the employer to pay the compensation later. The earned but unpaid compensation cannot be put in an escrow account or trust for the worker, who, in consequence, becomes a general creditor of his boss for the amount of the deferred compensation.

Unit Participation Plans. Certain deferred compensation plans provide employees, not with cash allocations, but rather with "units of participation" such as "stock appreciation rights" (SARs), which do not represent cash value. They are used to calculate the deferred compensation that is usually based on future appreciation of the company's stock. The increase in value of the units or rights is paid in the future, when the employee is in a lower bracket.

Phantom Stock. "Phantom," "shadow," or "stockless" stock is another way of calculating deferred compensation. It takes into account changes in value of the employer's stock. All capital adjustments, stock splits, cash, or stock dividends are recorded, and interest equivalents may be calculated also, so that on retirement an employee is credited with what would have been distributable if real stock actually had been set aside for him or her.

21
The Final Word

Perhaps you may feel that the melodrama of taxes is like an antique morality play (with Everyman-Taxpayer unsuccessfully tempted by malign forces) or a Punch-and-Judy show (in which Mr. Punch, our taxpayer, is financially battered soundly). The good news is that you may have a hand in writing significant parts of the script. Here is how.

Sowing, Reaping, and Timing

If you have read this text reasonably closely, you understand by now that knowledge of the eventual tax effect of a proposed activity or transaction is the best kind of tax planning. You know not to give cash to a charity if you can effect a better tax result by donating appreciated securities. You know whether to recover capital costs evenly over a straight line or more rapidly. You can decide whether there's a tax benefit in selling the old homestead now, or waiting until you are older.

Skillful taxpayers share with symphony conductors, skeet shooters, and stand-up comics an adroit sense of timing. In a time of annual reductions in tax rates, of course, it should be instinctive to consider accelerating deductions at year-end, while postponing the receipt of income until the strains of "Auld Lang Syne" die out.

Under the rules of constructive receipt, to be sure, tax

cannot be avoided on income already under the control of the taxpayer, but there are appropriate ways to smooth fluctuations in income or deductions, or to take advantage of rules that are applicable only in specific years.

Timing Ordinary Income. For a cash-basis taxpayer, advance payment for work to be performed later is taxable in the year the payment is received, rather than later, when the job is done. Conversely, arrangements may be made in advance to be paid in a year, or years, subsequent to the performance of work.

Some kinds of interest income may be accelerated or deferred by agreeing with a debtor to accept prepayments, or by extending interest due dates.

Dividend payments are not normally under a stockholder's control, but a closely held corporation may declare its year-end dividend and make it payable either in December or in the following January.

Bills for services performed near the end of the year may be delayed if you don't want to recognize any more income during the year. But if that's not the case, perhaps arrangements for advance billing can be made.

Timing Capital Gains or Losses. Gains or losses that are recognized in a given tax year are largely under your control. Simply sell now or hold off until next year.

Remember, net short-term gains in excess of long-term losses are taxed at full rates. So first try to use up short-term gains with short-term losses, then try to use up long-term gains with long (or short) losses.

Suppose that in December you take a capital loss in a particular security. Before the year is over, you find out that the loss is too big and it exceeds gains. Within thirty days of the sale, simply buy the same security back. That's a wash sale. The loss won't be recognized. It will be added to your new purchase price. You can sell in January and use the loss to offset next year's gains.

Another example: you hold a long-term bond with a low interest rate. Because of current high interest rates, this bond represents a paper capital loss. It may be worthwhile to switch to a similar, but not substantially identical, bond. (Remember that switching substantially identical securities will be a wash sale). The loss will be recognized. You'll have a higher cost basis (because you paid more for the new bond). Your interest income won't suffer, because the new bond probably pays more than the old one.

An installment sale may be helpful, especially if you are selling property late in the year.

> EXAMPLE: Lucy Anna Perchess is going to sell her business in December. She expects to realize $40,000 in long-term gain on the sale. She decides to sell on the installment basis. She will accept a quarter of the sale price in December and three more equal installments (plus interest) in each January thereafter for the next three years. The long-term gain each year will be $10,000. Lucy Anna will spread the gain over four years, but she will have to wait only a little more than two years for her money—from this December to the January twenty-five months later.

Timing Deductions and Credits. For a cash-basis taxpayer, it may be easier to choose the tax year for deductions than for the recognition of income. Deductible expenses are deductible when paid. In a high tax year, don't defer payments. If you've got an oil well, pay for the intangible drilling costs now under a contract requiring you to do so even if the hole isn't punched into the ground until next year.

Even if you don't own an oil well, there's still lots that can be done. Make charitable contributions in a high tax year. You can even use your credit card. Some deductible taxes may be prepaid.

There's a special rule regarding prepaid interest. It normally must be deducted evenly over the term of the loan. But interest that has been deferred (rather than prepaid) may be paid early to yield an accelerated deduction. (Watch out for "excess investment interest," though.)

Medical expenses are deductible only to the extent that they exceed a percentage of adjusted gross income. It may be worthwhile to pay such expenses in two-year cycles—if the medicos are sympathetic, of course. Married taxpayers might even consider whether it is cheaper to file separately.

> EXAMPLE: In 1983, Maxie and Minnie Mize have adjusted gross incomes of $40,000 each, and except for medical expenses, they have essentially equal deduc-

tions. Maxie's medical expenses are $1,800, and Minnie has received a doctor's bill of $2,000. If they file a joint return they won't have a medical deduction at all, because the combined expenses of $3,800 is less than 5 percent of the combined adjusted gross income of $80,000. (Remember, the floor is raised from 3 percent to 5 percent in 1983.) Maxie decides to pay his wife's doctor bill, and the Mizes file separate returns. He may deduct $1,800 ($3,800, less 5 percent of $40,000, which is $2,000). Perhaps that will make Maxie and Minnie feel better.

The timing of credits is also important, because a dollar's credit is a dollar in the pocket. Take a credit in the first year possible. It may be worthwhile, for example, to make an investment that will yield an investment credit or an energy credit before the year closes.

Return Preparation Time

The end of the tax year signals the start of "tax season," when the voice of the tax pro is heard in the land. From the first of January through the middle of April, the families of tax preparers tread softly during the few hours the breadwinner is home. Not for them the February vacation to Florida or Mexico.

All *you* have to worry about is your own return. Do you need the ministrations of a professional? Actually, the IRS instruction pamphlets are not bad guides in the preparation of many returns. They tell you where to put various figures, remind you to attach your W-2 forms and sign the return, and give you the proper address to which the whole abhorrent package may be sent. A short form or a relatively simple long form may certainly be prepared by the taxpayer. It's supposed to work that way. Maybe this book has been some encouragement in the composition of a return in the first person. (The IRS, by the way, will do the tax computation on the short form, 1040A, if the taxpayer fills out the rest of the form.)

Nevertheless, investment in professional preparation may often be worthwhile. Your financial affairs may be becoming more complex each year, you may be interested in a shelter, or you may simply be filled with fear and loathing.

Much of what you've learned in this text is best applied during the tax year, rather than at the time for reporting. It is sensible, if it's been an intricate tax year, to consult with a tax adviser before year-end. A professional analysis can be made, and perhaps some palliative tax action taken, before it's too late. That implies, of course, that you choose an adviser of reasonable sophistication and current learning.

The great majority of tax return preparers are honest and reputable, but finding an appropriate preparer for your own situation may take a bit of investigation. Talk to friends in the same financial condition. Perhaps someone can be found through work. The senior executives of many corporations are advised on tax matters as a perquisite. For other taxpayers, a union may be able to help. Try your lawyer, banker, or insurance agent. A recommendation is a better way to find a tax adviser than an ad in a tabloid. Make sure your preparer does not disappear after April 15; where will he or she be when you need him or her?

There are all kinds of tax professionals with various degrees of expertise and correspondingly varied price ranges.

- The IRS tries to respond to questions. During the 1980 tax season, they answered the phone more than 20 million times, received more than 36,000 written inquiries, and faced more than 5 million questioners in person. They won't answer questions over the phone anymore, but you may visit or write them. The help is free. You get what you pay for, some customers say, but they try hard. Because of the nature of the IRS business, don't expect them to stand behind their preparation advice. They won't.
- Commercial preparers, found in department stores and bank lobbies, or on late-night television commercials, are inexpensive. They may charge between $30 and $100 for easy returns, and they may not do any other kind. They put the figures in the right places and do the arithmetic properly. Most of the time. Such chain store operations might be necessary for those who have trouble with the language or simple math.

- There are also individual commercial preparers, working out of permanent offices, or out of barbershops or their basements part-time. They may be moonlighting accountants or former IRS agents. Their talents vary. Some may be excellent practitioners, but make sure of a preparer's reputation before making an appointment. One good way is to find out if the preparer is an "enrolled agent." The Service periodically administers a rugged examination to tax acolytes. If they pass, they are qualified to represent taxpayers before the IRS, and are competent tax preparers indeed. Their fees vary widely.
- Some banks have tax departments that are available to qualified customers, especially those of trust departments. They are generally solid, proficient preparers and offer continuity and close working relationships with their clientele. Banks are reasonably expensive, and don't cater very often to walk-in trade. Similar services may be offered to their customers by brokerage firms and other financial institutions.
- Certified public accountants are geared to take on any kind of tax preparation. A CPA may practice as an individual or in a small partnership. There are also giant international accounting firms with the most substantial return preparation resources. Most CPAs charge by the hour, and the fee for return preparation may range from $100 to thousands.
- Tax lawyers also charge by the hour—sometimes a lot. If you are not already a client, it may not be worthwhile to employ a tax lawyer for the simple preparation of your return. Many like to handle returns only as an accommodation—for a fee—for clients. What tax lawyers like best are complex problems of tax law. Rulings and court cases, corporate reorganizations and estate planning, new business arrangements and advance planning, and similar matters are what tax lawyers are trained for.

There are IRS exams for the enrollment of agents, while lawyers and CPAs may practice *ex officio* before the Service. There are no other rules regarding the qualification of tax return preparers. Anyone may fill out tax returns.

There are, nevertheless, standards that must be conformed to by anyone who prepares a tax return for money. Preparers are required to meet certain obligations under the law, or be subject to penalties. This doesn't mean that your preparer must tell confidential information to the other side. Tax information is confidential, and preparers of returns who improperly use or disclose information obtained in the preparation of tax returns are subject to criminal penalties.

A recent commissioner urged before he left office that preparers be obliged to "red flag" any item on a return about which there was a substantial legal question. That notion was roundly resisted by the tax bar. Under the latest rules, however, a taxpayer may be subject to penalties for substantial understatement of tax unless all of the relevant facts are shown on the return or there is real authority for the tax position claimed. Tax shelter items are held to an even higher standard. Tax preparers are subject to penalties for having anything to do with the preparation or presentation of any tax document which they know will result in the understatement of anybody's tax bill.

Make sure your preparer places his or her identifying number on the return, along with his or her business address (or home address, if there is no year-round business address). A preparer is also required to furnish you with a completed copy of any return or claim for refund prepared on your behalf—and not later than the time the original is presented to you for signing. An individual preparer must sign the return or claim by hand. (A stamp or label won't do.) Steer clear of anyone who charges to prepare returns but who won't do these things.

Don't deal with a preparer who promises to get you a refund before you even present your figures. Have nothing to do with anyone who takes a share of any refund as a fee.

If there's an understatement of a tax liability due to the preparer's "negligent or intentional disregard of rules and regulations," the preparer is subject to a penalty. That doesn't mean that a good-faith interpretation of the law in your favor can be considered "intentional disregard," though. "Willful understatement" of a tax liability is reason for another penalty that could take place if information regarding a taxpayer's tax liability is intentionally disregarded by a preparer.

The Service may seek injunctions or criminal sanctions against preparers who misbehave. Don't expect or ask your tax preparer to play games. It's simply not worth it.

If your preparer makes an honest mistake and you have to pay some more in tax, don't expect that he or she will pay your tax for you. It's *your* tax, which should have been paid in the first place. Interest or penalties on the underpayment are another matter. If interest or penalties are assessed strictly because of a preparer's goof, ask that those charges, aside from the increase in tax itself, be picked up by the preparer. You'll be surprised how many preparers, protective of their reputations, will do so, or make some other satisfactory arrangement. Just don't try to blame your faithful tax preparer for your own error. They've heard it all before.

Just Biding Time

The Pipeline and Audits. The commissioner has provided us with a charming graphic display of the travels of a return upon arrival at one of the ten Service Centers. It moves, along with tons of other forms, through what the IRS chooses to call its "pipeline," which is simply a series of largely automated processing steps.

In 1980, nearly 100 million individual income tax returns were filed and just about 89 million were checked by IRS computers for math errors. Approximately 73 out of every 1,000 checked contained such mistakes. Increases in tax, averaging $315, were indicated on about 40 of those. Refunds, averaging $203, were indicated for the other 33 out of the 1,000.

A math check is routine. An audit is not. In 1980, fewer than 2 million individual returns were examined. Coverage by field agents, office auditors, and Service Center personnel was just about 2 percent, therefore, but the coverage varied. For example, one out of a hundred returns (without business schedules) that showed adjusted gross income below $10,000 was audited. But one out of twenty of those showing business income and adjusted gross income over $30,000 was audited. (That's not too bad; more than three-quarters of corporations

Processing Pipeline

Returns are delivered to the Regional Service Centers.

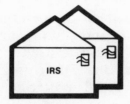

Envelopes are opened and counted.

Returns are sorted by type of return.

Tax returns and accompanying checks are compared.

Returns are edited and coded for computer processing.

Tax return information is placed on magnetic tape for computer processing.

IRS computers check returns for mathematical accuracy.

Tapes are sent to the National Computer Center for Account Posting and Settlement.

Tapes of Refunds are sent to the Treasury Department Disbursing Center for issuance of checks directly to taxpayers.

Once a tax return reaches one of ten IRS Service Centers, it travels through a series of processing steps known as "the pipeline."

While many parts of the pipeline shown here are automated for faster processing and faster refunds, people are involved every step of the way.

filing returns reporting balance sheet assets of more than $100 million were visited by the tax auditors.)

There are firm restrictions on the disclosure of information contained in individual returns (which is why the IRS won't talk to anyone else about your return without proper authorization). Until recently, though, there were no restrictions on general tax information. That comes under the rubric of freedom of information. Or so thought an energetic lady who sued the IRS for information and data used to develop secret audit-selection computer programs. Those programs identify returns with real potential for fruitful audit. She won her argument all the way up to the Supreme Court, which held off making a decision until Congress could react. And it did react. Except for the accustomed statistics, the law now provides that nothing can make the IRS reveal data or standards used for the selection of returns to be audited if it doesn't want to. It certainly doesn't want to, but at least we know some of the things the IRS simply doesn't like to see in tax returns.

Obviously, tax shelters are likely to cause audits. Those in particular occupations, like doctors or airline pilots, those who deal in cash, and those in the public eye are more likely to file more interesting returns. Large home office or travel and entertainment expenditures may attract an audit. Family transactions or overly complex self-prepared returns could trigger audits. Finally, it seems that a full-scale audit may be instigated just for the hell of it, because the computer needs statistics for the "taxpayer compliance measurement program." Just remember, though, if you file a clean return, the odds are substantially in your favor. (Remember also that the Service has recently contracted with Dun & Bradstreet, the private intelligence agency, to provide credit information. As needed, D&B will supply information on such matters as taxpayers' business history and bank accounts.)

One way to insure a draconian audit is to skirt the tax law in an attempt to demonstrate its inapplicability to you. If your contemplative world view doesn't countenance taxation, be warned.

Instead of the filing of a normal tax return, the submission of a thirty-two-page preprinted "Petition for Redress of Grievances," complete with objections, statements, affidavits, the

Declaration of Independence, and the Constitution, as well as a Form W-2—but without other sufficient data—is not a satisfactory return, in the opinion of the Tax Court. This unsanctioned method of filing was, of course, learned at a tax protest school and rather deliberate.

Such protests are often based on a putative constitutional right to file a virtually blank return. Sometimes a tax protester may report only a percentage of his or her income, remonstrating with Uncle Sam that inflation has already confiscated the rest. A protester may take a discount for the portion of the levy deemed to be collectible for improper governmental expenditures. Or a return may simply be omitted altogether.

The hopefully denominated Tax Equity and Fiscal Responsibility Act of 1982 provides countermeasures against tax protesters. It slaps a flat $500 penalty against anyone who files a "frivolous" return. A return may be characterized as frivolous if it doesn't contain enough information to calculate the tax or if it contains information which is obviously wrong and it is filed either with an intent to delay or impede Uncle Sam's collection of taxes or is essentially frivolous. (That last little bit may lead to some litigation, one supposes.)

If no return is filed, a new penalty is provided, even if no tax is due in the first place. Unless reasonable cause can be demonstrated for "extended failure to file," which may cover a period as short as sixty days, the penalty is set at no less than $100. The usual penalties mount, of course, according to tax due but not reported, but the IRS also wants you to pay for being searched out if you should have filed, but didn't because you were paid up anyway.

If you are audited, you may or may not agree with the result. If you do, you can simply pay up. If not, you can appeal. The IRS has provided a schematic diagram, resembling a board game but less fun, which shows the procedure. By the time the appeal gets very far, you may need the help of a tax lawyer, a lot of time, and perhaps a small war chest, so play only so far as is reasonable under the circumstances. Don't appeal simply out of anger—they have more time and money than you do.

An audit will probably be an "office audit" at the IRS, but it may be a "field audit" at your place. Either way, remember this: if an agent is identified as a "special agent" or is from

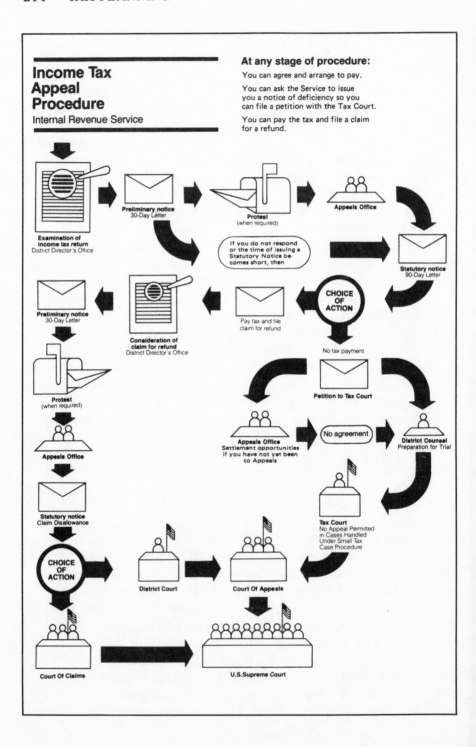

Income Tax Appeal Procedure
Internal Revenue Service

At any stage of procedure:
You can agree and arrange to pay.

You can ask the Service to issue you a notice of deficiency so you can file a petition with the Tax Court.

You can pay the tax and file a claim for a refund.

Examination of income tax return
District Director's Office

Preliminary notice
30-Day Letter

Protest
(when required)

Appeals Office

If you do not respond or the time of issuing a Statutory Notice becomes short, then

Statutory notice
90-Day Letter

Preliminary notice
30-Day Letter

Consideration of claim for refund
District Director's Office

Pay tax and file claim for refund

CHOICE OF ACTION

No tax payment

Protest
(when required)

Appeals Office

Petition to Tax Court

Appeals Office
Settlement opportunities if you have not yet been to Appeals

No agreement

District Counsel
Preparation for Trial

Statutory notice
Claim Disallowance

Tax Court
No Appeal Permitted in Cases Handled Under Small Tax Case Procedure

CHOICE OF ACTION

District Court

Court Of Appeals

Court Of Claims

U.S.Supreme Court

"Intelligence," don't wait. Get a lawyer. The presence of such an agent means that there is a criminal investigation afoot. Beware!

Refunds. More than half of all returns filed result in refunds, primarily because of excessive prepayments. If the bottom line of your return indicates that the IRS owes you money, don't be apprehensive that it will cause an audit. Just double-check the math and wait for that Treasury Department check. You should be receiving it around June, if you filed by April 15. If you don't, the refund will earn interest.

Interest is allowed (at the prime rate) until thirty days before the refund. No interest is due, however, on a refund made within forty-five days after the return is due, or, if later, when the return is actually filed. If you underpay *them*, you understand, interest starts running on the due date of the return, and you get no interest on excessive prepayments.

Suppose you find, after the return has been filed, that you made an error. Simply file an amended return. Form 1040X is used to indicate any change, upward or downward, on an individual tax return. It's necessary only to detail the changes from the original return; an entire corrected return isn't required. The 1040X is used to claim refunds.

Generally, a claim for refund must be filed within three years from the date the original return was due or filed, or two years from the date the overpayment was made, whichever is later. (If no return was filed, then the period is two years.) Longer time periods may be available if you and the IRS agree to extend the period, which, of course, gives them more time to assess more taxes, too. Net operating losses, net capital losses, certain credits, and losses from bad debts or worthless securities also extend the period during which claims may be made.

Record Keeping. You are required to keep "books and records" available for inspection by the IRS. You'll need to keep your tax records for your own purposes anyway. It's all very well to say that you should keep records as long as the contents are material, but how long is that?

For income tax returns, generally, keep all the necessary papers and documentation at least until the statute of limitations for assessment of tax expires for that kind of return. For income, estate, and gift taxes, that's normally three years after the return is filed (but not earlier than three years after the due date, if it's filed early). If more than a quarter of the taxpayer's true gross income is omitted from the return, the period is extended to six years. There's no statute of limitations at all if there's a willful or fraudulent attempt to evade tax, or if no return was ever filed.

While for most practical purposes three years will be long enough to retain all those pieces of paper, there are reasons why some records should be kept longer.

Documents pertaining to the cost bases and acquisition dates of assets should be kept as long as necessary. Gain or loss on the sale or disposition of capital assets depends on the cost bases and the periods held. Documents concerning loans, inventory, and other transactions should be retained as long as they are material. For example, special rules regarding net operating losses, bad debts or such past problems, may require holding on to records longer than usual. The possibility of income averaging dictates a little more filing space, too.

Cash payments should be avoided, since canceled checks or other documentation, such as credit card charges, provide substantiation of deductions. If you are in a trade or business that involves cash receipts, set up your books in an orderly and clear fashion. Tax auditors are particularly interested in cash businesses. If you have more than one business, maintain a separate set of books, including separate bank accounts, for each separate business.

In *David Copperfield*, Dickens mused, "It was as true as taxes. And nothing's truer than them." Just do your honest best with such ultimate truth. Nobody, not even Uncle Sam, can ask for more. We hope.

APPENDICES

A
Tax Rate Schedules

MARRIED INDIVIDUALS FILING JOINT RETURNS AND SURVIVING SPOUSES

1. For taxable years beginning in 1982—

If taxable income is:	The tax is:
Not over $3,400	No tax.
Over $3,400 but not over $5,500.......	12% of the excess over $3,400.
Over $5,500 but not over $7,600.......	$252, plus 14% of the excess over $5,500.
Over $7,600 but not over $11,900......	$546, plus 16% of the excess over $7,600.
Over $11,900 but not over $16,000.....	$1,234, plus 19% of the excess over $11,900.
Over $16,000 but not over $20,200.....	$2,013, plus 22% of the excess over $16,000.
Over $20,200 but not over $24,600.....	$2,937, plus 25% of the excess over $20,200.
Over $24,600 but not over $29,900.....	$4,037, plus 29% of the excess over $24,600.
Over 29,900 but not over $35,200......	$5,574, plus 33% of the excess over $29,900.
Over $35,200 but not over $45,800.....	$7,323, plus 39% of the excess over $35,200.
Over $45,800 but not over $60,000.....	$11,457, plus 44% of the excess over 45,800.
Over $60,000 but not over $85,500.....	$17,705, plus 49% of the excess over $60,000.
Over $85,600	$30,249, plus 50% of the excess over $85,600.

2. For taxable years beginning in 1983—

If taxable income is:	The tax is:
Not over $3,400	No tax.
Over $3,400 but not over $5,500.......	11% of the excess over $3,400.
Over $5,500 but not over $7,600.......	$231, plus 13% of the excess over $5,500.
Over $7,600 but not over $11,900......	$504, plus 15% of the excess over $7,600.
Over $11,900 but not over $16,000.....	$1,149, plus 17% of the excess over $11,900.
Over $16,000 but not over $20,200.....	$1,846, plus 19% of the excess over $16,000.
Over $20,200 but not over $24,600.....	$2,644, plus 23% of the excess over $20,200.
Over $24,600 but not over $29,900.....	$3,656, plus 26% of the excess over $24,600.
Over $29,900 but not over $35,200.....	$5,034, plus 30% of the excess over $29,900.
Over $35,200 but not over $45,800.....	$6,624, plus 35% of the excess over $35,200.
Over $45,800 but not over $60,000.....	$10,334, plus 40% of the excess over $45,800.
Over $60,000 but not over $85,600.....	$16,014, plus 44% of the excess over $60,000.

Over $85,600 but not over $109,400. . . .$27,278, plus 48% of the excess over
$85,600.
Over $109,400 . . . .$38,702, plus 50% of the excess over
$109,400.

3. For taxable years beginning after 1983—

If taxable income is:	The tax is:

Not over $3,400 . . . . , ...No tax.
Over $3,400 but not over $5,500. . . . . . .11% of the excess over $3,400.
Over $5,500 but not over $7,600. . . . . . .$231, plus 12% of the excess over $5,500.
Over $7,600 but not over $11,900 . . . .$483, plus 14% of the excess over $7,600.
Over $11,900 but not over $16,000 . . .$1,085 plus 16% of the excess over $11,900.
Over $16,000 but not over $20,200 . . .$1,741 plus 18% of the excess over $16,000.
Over $20,200 but not over $24,600 . . .$2,497, plus 22% of the excess over $20,200.
Over $24,600 but not over $29,900 . . .$3,465, plus 25% of the excess over $24,600
Over $29,900 but not over $35,200 . . .$4,790, plus 28% of the excess over $29,900.
Over $35,200 but not over $45,800 . . .$6,274, plus 33% of the excess over $35,200.
Over $45,800 but not over $60,000 . . .$9,772, plus 38% of the excess over $45,800.
Over $60,000 but not over $85,600 . . .$15,168, plus 42% of the excess over
$60,000.
Over $85,600 but not over $109,400 . .$25,920, plus 45% of the excess over
$85,600.
Over $109,400 but not over $162,400 .$36,630, plus 49% of the excess over
$109,400.
Over $162,400. . . . .$62,600, plus 50% of the excess over
$162,400.

HEADS OF HOUSEHOLDS

1. For taxable years beginning in 1982—

If taxable income is:	The tax is:

Not over $2,300 . . . . .No tax.
Over $2,300 but not over $4,400. . . . . . .12% of the excess over $2,300.
Over $4,400 but not over $6,500. . . . . . .$252, plus 14% of the excess over $4,400.
Over $6,500 but not over $8,700. . . . . . .$546, plus 16% of the excess over $6,500.
Over $8,700 but not over $11,800 . . . .$898, plus 20% of the excess over $8,700.
Over $11,800 but not over $15,000 . . .$1,518, plus 22% of the excess over $11,800.
Over $15,000 but not over $18,200 . . .$2,222, plus 23% of the excess over $15,000.
Over $18,200 but not over $23,500 . . .$2,958, plus 28% of the excess over $18,200.
Over $23,500 but not over $28,800 . . .$4,442, plus 32% of the excess over $23,500.
Over $28,800 but not over $34,100 . . .$6,138, plus 38% of the excess over $28,800.
Over $34,100 but not over $44,700 . . .$8,152, plus 41% of the excess over $34,100.
Over $44,700 but not over $60,600 . . .$12,498, plus 49% of the excess over
$44,700.
Over $60,600. . . . .$20,289, plus 50% of the excess over
$60,600.

2. For taxable years beginning in 1983—

If taxable income is:	The tax is:

Not over $2,300 . . . . .No tax.
Over $2,300 but not over $4,400. . . . . . .11% of the excess over $2,300.
Over $4,400 but not over $6,500. . . . . . .$231, plus 13% of the excess over $4,400.
Over $6,500 but not over $8,700. . . . . . .$504, plus 15% of the excess over $6,500.
Over $8,700 but not over $11,800 . . . .$834, plus 18% of the excess over $8,700.
Over $11,800 but not over $15,000 . . .$1,392, plus 19% of the excess over $11,800.
Over $15,000 but not over $18,200 . . .$2,000, plus 21% of the excess over $15,000.

Over $18,200 but not over $23,500 ...$2,672, plus 25% of the excess over $18,200.
Over $23,500 but not over $28,800 ...$3,997, plus 29% of the excess over $23,500.,
Over $28,800 but not over $34,100 ...$5,534, plus 34% of the excess over $28,800.
Over $34,100 but not over $44,700 ...$7,336, plus 37% of the excess over $34,100.
Over $44,700 but not over $60,600 ...$11,258, plus 44% of the excess over $44,700.
Over $60,600 but not over $81,800 ...$18,254, plus 48% of the excess over $60,600.
Over $81,800 .... $28,430, plus 50% of the excess over $81,800.

3. For taxable years beginning after 1983—

If taxable income is: **The tax is:**

Not over $2,300 .... No tax.
Over $2,300 but not over $4,400 ..... 11% of the excess over $2,300.
Over $4,400 but not over $6,500 ..... $231, plus 12% of the excess over $4,400.
Over $6,500 but not over $8,700 ..... $483, plus 14% of the excess over $6,500.
Over $8,700 but not over $11,800 .... $791, plus 17% of the excess over $8,700.
Over $11,800 but not over $15,000 ...$1,318, plus 18% of the excess over $11,800.
Over $15,000 but not over $18,200 ...$1,894, plus 20% of the excess over $15,000.
Over $18,200 but not over $23,500 ...$2,534, plus 24% of the excess over $18,200.
Over $23,500 but not over $28,800 ...$3,806, plus 28% of the excess over $23,500.
Over $28,800 but not over $34,100 ...$5,290, plus 32% of the excess over $28,800.
Over $34,100 but not over $44,700 ...$6,986, plus 35% of the excess over $34,100.
Over $44,700 but not over $60,600 ...$10,696, plus 42% of the excess over $44,700.
Over $60,600 but not over $81,800 ...$17,374, plus 45% of the excess over $60,600.
Over $81,800 but not over $108,300 ..$26,914, plus 48% of the excess over $81,800.
Over $108,300 .... $39,634, plus 50% of the excess over $108,300.

UNMARRIED INDIVIDUALS (OTHER THAN SURVIVING SPOUSES AND HEADS OF HOUSEHOLDS)

1. For taxable years beginning in 1982—

If taxable income is: **The tax is:**

Not over $2,300 .... No tax.
Over $2,300 but not over $3,400 ..... 12% of the excess over $2,300.
Over $3,400 but not over $4,400 ..... $132, plus 14% of the excess over $3,400.
Over $4,400 but not over $6,500 ..... $272, plus 16% of the excess over $4,400.
Over $6,500 but not over $8,500 ..... $608, plus 17% of the excess over $6,500.
Over $8,500 but not over $10,800 .... $948, plus 19% of the excess over $8,500.
Over $10,800 but not over $12,900 ...$1,385, plus 22% of the excess over $10,800.
Over $12,900 but not over $15,000 ...$1,847, plus 23% of the excess over $12,900.
Over $15,000 but not over $18,200 ...$2,330, plus 27% of the excess over $15,000.
Over $18,200 but not over $23,500 ...$3,194, plus 31% of the excess over $18,200.
Over $23,500 but not over $28,800 ...$4,837, plus 35% of the excess over $23,500.
Over $28,800 but not over $34,100 ...$6,692, plus 40% of the excess over $28,800.
Over $34,100 but not over $41,500 ...$8,812, plus 44% of the excess over $34,100.
Over $41,500 .... $12,068, plus 50% of the excess over $41,500.

2. For taxable years beginning in 1983—

If taxable income is:	The tax is:
Not over $2,300	No tax.
Over $2,300 but not over $3,400.	11% of the excess over $2,300.
Over $3,400 but not over $4,400.	$121, plus 13% of the excess over $3,400.
Over $4,400 but not over $8,500.	$251, plus 15% of the excess over $4,400.
Over $8,500 but not over $10,800	$866, plus 17% of the excess over $8,500.
Over $10,800 but not over $12,900 . . .	$1,257, plus 19% of the excess over $10,800.
Over $12,900 but not over $15,000 . . .	$1,656, plus 21% of the excess over $12,900.
Over $15,000 but not over $18,200 . . .	$2,097, plus 24% of the excess over $15,000.
Over $18,200 but not over $23,500 . . .	$2,865, plus 28% of the excess over $18,200.
Over $23,500 but not over $28,800 . . .	$4,349, plus 32% of the excess over $23,500.
Over $28,800 but not over $34,100 . . .	$6,045, plus 36% of the excess over $28,800.
Over $34,100 but not over $41,500 . . .	$7,953, plus 40% of the excess over $34,100.
Over $41,500 but not over $55,300 . . .	$10,913, plus 45% of the excess over $41,500.
Over $55,300	$17,123, plus 50% of the excess over $55,300.

3. For taxable years beginning after 1983—

If taxable income is:	The tax is:
Not over $2,300	No tax.
Over $2,300 but not over $3,400.	11% of the excess over $3,400.
Over $3,400 but not over $4,400.	$121, plus 12% of the excess over $3,400.
Over $4,400 but not over $6,500.	$241, plus 14% of the excess over $4,400.
Over $6,500 but not over $8,500.	$535, plus 15% of the excess over $6,500.
Over $8,500 but not over $10,800	$835, plus 16% of the excess over $8,500.
Over $10,800 but not over $12,900 . . .	$1,203, plus 18% of the excess over $10,800.
Over $12,900 but not over $15,000 . . .	$1,581, plus 20% of the excess over $12,900.
Over $15,000 but not over $18,200 . . .	$2,001, plus 23% of the excess over $15,000.
Over $18,200 but not over $23,500 . . .	$2,737, plus 26% of the excess over $18,200.
Over $23,500 but not over $28,800 . . .	$4,115, plus 30% of the excess over $23,500.
Over $28,800 but not over $34,100 . . .	$5,705, plus 34% of the excess over $28,800.
Over $34,100 but not over $41,500 . . .	$7,057, plus 38% of the excess over $34,100.
Over $41,500 but not over $55,300 . . .	$10,319, plus 42% of the excess over $41,500.
Over $55,300 but not over $81,800 . . .	$16,115, plus 48% of the excess over $55,300.
Over $81,800	$28,835, plus 50% of the excess over $81,800.

MARRIED INDIVIDUALS FILING SEPARATE RETURNS

1. For taxable years beginning in 1982—

If taxable income is:	The tax is:
Not over $1,700	No tax.
Over $1,700 but not over $2,750.	12% of the excess over $1,700.
Over $2,750 but not over $3,800.	$126, plus 14% of the excess over $2,750.
Over $3,800 but not over $5,950.	$273, plus 16% of the excess over $3,800.
Over $5,950 but not over $8,000.	$617, plus 19% of the excess over $5,950.
Over $8,000 but not over $10,100	$1,006, plus 22% of the excess over $8,000.
Over $10,100 but not over $12,300 . . .	$1,468, plus 25% of the excess over $10,100.
Over $12,300 but not over $14,950 . . .	$2,018, plus 29% of the excess over $12,300.

Over $14,950 but not over $17,600 . . .$2,787, plus 33% of the excess over $14,950.
Over $17,600 but not over $22,900 . . .$3,661, plus 39% of the excess over $17,600.
Over $22,900 but not over $30,000 . . .$5,728, plus 44% of the excess over $22,900.
Over $30,000 but not over $42,800 . . .$8,852, plus 49% of the excess over $30,000.
Over $42,800 . . . .$15,124, plus 50% of the excess over
$42,800.

2. For taxable years beginning in 1983—

If taxable income is: **The tax is:**
Not over $1,700 . . . . .No tax.
Over $1,700 but not over $2,750. . . . . .11% of the excess over $1,700.
Over $2,750 but not over $3,800. . . . . .$115, plus 13% of the excess over $2,750.
Over $3,800 but not over $5,950. . . . . .$252, plus 15% of the excess over $3,800.
Over $5,950 but not over $8,000. . . . . .$574, plus 17% of the excess over $5,950.
Over $8,000 but not over $10,100 . . . .$923, plus 19% of the excess over $8,000.
Over $10,100 but not over $12,300 . . .$1,322, plus 23% of the excess over $10,100.
Over $12,300 but not over $14,950 . . .$1,828, plus 26% of the excess over $12,300.
Over $14,950 but not over $17,600 . . .$2,517, plus 30% of the excess over $14,950.
Over $17,600 but not over $22,900 . . .$3,312, plus 35% of the excess over $17,600.
Over $22,900 but not over $30,000 . . .$5,167, plus 40% of the excess over $22,900.
Over $30,000 but not over $42,800 . . .$8,007, plus 44% of the excess over $30,000.
Over $42,800 but not over $54,700 . . .$13,639, plus 48% of the excess over
$42,800.
Over $54,700 . . . .$19,351, plus 50% of the excess over
$54,700.

3. For taxable years beginning after 1983—

If taxable income is: **The tax is:**
Not over $1,700 . . . . .No tax.
Over $1,700 but not over $2,750. . . . . .11% of the excess over $1,700.
Over $2,750 but not over $3,800. . . . . .$115, plus 12% of the excess over $2,750.
Over $3,800 but not over $5,950. . . . . .$241, plus 14% of the excess over $3,800.
Over $5,950 but not over $8,000. . . . . .$542, plus 16% of the excess over $5,950.
Over $8,000 but not over $10,100 . . . .$870, plus 18% of the excess over $8,000.
Over $10,100 but not over $12,300 . . .$1,248, plus 22% of the excess over $10,100.
Over $12,300 but not over $14,950 . . .$1,732, plus 25% of the excess over $12,300.
Over $14,950 but not over $17,600 . . .$2,395, plus 28% of the excess over $14,950.
Over $17,600 but not over $22,900 . . .$3,137, plus 33% of the excess over $17,600.
Over $22,900 but not over $30,000 . . .$4,886, plus 38% of the excess over $22,900.
Over $30,000 but not over $42,800 . . .$7,584, plus 42% of the excess over $30,000.
Over $42,800 but not over $54,700 . . .$12,960, plus 45% of the excess over
$42,800.
Over $54,700 but not over $81,200 . . .$18,315, plus 49% of the excess over
$54,700.
Over $81,200 . . . .$31,300, plus 50% of the excess over
$81,200.

ESTATES AND TRUSTS

1. For taxable years beginning in 1982—

If taxable income is: **The tax is:**
Not over $1,050 . . . . .12% of taxable income.
Over $1,050 but not over $2,100. . . . . . .$126, plus 14% of the excess over $1,050.
Over $2,100 but not over $4,250. . . . . . .$273, plus 16% of the excess over $2,100.
Over $4,250 but not over $6,300. . . . . . .$617, plus 19% of the excess over $4,250.

Over $6,300 but not over $8,400. . . . . . .$1,006, plus 22% of the excess over $6,300.
Over $8,400 but not over $10,600. . . . . .$1,468, plus 25% of the excess over $8,400.
Over $10,600 but not over $13,250. . . . .$2,018, plus 29% of the excess over $10,600.
Over $13,250 but not over $15,900. . . . .$2,787, plus 33% of the excess over $13,250.
Over $15,900 but not over $21,200. . . . .$3,661, plus 39% of the excess over $15,900.
Over $21,200 but not over $28,300. . . . .$5,728, plus 44% of the excess over $21,200.
Over $28,300 but not over $41,100. . . . .$8,852, plus 49% of the excess over $28,300.
Over $41,100 . . . .$15,124, plus 50% of the excess over
$41,100.

2. For taxable years beginning in 1983—

If taxable income is: **The tax is:**
Not over $1,050 . . . . .11% of taxable income.
Over $1,050 but not over $2,100. . . . . .$115, plus 13% of the excess over $1,050.
Over $2,100 but not over $4,250. . . . . .$252, plus 15% of the excess over $2,100.
Over $4,250 but not over $6,300. . . . . .$574, plus 17% of the excess over $4,250.
Over $6,300 but not over $8,400. . . . . .$923, plus 19% of the excess over $6,309.
Over $8,400 but not over $10,600 . . . .$1,322, plus 23% of the excess over $8,400.
Over $10,600 but not over $13,250 . . .$1,828, plus 26% of the excess over $10,600.
Over $13,250 but not over $15,900 . . .$2,517, plus 30% of the excess over $13,250.
Over $15,900 but not over $21,200 . . .$3,312, plus 35% of the excess over $15,900.
Over $21,200 but not over $28,300 . . .$5,167, plus 40% of the excess over $21,200.
Over $28,300 but not over $41,100 . . .$8,007, plus 44% of the excess over $28,300.
Over $41,100 but not over $53,000 . . .$13,639, plus 48% of the excess over
$41,100.
Over $53,000 . . . .$19,351, plus 50% of the excess over
$53,000.

3. For taxable years beginning after 1983—

If taxable income is: **The tax is:**
Not over $1,050 . . . . .11% of taxable income.
Over $1,050 but not over $2,100. . . . . .$115, plus 12% of the excess over $1,050.
Over $2,100 but not over $4,250. . . . . .$241, plus 14% of the excess over $2,100.
Over $4,250 but not over $6,300. . . . . .$542, plus 16% of the excess over $4,250.
Over $6,300 but not over $8,400. . . . . .$870, plus 18% of the excess over $6,300.
Over $8,400 but not over $10,600 . . . .$1,248, plus 22% of the excess over $8,400.
Over $10,600 but not over $13,250 . . .$1,732, plus 25% of the excess over $10,600.
Over $13,250 but not over $15,900 . . .$2,395, plus 28% of the excess over $13,250.
Over $15,900 but not over $21,200 . . .$3,137, plus 33% of the excess over $15,900.
Over $21,200 but not over $28,300 . . .$4,886, plus 38% of the excess over $21,200.
Over $28,300 but not over $41,100 . . .$7,584, plus 42% of the excess over $28,300.
Over $41,100 but not over $53,000 . . .$12,960, plus 45% of the excess over
$41,100.
Over $53,000 but not over $79,500 . . .$18,315, plus 49% of the excess over
$53,000.
Over $79,500 . . . .$31,300, plus 50% of the excess over
$79,500.

B
Tax/Tax-Exempt Equivalent Chart

A RETURN ON A TAX-EXEMPT INVESTMENT YIELDING:

Tax Rate	6%	7%	8%	9%	10%*
	Is Equivalent to a Taxable Return of:				
16%	7.14	8.33	9.52	10.71	11.90
17	7.23	8.43	9.64	10.84	12.05
19	7.41	8.64	9.88	11.11	12.35
20	7.50	8.75	10.00	11.25	12.50
22	7.69	8.97	10.26	11.54	12.82
23	7.79	9.09	10.39	11.69	12.99
25	8.00	9.33	10.67	12.00	13.33
27	8.22	9.59	10.96	12.33	13.70
28	8.33	9.72	11.11	12.50	13.89
29	8.45	9.86	11.27	12.68	14.08
30	8.57	10.00	11.43	12.86	14.29
31	8.70	10.14	11.59	13.04	14.49
32	8.82	10.29	11.76	13.24	14.71
33	8.96	10.45	11.94	13.43	14.93
34	9.09	10.61	12.12	13.64	15.15
35	9.23	10.77	12.31	13.85	15.38
36	9.38	10.94	12.50	14.06	15.63
38	9.68	11.29	12.90	14.52	16.13
39	9.84	11.48	13.11	14.75	16.39
40	10.00	11.67	13.33	15.00	16.67
41	10.17	11.86	13.56	15.25	16.95
42	10.34	12.07	13.79	15.52	17.24
44	10.71	12.50	14.29	16.07	17.86
45	10.91	12.73	14.55	16.36	18.18
48	11.54	13.46	15.38	17.31	19.23
49	11.76	13.73	15.69	17.65	19.61
50	12.00	14.00	16.00	18.00	20.00

*The last column (by shifting the decimal one place to the left) may be used to calculate yields at other rates. For example: at 40% tax rate, what taxable income is equivalent to 7½% tax-free? Answer: 12½% (7½% × 1.667 = 12.5). Or, at 40% tax rate, what tax-free income is equivalent to a thousand taxable dollars? Answer: $600 (1000 ÷ 1.667 = 599.88).

C
Federal Tax Forms
(Taxpayer to Uncle Sam)

See forms on following pages.

Form **1040** Department of the Treasury—Internal Revenue Service

U.S. Individual Income Tax Return 1982

For the year January 1—December 31, 1982, or other tax year beginning ____ 1982, ending ____ 19 ____ | OMB No. 1545-0074

Use IRS label. Otherwise, please print or type.

Your first name and initial (if joint return, also give spouse's name and initial) | Last name | Your social security number

Present home address (Number and street, including apartment number, or rural route) | Spouse's social security no.

City, town or post office, State and ZIP code

Your occupation ▲
Spouse's occupation ▲

Presidential Election Campaign ▲

Do you want $1 to go to this fund? . . . . | Yes ▨ | No | Note: Checking "Yes" will not increase your tax or reduce your refund.
If joint return, does your spouse want $1 to go to this fund? . . . | Yes ▨ | No

For Privacy Act and Paperwork Reduction Act Notice, see Instructions.

Filing Status
Check only one box.

1 ☐ Single
2 ☐ Married filing joint return (even if only one had income)
3 ☐ Married filing separate return. Enter spouse's social security no. above and full name here ▲ ____
4 ☐ Head of household (with qualifying person). (See page 6 of Instructions.) If the qualifying person is your unmarried child but not your dependent, enter child's name ▲ ____
5 ☐ Qualifying widow(er) with dependent child (Year spouse died ▲ 19 ____). (See page 6 of Instructions.)

Exemptions
Always check the box labeled Yourself.
Check other boxes if they apply.

6a ☐ Yourself | ☐ 65 or over | ☐ Blind
b ☐ Spouse | ☐ 65 or over | ☐ Blind

Enter number of boxes checked on 6a and b ▲ ☐

c First names of your dependent children who lived with you ▲ ____

Enter number of children listed on 6c ▲ ☐

d Other dependents:

(1) Name	(2) Relationship	(3) Number of months lived in your home	(4) Did dependent have income of $1,000 or more?	(5) Did you provide more than one-half of dependent's support?

Enter number of other dependents ▲ ☐

e Total number of exemptions claimed . . . .

Add numbers entered in boxes above ▲ ☐

Income
Please attach Copy B of your Forms W-2 here.

7 Wages, salaries, tips, etc. . . . . | 7 ____
8 Interest income (attach Schedule B if over $400 or you have any All-Savers interest) . . . . | 8 ____
9a Dividends (attach Schedule B if over $400) ____ , 9b Exclusion ____
c Subtract line 9b from line 9a . . . . | 9c ▨

If you do not have a W–2, see page 5 of Instructions.	**10** Refunds of State and local income taxes (do not enter an amount unless you deducted those taxes in an earlier year—see page 9 of Instructions)	**10**
	11 Alimony received ▲	**11**
	12 Business income or (loss) (attach Schedule C)	**12**
	13 Capital gain or (loss) (attach Schedule D)	**13**
	14 40% capital gain distributions not reported on line 13 (See page 9 of Instructions)	**14**
	15 Supplemental gains or (losses) (attach Form 4797)	**15**
	16 Fully taxable pensions, IRA distributions, and annuities not reported on line 17	**16**
	17a Other pensions and annuities. Total received . . . . 17a |	**17b**
	b Taxable amount, if any, from worksheet on page 10 of Instructions	**18**
	18 Rents, royalties, partnerships, estates, trusts, etc. (attach Schedule E)	**19**
	19 Farm income or (loss) (attach Schedule F) . . ▲	
	20a Unemployment compensation (insurance). Total received | 20a |	**20b**
Please attach check or money order here.	**b** Taxable amount, if any, from worksheet on page 10 of Instructions	
	21 Other income (state nature and source—see page 10 of Instructions) ▲	**21**
	22 **Total income.** Add amounts in column for lines 7 through 21 . . ▲	**22**
Adjustments to Income (See Instructions on page 11)	**23** Moving expense (attach Form 3903 or 3903F) . . . | 23 |	
	24 Employee business expenses (attach Form 2106) . . | 24 |	
	25 Payments to an IRA. You must enter code from page 11 (.......) . . . . | 25 |	
	26 Payments to a Keogh (H.R. 10) retirement plan . . | 26 |	
	27 Penalty on early withdrawal of savings . . . . . | 27 |	
	28 Alimony paid . . . . | 28 |	
	29 Deduction for a married couple when both work (attach Schedule W) . . . . | 29 |	
	30 Disability income exclusion (attach Form 2440) . . . | 30 |	
	31 Total adjustments. Add lines 23 through 30. . . . ▲	**31**
Adjusted Gross Income	**32** **Adjusted gross income.** Subtract line 31 from line 22. If this line is less than $10,000, see "Earned Income Credit" (line 62) on page 15 of Instructions. If you want IRS to figure your tax, see page 3 of Instructions . . . ▲	**32**

363–062–2

Form 1040 (1982) | Page 2

Tax Computation

(See Instructions on page 12)

33	Amount from line 32 (adjusted gross income)	33	
34a	If you itemize, complete Schedule A (Form 1040) and enter the amount from Schedule A, line 30	34a	
	Caution: If you have unearned income and can be claimed as a dependent on your parent's return, check here ▲ ☐ and see page 12 of the Instructions. Also see page 12 of the Instructions if:		
	● You are married filing a separate return and your spouse itemizes deductions, OR		
	● You file Form 4563, OR ● You are a dual-status alien.		
34b	If you do not itemize, complete the worksheet on page 13. Then enter the allowable part of your charitable contributions here	34b	
35	Subtract line 34a or 34b, whichever applies, from line 33	35	
36	Multiply $1,000 by the total number of exemptions claimed on Form 1040, line 6e . .	36	
37	Taxable Income. Subtract line 36 from line 35	37	
38	Tax. Enter tax here and check if from ☐ Tax Table, ☐ Tax Rate Schedule X, Y, or Z, or ☐ Schedule G	38	
39	Additional Taxes. (See page 13 of Instructions.) Enter here and check if from ☐ Form 4970, ☐ Form 4972, ☐ Form 5544, or ☐ section 72 penalty taxes . . . . . }	39	
40	**Total.** Add lines 38 and 39 . . . . ▲	40	

Credits

(See Instructions on page 13)

41	Credit for the elderly (attach Schedules R&RP) . . .	41	
42	Foreign tax credit (attach Form 1116)	42	
43	Investment credit (attach Form 3468)	43	
44	Partial credit for political contributions	44	
45	Credit for child and dependent care expenses (attach Form 2441) .	45	
46	Jobs credit (attach Form 5884)	46	
47	Residential energy credit (attach Form 5695) . . .	47	
48	Other credits—see page 14 ▲	48	
49	**Total credits.** Add lines 41 through 48	49	
50	**Balance.** Subtract line 49 from line 40 and enter difference (but not less than zero) . ▲	50	

Other Taxes

51	Self-employment tax (attach Schedule SE)	51	
52	Minimum tax (attach Form 4625)	52	
53	Alternative minimum tax (attach Form 6251)	53	

06 (Including Advance EIC Payments)

54	Tax from recapture of investment credit (attach Form 4255)	54
55	Social security (FICA) tax on tip income not reported to employer (attach Form 4137) .	55
56	Uncollected employee FICA and RRTA tax on tips (from Form W–2)	56
57	Tax on an IRA (attach Form 5329)	57
58	Advance earned income credit (EIC) payments received (from Form W–2) . . .	58
59	**Total tax. Add lines 50 through 58** . . . . ▮	**59**

Payments

Attach Forms W–2, W–2G, and W–2P to front.

60	Total Federal income tax withheld	60	
61	1982 estimated tax payments and amount applied from 1981 return .	61	
62	Earned income credit. If line 33 is under $10,000, see page 15 of Instructions	62	
63	Amount paid with Form 4868	63	
64	Excess FICA and RRTA tax withheld (two or more employers) .	64	
65	Credit for Federal tax on special fuels and oils (attach Form 4136)	65	
66	Regulated Investment Company credit (attach Form 2439)	66	
67	**Total. Add lines 60 through 66** . . . . ▲	**67**

Refund or Amount You Owe

68	If line 67 is larger than line 59, enter amount **OVERPAID** . . . . ▲	68
69	Amount of line 68 to be **REFUNDED TO YOU** . . . . . . ▲	69
70	Amount of line 68 to be applied to your 1983 estimated tax . . . ▲	70	
71	If line 59 is larger than line 67, enter **AMOUNT YOU OWE.** Attach check or money order for full amount payable to Internal Revenue Service. Write your social security number and "1982 Form 1040" on it. ▲ (Check ▲ ☐ if Form 2210 (2210F) is attached. See page 16 of Instructions.) ▲ $	71

Please Sign Here

Under penalties of perjury, I declare that I have examined this return, including accompanying schedules and statements, and to the best of my knowledge and belief, it is true, correct, and complete. Declaration of preparer (other than taxpayer) is based on all information of which preparer has any knowledge.

▲ Your signature _____ Date _____

▲ Spouse's signature (if filing jointly, BOTH must sign) _____ Date _____

Paid Preparer's Use Only

Preparer's signature ▲ _____ Date _____

Check if self-employed ☐

Preparer's social security no. _____

Firm's name (or yours, if self-employed) and address ▲ _____

E.I. No. ▲ _____

ZIP code ▲ _____

Schedules A&B (Form 1040)

Department of the Treasury
Internal Revenue Service

Schedule A—Itemized Deductions

(Schedule B is on back)

▶ Attach to Form 1040.　▶ See Instructions for Schedules A and B (Form 1040).

OMB No. 1545-0074

19**82**
07

Name(s) as shown on Form 1040

Your social security number

Medical and Dental Expenses

(Do not include expenses reimbursed or paid by others.)

(See page 17 of Instructions.)

1 Medicines and drugs	1	
2 Write 1% of Form 1040, line 33	2	
3 Subtract line 2 from line 1. If line 2 is more than line 1, write zero .	3	
4 Total insurance premiums you paid for medical and dental care .	4	
5 Other medical and dental expenses:		
a Doctors, dentists, nurses, hospitals, etc	5a	
b Transportation	5b	
c Other (list—include hearing aids, dentures, eyeglasses, etc.)		
▲		
....	5c	
6 Add lines 3 through 5c	6	
7 Multiply amount on Form 1040, line 33, by 3% (.03) . . .	7	
8 Subtract line 7 from line 6. If line 7 is more than line 6, write zero .	8	
9 Write one-half of amount on line 4, but not more than $150 .	9	
10 COMPARE amounts on line 8 and line 9, and write the LARGER amount here . . ▲	10	

Taxes

(See page 18 of Instructions.)

11 State and local income	11	
12 Real estate	12	
13 a General sales (see sales tax tables)	13a	
b General sales on motor vehicles	13b	
14 Other (list—include personal property) ▶	14	
15 Add lines 11 through 14. Write your answer here . . . . . ▲	15	

(See page 19 of Instructions.)

b Home mortgage interest paid to individuals (show that person's name and address) ▶ _____ | 16b |
17 Credit cards and charge accounts . . . . . | 17 |
18 Other (list) ▶ _____
_____ | 18 |
19 Add lines 16a through 18. Write your answer here . . . . . . ▲ | 19 |

Contributions

(See page 19 of Instructions.)

20 a Cash contributions. (If you gave $3,000 or more to any one organization, report those contributions on line 20b.) . . . . | 20a |
b Cash contributions totaling $3,000 or more to any one organization. (Show to whom you gave and how much you gave.)
▲
_____ | 20b |
21 Other than cash (see page 19 of Instructions for required statement) . . | 21 |
22 Carryover from prior years. . . . . . . | 22 |
23 Add lines 20a through 22. Write your answer here . . . . . . ▲ | 23 |

Casualty and Theft Losses and Miscellaneous Deductions

(See page 20 of Instructions.)

24 Total casualty or theft loss(es) (attach Form 4684) . . . . | 24 |
25 a Union and professional dues . . . . . | 25a |
b Tax return preparation fee . . . . . | 25b |
26 Other (list) ▶ _____
_____ | 26 |
27 Add lines 24 through 26. Write your answer here . . . . . . ▲ | 27 |

Summary of Itemized Deductions

(See page 20 of Instructions.)

28 Add lines 10, 15, 19, 23, and 27 . . . . | 28 |
29 If you checked Form 1040, Filing Status box { 2 or 5, write $3,400 . . 1 or 4, write $2,300 . . 3, write $1,700 . . } | 29 |
30 Subtract line 29 from line 28. Write your answer here and on Form 1040, line 34a. (If line 29 is more than line 28, see the Instructions for line 30 on page 20.) . . ▲ | 30 |

232 • APPENDICES

Schedules A&B (Form 1040) 1982 | **Schedule B—Interest and Dividend Income** | OMB No. 1545-0074 | Page **2**

Name(s) as shown on Form 1040 (Do not enter name and social security number if shown on other side) | Your social security number

Part I
Interest Income

(See pages 8 and 20 of Instructions.)

Also complete Part III if you received more than $400 in interest.

If you received more than $400 in interest or you received any interest from an All-Savers Certificate, you must complete Part I and list ALL interest received. If you received interest as a nominee for another, or you received or paid accrued interest on securities transferred between interest payment dates, please see page 20.

Interest income other than interest from All-Savers Certificates

	Amount
1 Interest income from seller-financed mortgages. (See Instructions and show name of payer.)	1
2 Other interest income (list name of payer)	
3 Add lines 1 and 2 . . .	3

Interest from All-Savers Certificates (ASCs). (See page 21.)

	Amount
4	
5 Add amounts on line 4 . . .	5
6 Write the amount of your ASC exclusion from the worksheet on page 21 of Instructions . .	6
7 Subtract line 6 from line 5 . . .	7
8 Add lines 3 and 7. Write your answer here and on Form 1040, line 8 . . . ▲	8

Part II
Dividend
Income

(See pages 9 and 21 of Instructions.)

Also complete Part III if you received more than $400 in dividends.

If you received more than $400 in gross dividends (including capital gain distributions) and other distributions on stock, or you are electing to exclude qualified reinvested dividends from a public utility, complete Part II. If you received dividends as a nominee for another, see page 21.

Name of payer	Amount
9	
	B

10 Add amounts on line 9 10

11 Capital gain distributions. Enter here and on line 13, Schedule D.* 11

12 Nontaxable distributions. (See Instructions for adjustment to basis.) . 12

13 Exclusion of qualified reinvested dividends from a public utility. (See Instructions.) 13

14 Add lines 11, 12, and 13 14

15 Subtract line 14 from line 10. Write your answer here and on Form 1040, line 9a . ▶ 15

*If you received capital gain distributions for the year and you do not need Schedule D to report any other gains or losses, do not file that schedule. Instead, enter 40% of your capital gain distributions on Form 1040, line 14.

Part III
Foreign
Accounts
and
Foreign
Trusts
(See page 21 of Instructions.)

If you received more than $400 of interest or dividends, OR if you had a foreign account or were a grantor of, or a transferor to, a foreign trust, you must answer both questions in Part III.

	Yes	No
16 At any time during the tax year, did you have an interest in or a signature or other authority over a bank account, securities account, or other financial account in a foreign country?		
17 Were you the grantor of, or transferor to, a foreign trust which existed during the current tax year, whether or not you have any beneficial interest in it? If "Yes," you may have to file Forms 3520, 3520-A, or 926 . .		

SCHEDULE C (Form 1040)
Department of the Treasury
Internal Revenue Service

Profit or (Loss) From Business or Profession

(Sole Proprietorship)

Partnerships, Joint Ventures, etc., Must File Form 1065.

▶ Attach to Form 1040 or Form 1041. ▶ See Instructions for Schedule C (Form 1040).

OMB. No. 1545-0074

1982 08

Name of proprietor | Social security number of proprietor

A Main business activity (see Instructions) ▶ _____ ; product ▶ _____

B Business name ▶ _____

C Employer identification number

D Business address (number and street) ▶ _____
City, State and ZIP Code ▶

E Accounting method: (1) ☐ Cash   (2) ☐ Accrual   (3) ☐ Other (specify) ▶ _____

F Method(s) used to value closing inventory:
(1) ☐ Cost   (2) ☐ Lower of cost or market   (3) ☐ Other (if other, attach explanation)

G Was there any major change in determining quantities, costs, or valuations between opening and closing inventory? · · · · · · · ☐ Yes ☐ No

H Did you operate this business at the end of 1982? ·

I Did you operate this business at the end of 1982? · · · · ·
If "Yes," attach explanation.

J How many months in 1982 did you actively operate this business? ▶

Part I Income

1 a Gross receipts or sales · · · · · · · · · · 1a
   b Returns and allowances · · · · · · · · · 1b
   c Balance (subtract line 1b from line 1a) · 1c
2 Cost of goods sold and/or operations (Schedule C–1, line 8) · · · · · · · · · · · · · 2
3 Gross profit (subtract line 2 from line 1c) · 3
4 a Windfall Profit Tax Credit or Refund received in 1982 (see Instructions) · · · · · · 4a
   b Other income · 4b
5 Total income (add lines 3, 4a, and 4b) · ▶ 5

Part II Deductions

6 Advertising . · · · · · · · · ·
7 Bad debts from sales or services (Cash method taxpayers, see Instructions) · · · · ·
8 Bank service charges . · · · ·
9 Car and truck expenses . · · · ·
10 Commissions · · · · · · · · ·
25 Taxes (Do not include Windfall Profit Tax here. See line 29.) · ·
26 Travel and entertainment · · ·
27 Utilities and telephone · · · ·
28 a Wages . · · · ·
   b Jobs credit
   c Subtract line 28b from 28a .

12 Depreciation, including Section 179 expense deduction (from Form 4562) . . . .

1982

30 Other expenses (specify):

a
b
c
d
e
f
g
h
i
j
k
m

13 Dues and publications . . . .
14 Employee benefit programs . .
15 Freight (not included on Schedule C-1) .
16 Insurance . . . . . .
17 Interest on business indebtedness
18 Laundry and cleaning . . . .
19 Legal and professional services .
20 Office supplies and postage . . .
21 Pension and profit-sharing plans .
22 Rent on business property . . .
23 Repairs . . . . .
24 Supplies (not included on Schedule C-1) .

31 **Total deductions** (add amounts in columns for lines 6 through 30m) . . . . . ▲ | 31

32 Net profit or (loss) (subtract line 31 from line 5). If a profit, enter on Form 1040, line 12, and on Schedule SE, Part I, line 2 (or Form 1041, line 6). If a loss, go on to line 33. . . . | 32

33 If you have a loss, do you have amounts for which you are not "at risk" in this business (see Instructions)? . . ☐ **Yes** ☐ **No**
If you checked "No," enter the loss on Form 1040, line 12, and on Schedule SE, Part I, line 2 (or Form 1041, line 6).

SCHEDULE C-1.—Cost of Goods Sold and/or Operations (See Schedule C Instructions for Part I, line 2)

1 Inventory at beginning of year (if different from last year's closing inventory, attach explanation) . | 1

2 Purchases (less cost of items withdrawn for personal use) . . . . . . | 2

3 Cost of labor (do not include salary paid to yourself) . . . . . . | 3

4 Materials and supplies . . . . | 4

5 Other costs . . . . | 5

6 Add lines 1 through 5 . . . . | 6

7 Inventory at end of year . . . . | 7

8 **Cost of goods sold and/or operations** (subtract line 7 from line 6). Enter here and on Part I, line 2 . ▲ | 8

SCHEDULE D (FORM 1040)
Department of the Treasury
Internal Revenue Service

Capital Gains and Losses (Examples of property to be reported on this Schedule are gains and losses on stocks, bonds, and similar investments, and gains (but not losses) on personal assets such as a home or jewelry.)
▶ Attach to Form 1040.   ▶ See Instructions for Schedule D (Form 1040).

OMB No. 1545-0074

1982
14

Name(s) as shown on Form 1040

Your social security number

Part I   **Short-term Capital Gains and Losses—Assets Held One Year or Less**

a. Kind of property and description (Example, 100 shares 7% preferred of "Z" Co.)	b. Date acquired (Mo., day, yr.)	c. Date sold (Mo., day, yr.)	d. Gross sales price less expense of sale	e. Cost or other basis, as adjusted (see instructions page 23)	f. LOSS If column (e) is more than (d) subtract (d) from (e)	g. GAIN If column (d) is more than (e) subtract (e) from (d)
1						

2a Gain from sale or exchange of a principal residence held one year or less, from Form 2119, lines 7 or 11 . . . . | **2a** |

b Short-term capital gain from installment sales from Form 6252, line 21 or 29 . | **2b** |

3 Net short-term gain or (loss) from partnerships and fiduciaries . . . . . | **3** |

4 Add lines 1 through 3 in column f and column g . . . . | **4** ( ) |

5 Combine line 4, column f and line 4, column g and enter the net gain or (loss) . . . . . . | **5** |

6 Short-term capital loss carryover from years beginning after 1969 . . . . . . | **6** ( ) |

7 Net short-term gain or (loss), combine lines 5 and 6 . . . . | **7** |

Part II Long-term Capital Gains and Losses—Assets Held More Than One Year

8

9a Gain from sale or exchange of a principal residence held more than one year, from Form 2119, lines 7, 11, 16 or 18 . . . . **9a**

b Long-term capital gain from installment sales from Form 6252, line 21 or 29 . **9b**

10 Net long-term gain or (loss) from partnerships and fiduciaries **10**

11 Add lines 8 through 10 in column f and column g . . . . **11** ( )

12 Combine line 11, column f and line 11, column g and enter the net gain or (loss) **12**

13 Capital gain distributions **13**

14 Enter gain from Form 4797, line 5(a)(1) **14**

15 Enter your share of net long-term gain from small business corporations (Subchapter S) . **15**

16 Combine lines 12 through 15 . . . . **16**

17 Long-term capital loss carryover from years beginning after 1969 . . . . **17** ( )

18 Net long-term gain or (loss), combine lines 16 and 17 . . . . **18**

Note: Complete this form on reverse. However, if you have capital loss carryovers from years beginning before 1970, do not complete Parts III or V. See Form 4798 instead.

Schedule D (Form 1040) 1982

Page **2**

Part III Summary of Parts I and II

19 Combine lines 7 and 18, and enter the net gain or (loss) here . . . .
Note: *If line 19 is a loss, skip lines 20 through 22 and complete lines 23 and 24. If line 19 is a gain complete lines 20 through 22 and skip lines 23 and 24* . . . . | **19**

20 If line 19 shows a gain, enter the smaller of line 18 or line 19. Enter zero if there is a loss or no entry on line 18 . . . . | **20** |

21 Enter 60% of line 20 . . . . | **21**

If line 21 is more than zero, you may be liable for the alternative minimum tax. See Form 6251.

22 Subtract line 21 from line 19. Enter here and on Form 1040, line 13 . . . . | **22**

23 If line 19 shows a loss, enter one of the following amounts:
   (i)   If line 7 is zero or a net gain, enter 50% of line 19;
   (ii) If line 18 is zero or a net gain, enter line 19; or
   (iii) If line 7 and line 18 are net losses, enter amount on line 7 added to 50% of the amount on line 18 | **23**

24 Enter here and as a loss on Form 1040, line 13, the smallest of:
   (i)   The amount on line 23;
   (ii) $3,000 ($1,500 if married and filing a separate return); or
   (iii) Taxable income, as adjusted . . . . | **24**

Part IV Complete this Part Only if You Elect Out of the Installment Method And Report a Note or Other Obligation at Less Than Full Face Value

☐ Check here if you elect out of the installment method.

Enter the face amount of the note or other obligation ▶ --------------------------------
Enter the percentage of valuation of the note or other obligation ▶

Part V Computation of Post-1969 Capital Loss Carryovers from 1982 to 1983

(Complete this part if the loss on line 23 is more than the loss on line 24)
Note: You do not have to complete Part V on the copy you file with IRS.

Section A.—Short-term Capital Loss Carryover

25	Enter loss shown on line 7; if none, enter zero and skip lines 26 through 30—then go to line 31 . .	
26	Enter gain shown on line 18. If that line is blank or shows a loss, enter zero	
27	Reduce any loss on line 25 to the extent of any gain on line 26	
28	Enter amount shown on line 24	
29	Enter smaller of line 27 or 28	
30	Subtract line 29 from line 27. This is your short-term capital loss carryover from 1982 to 1983 . .	

Section B.—Long-term Capital Loss Carryover

31	Subtract line 29 from line 28 (**Note:** *If you skipped lines 26 through 30, enter amount from line 24*) .	
32	Enter loss from line 18; if none, enter zero and skip lines 33 through 36	
33	Enter gain shown on line 7. If that line is blank or shows a loss, enter zero	
34	Reduce any loss on line 32 to the extent of any gain on line 33	
35	Multiply amount on line 31 by 2	
36	Subtract line 35 from line 34. This is your long-term capital loss carryover from 1982 to 1983 . .	

SCHEDULE F (Form 1040)

Department of the Treasury
Internal Revenue Service

Farm Income and Expenses

▲ Attach to Form 1040, Form 1041, or Form 1065.
▲ See Instructions for Schedule F (Form 1040).

OMB No. 1545-0074

1982
16

Name of proprietor(s)

Social security number

Farm name and address ▲

Employer identification number

Part I Farm Income—Cash Method

Do not include sales of livestock held for draft, breeding, sport, or dairy purposes; report these sales on Form 4797.

Sales of Livestock and Other Items You Bought for Resale

a. Description	b. Amount	c. Cost or other basis
1 Livestock ▲		
2 Other items ▲		
3 Totals		

4 Profit or (loss), subtract line 3, column c, from line 3, column b . . . . . . ▲

Sales of Livestock and Produce You Raised and Other Farm Income

Kind	Amount
5 Cattle and calves . . .	
6 Sheep.	
7 Swine.	
8 Poultry	
9 Dairy products . . .	
10 Eggs	

Part II Farm Deductions—Cash and Accrual Method

Do not include personal or living expenses (such as taxes, insurance, repairs, etc., on your home), which do not produce farm income. Reduce the amount of your farm deductions by any reimbursement before entering the deduction below.

Items	Amount
32 a Labor hired	
b Jobs credit	
c Balance (subtract line 32b from line 32a) .	
33 Repairs, maintenance .	
34 Interest	
35 Rent of farm, pasture .	
36 Feed purchased . .	
37 Seeds, plants purchased .	
38 Fertilizers, lime, chemicals	
39 Machine hire . . .	
40 Supplies purchased .	
41 Breeding fees . . .	
42 Veterinary fees, medicine .	
43 Gasoline, fuel, oil . .	

F

11 Wool . . . .
12 Cotton . . . .
13 Tobacco . . . .
14 Vegetables . . . . . .
15 Soybeans . . . .
16 Corn . . . .
17 Other grains . . . . . .
18 Hay and straw . . . . .
19 Fruits and nuts . . . . .
20 Machine work . . . . .
21 a Patronage dividends . .
   b Less: Nonincome items
   c Net patronage dividends . . . .
22 Per-unit retains . . . .
23 Nonpatronage distributions from exempt cooperatives . .
24 Agricultural program payments: a Cash . . . . . .
   b Materials and services . . . .
25 Commodity credit loans under election (or forfeited) . . .
26 Federal gasoline tax credit . . . .
27 State gasoline tax refund . . . . . .
28 Crop insurance proceeds . . . . . .
29 Other (specify) ▲
30 Add amounts in column for lines 5 through 29 .
31 Gross profits* (add lines 4 and 30). . . . ▲

44 Storage, warehousing . . . .
45 Taxes . . . . .
46 Insurance . . . .
47 Utilities . . . . .
48 Freight, trucking . . .
49 Conservation expenses .
50 Land clearing expenses .
51 Pension and profit-sharing plans . . . .
52 Employee benefit programs other than line 51 . . .
53 Other (specify) ▲

54 Total (add lines 32c through 53) . . . .
55 Depreciation, including Section 179 expense deduction (from Form 4562) . . .
56 Total deductions (add lines 54 and 55) . . .

57 Net farm profit or (loss) (subtract line 56 from line 31). If a profit, enter on Form 1040, line 19, and on Schedule SE, Part I, line 1. If a loss, go on to line 58. (Fiduciaries and partnerships, see the Instructions.). . . . . ▮ 57

58 If you have a loss, do you have amounts for which you are not "at risk" in this farm (see instructions)? . . ☐ Yes ☐ No
If you checked "No," enter the loss on Form 1040, line 19, and on Schedule SE, Part I, line 1.

*Use amount on line 31 for optional method of computing net earnings from self-employment. (See Schedule SE, Part II, line 4.)

Schedule F (Form 1040) 1982   17   Page **2**

Part III   Farm Income—Accrual Method (Do not include sales of livestock held for draft, breeding, sport, or dairy purposes; report these sales on Form 4797 and omit them from "Inventory at beginning of year" column.)

a. Kind	b. Inventory at beginning of year	c. Cost of items purchased during year	d. Sales during year	e. Inventory at end of year
59 Cattle and calves				
60 Sheep				
61 Swine				
62 Poultry				
63 Dairy products				
64 Eggs				
65 Wool				
66 Cotton				
67 Tobacco				
68 Vegetables				
69 Soybeans				
70 Corn				
71 Other grains				
72 Hay and straw				
73 Fruits and nuts				
74 Machine Work				
75 Other (specify) ▶				
76 Totals (enter here and in Part IV				

Part IV Summary of Income and Deductions—Accrual Method

77 Inventory of livestock, crops, and products at end of year (line 76, column e)

78 Sales of livestock, crops, and products during year (line 76, column d)

79 Agricultural program payments: a Cash
b Materials and services

80 Commodity credit loans under election (or forfeited)

81 Federal gasoline tax credit

82 State gasoline tax refund

83 Other farm income (specify) ▶

84 Add lines 77 through 83

85 Inventory of livestock, crops, and products at beginning of year (line 76, column b)

86 Cost of livestock and products purchased during year (line 76, column c)

87 Total (add lines 85 and 86)

88 **Gross profits*** (subtract line 87 from line 84)

89 Total deductions from Part II, line 56

90 Net farm profit or (loss) (subtract line 89 from line 88). If a profit, individuals enter on Form 1040, line 19, and on Schedule SE, Part I, line 1. If a loss, go on to line 91. (Fiduciaries and partnerships, see the Instructions.)   90

91 If you have a loss, do you have amounts for which you are not "at risk" in this farm (see Instructions)? · ☐ Yes ☐ No
If you checked "No," enter the loss on Form 1040, line 19, and on Schedule SE, Part I, line 1.

*Use amount on line 88 for optional method of computing net earnings from self-employment. (See Schedule SE, Part II, line 4.)

Schedule G
(Form 1040)

Department of the Treasury
Internal Revenue Service

Income Averaging

▶ See instructions on back.   ▶ Attach to Form 1040.

OMB No. 1545-0074

1982
20

Name(s) as shown on Form 1040

Your social security number

Step 1   Figure your income for 1978-1981

1978

1 Fill in the amount from your 1978 Form 1040 (line 34) or Form 1040A (line 10) 1

2 Multiply your total exemptions in 1978 by $750 2

3 Subtract line 2 from line 1. If less than zero, enter zero 3

1979

4 Fill in the amount from your 1979 Form 1040 (line 34) or Form 1040A (line 11) 4

5 Multiply your total exemptions in 1979 by $1,000 . . . 5

6 Subtract line 5 from line 4. If less than zero, enter zero 6

1980

7 Fill in the amount from your 1980 Form 1040 (line 34) or Form 1040A (line 11) 7

8 Multiply your total exemptions in 1980 by $1,000 . . . 8

9 Subtract line 8 from line 7. If less than zero, enter zero 9

1981

10 Taxable income. Fill in the amount from your 1981 Form 1040 (line 34) or Form 1040A (line 12). If less than zero, enter zero 10

Total

11 Fill in all income earned outside of the United States or within U.S. possessions and excluded for 1978 through 1981 11

12 Add lines 3, 6, 9, 10 and 11 12

Step 2   Figure your averageable income

Multiply the amount on line 12 by 30% (.30) 13

13 Write in the answer 13

14 Fill in your taxable income for 1982 from Form 1040, line 37 . . 14

15 If you received a premature or excessive distribution subject to a penalty under
   section 72, see instructions . . . . |15|

16 Subtract line 15 from line 14 . . . . |16|

17 If you live in a community property state and are filing a separate return, see instructions . . |17|

18 Subtract line 17 from line 16. If less than zero, enter zero . . . . |18|

19 Write in the amount from line 13 above . . . . |19|

20 Subtract line 19 from line 18. This is your averageable income . . . . |20|

**If line 20 is $3,000 or less, do not complete the rest
of this form. You do not qualify for income averaging.**

Step 3   Figure your tax

21 Multiply the amount on line 20 by 20% (.20) . . . . |21|

22 Write in the answer . . . . |22|

23 Write in the amount from line 13 above . . . . |23|

24 Write in the amount from line 17 above . . . . |24|

25 Add lines 21 and 22 . . . . |25|

26 Add lines 23 and 24 . . . . |26|

27 Tax on amount on line 25 (from Tax Rate Schedule X, Y, or Z) . . . |27|

28 Tax on amount on line 23 (from Tax Rate Schedule X, Y, or Z) . . . |28|

29 Tax on amount on line 22 (from Tax Rate Schedule X, Y, or Z) . . . |29|

   Subtract line 28 from line 27 . . . .

   Multiply the amount on line 29 by 4 . . . .

30 Write in the answer . . . . |30|

   If you have no entry on line 15, skip lines 31 through 33 and go to line 34.

31 Tax on amount on line 14 (from Tax Rate Schedule X, Y, or Z) . . . |31|

32 Tax on amount on line 16 (from Tax Rate Schedule X, Y, or Z) . . . |32|

33 Subtract line 32 from line 31 . . . . |33|

34 Add lines 26, 30, and 33. Write the result here and on Form 1040, line 38. Be sure
   to check the Schedule G box on that line . . . . |34|

OMB No. 1545-0085

1982

Department of the Treasury — Internal Revenue Service

Form 1040A US Individual Income Tax Return

Step 1
Name and address

Use the IRS mailing label. Otherwise, print or type.

Your first name and initial (if joint return, also give spouse's name and initial) | Last name | Your social security no.

Present home address | Spouse's social security no.

City, town or post office, State, and ZIP code

Your occupation

Spouse's occupation

Presidential Election Campaign Fund

Do you want $1 to go to this fund? . . . . ☐ Yes ☐ No

If joint return, does your spouse want $1 to go to this fund? ☐ Yes ☐ No

Step 2
Filing status
(Check only one)
and Exemptions

1 ☐ Single (See if you can use Form 1040EZ.)
2 ☐ Married filing joint return (even if only one had income)
3 ☐ Married filing separate return. Enter spouse's social security no. above and full name here.
4 ☐ Head of household (with qualifying person). If the qualifying person is your unmarried child but not your dependent, write this child's name here.

Always check the exemption box labeled Yourself. Check other boxes if they apply.

5a ☐ Yourself ☐ 65 or over ☐ Blind

b ☐ Spouse ☐ 65 or over ☐ Blind

Write number of boxes checked on 5a and b ☐

c First names of your dependent children who lived with you

Write number of children listed on 5c ☐

Attach Copy B of Forms W-2 here

d Other dependents:

(1) Name	(2) Relationship	(3) Number of months lived in your home.	(4) Did dependent have income of $1,000 or more?	(5) Did you provide more than one-half of dependent's support?

Write number of other dependents listed on 5d ☐

e Total number of exemptions claimed . . . .

Add numbers entered in boxes above ☐

Step 3
Adjusted gross income

6 Wages, salaries, tips, etc. (*Attach Forms W-2*) . . . . 6 .

7 Interest income (*Complete page 2 if over $400 or you have any All-Savers interest*) . . . . 7 .

8a Dividends _____ . (Complete page 2 if over $400) 8b Exclusion _____ 8c .

9a Unemployment compensation (insurance). Total from Form(s) 1099-UC Subtract line 8b from 8a

b Taxable amount, if any, from worksheet on page 16 of Instructions . . . . 9b .

Step 4
Taxable income

10 Add lines 6, 7, 8c, and 9b. This is your total income. 10

11 Deduction for a married couple when both work. Complete the worksheet on page 17. 11

12 Subtract line 11 from line 10. This is your adjusted gross income. 12

13 Allowable part of your charitable contributions. Complete the worksheet on page 18. 13

14 Subtract line 13 from line 12 14

15 Multiply $1,000 by the total number of exemptions claimed in box 5e. 15

16 Subtract line 15 from line 14. This is your taxable income. 16

Step 5
Tax, credits, and payments

Attach check or money order here

17a Partial credit for political contributions. See page 19. . . . . . . ■ 17a

b Total Federal income tax withheld, from W-2 form(s). *(If line 6 is more than $32,400, see page 19.)* 17b

Stop Here and Sign Below if You Want IRS to Figure Your Tax

c Earned income credit, from worksheet on page 21 . . . . 17c

18 Add lines 17a, b, and c. These are your total credits and payments. 18

19a Find tax on amount on line 16. Use tax table, pages 26-31. . . . . . 19a

b Advance EIC payment *(from W-2 form(s))*. 19b

20 Add lines 19a and 19b. This is your total tax. 20

Step 6
Refund or amount you owe

21 If line 18 is larger than line 20, subtract line 20 from line 18. Enter the amount to be **refunded to you** 21

22 If line 20 is larger than line 18, subtract line 18 from line 20. Enter the **amount you owe.** Attach payment for full amount payable to "Internal Revenue Service." 22

Step 7
Sign your return

I have read this return and any attachments filed with it. Under penalties of perjury, I declare that to the best of my knowledge and belief, the return and attachments are correct and complete.

▲ _____   _____   _____
Your signature   Date   Spouse's signature (If filing jointly, BOTH must sign)

Paid preparer's   _____   _____   Check if self-   Preparer's social security no.
signature   Date   employed ☐

Firm's name (or   E.I. no.
yours, if self-employed)
Address and Zip code

For **Privacy Act and Paperwork Reduction Act Notice,** see page 34.

1982 Form 1040A

Caution: You may **NOT** file Form 1040A (you must file Form 1040 instead) if any of the following apply to you:

- You could be claimed as a dependent on your parent's return AND had interest, dividends, or other unearned income of $1,000 or more.

- You had a foreign financial account or were a grantor of, or transferor to, a foreign trust.

- You received interest or dividends as a nominee (in your name) for someone else.

- You received or paid accrued interest on securities transferred between interest payment dates.

- You received capital gain distributions or nontaxable distributions.

- You are choosing to exclude qualified reinvested dividends from a qualified public utility.
  Note: You may also be required to file Form 1040 for other reasons. See pages 4 through 6 of instructions.

Part I   Interest income

You must complete this part if you received over $400 in interest income, OR you received any interest from an All-Savers Certificate (ASC). Use lines 1 and 2 to report interest income other than ASC interest. Use lines 3 through 6 to report ASC interest. Use line 7 to add the totals from lines 2 and 6.

Interest income from sources other than All-Savers Certificates. (See page 14)

1 List names of payers	Amount
	$
	$
	$
	$
	$
	$
	$
	$

2 Add amounts on line 1. This is your total interest from other than ASCs. | 2 | . |

Interest income from All-Savers Certificates. (See page 14)

3 List names of payers   Amount

$

$

$

4 Add amounts on line 3.   4

5 Write the amount of your ASC exclusion from the worksheet on page
14 of the instructions.   5

6 Subtract line 5 from line 4. This is your taxable ASC interest.   6

7 Add lines 2 and 6 and write your answer here. This is your total taxable interest. Also write this
amount on line 7 of Form 1040A.   7

Part II   Dividend income

You must complete this part if you received over $400 in ordinary dividends. See page 15 for information on the dividend
exclusion.

8 List names of payers   Amount

$

$

$

$

$

$

9 Add amounts on line 8. Write your answer here and on line 8a of Form 1040A.   9

Form **5695**

Department of the Treasury
Internal Revenue Service

Residential Energy Credit

▲ Attach to Form 1040. ▲ See Instructions on back.

For Paperwork Reduction Act Notice, see instructions on back.

OMB No. 1545-0214

1982

33

Name(s) as shown on Form 1040

Your social security number

Enter in the space below the address of your principal residence on which the credit is claimed if it is different from the address shown on Form 1040.

If you have an energy credit carryover from a previous tax year and no energy savings costs this year, skip to Part III, line 24.

Part I   Fill in your energy conservation costs (but do not include repair or maintenance costs).

1 Was your principal residence substantially completed before April 20, 1977? . . . . . ▲ ☐ Yes   ☐ No

Note: You MUST answer this question. Failure to do so will delay the processing of your return. If you checked the "No" box, you CANNOT claim an energy credit under Part I and you should not fill in lines 2 through 12 of this form.

2 a Insulation	2a	
b Storm (or thermal) windows or doors	2b	
c Caulking or weatherstripping	2c	
d A replacement burner for your existing furnace that reduces fuel use . .	2d	
e A device for modifying flue openings to make a heating system more efficient .	2e	
f An electrical or mechanical furnace ignition system that replaces a gas pilot light .	2f	
g A thermostat with an automatic setback	2g	
h A meter that shows the cost of energy used	2h	
3 Total (add lines 2a through 2h)	3	
4 Enter the part of expenditures made from nontaxable government grants and subsidized financing .	4	
5 Subtract line 4 from line 3	5	
6 Maximum amount of cost on which credit can be figured	6	$2,000 00
7 Enter the total energy conservation costs for this residence. Add line 2 of your 1978, 1979, and 1980 Forms 5695 and line 3 of your 1981 Form 5695	7	
8 Subtract line 7 from line 6	8	
9 Enter the total nontaxable grants and subsidized financing used to purchase qualified energy items for this residence. Add the amount on line 4 of this form and the amount on line 4 of your 1981 Form 5695 .	9	

10 Subtract line 9 from line 8. If zero or less, do not complete the rest of this part	**10**	
11 Enter the amount on line 5 or line 10, whichever is less	**11**	
12 Enter 15% of line 11 here and include in amount on line 23 below	**12**	

Part II   Fill in your renewable energy source costs (but do not include repair or maintenance costs).

13 a Solar _____ 13 b Geothermal _____ 13 c Wind _____ Total ▲	**13d**	
14 Enter the part of expenditures made from nontaxable government grants and subsidized financing . .	**14**	
15 Subtract line 14 from line 13	**15**	
16 Maximum amount of cost on which the credit can be figured	**16**	$10,000	00
17 Enter the total renewable energy source costs for this residence. Add line 5 of your 1978 Form 5695, line 9 of your 1979 and 1980 Forms 5695, and line 13d of your 1981 Form 5695	**17**	
18 Subtract line 17 from line 16	**18**	
19 Enter the total nontaxable grants and subsidized financing used to purchase qualified energy items for this residence. Add the amount on line 14 of this form and the amount on line 14 of your 1981 Form 5695	**19**	
20 Subtract line 19 from line 18. If zero or less, do not complete the rest of this part	**20**	
21 Enter the amount on line 15 or line 20, whichever is less	**21**	
22 Enter 40% of line 21 here and include in amount on line 23 below	**22**	

Part III   Fill in this part to figure the limitation.

23 Add lines 12 and 22. If less than $10, enter zero	**23**	
24 Enter your energy credit carryover from a previous tax year. Caution—Do not make an entry on this line if your 1981 Form 1040, line 47, showed an amount of more than zero	**24**	
25 Add lines 23 and 24	**25**	
26 Enter the amount of tax shown on Form 1040, line 40	**26**	
27 Add lines 41 through 46 from Form 1040 and enter the total	**27**	
28 Subtract line 27 from line 26. If zero or less, enter zero	**28**	
29 Residential energy credit. Enter the amount on line 25 or line 28, whichever is less. Also, enter this amount on Form 1040, line 47. Complete Part IV below if this line is less than line 25	**29**	

Part IV   Fill in this part to figure your carryover to 1983 (Complete only if line 29 is less than line 25).

30 Enter amount from Part III, line 25	**30**	
31 Enter amount from Part III, line 29	**31**	
32 Credit carryover to 1983 (subtract line 31 from line 30)	**32**	

D
Federal Tax Forms
(Uncle Sam to Taxpayer)

See forms on following pages.

Request for Missing Information or Papers to Complete Return

We are sending back your tax return because we need more information to process it.
Please supply all the items asked for in the boxes checked on both sides of this form. When you reply, be sure to include your return and this form as well as any other information requested.
Thank you for your cooperation.

Enclosures: Notice 610

☐ Form 1040, OMB NO. 1545-0074   ☐ Form 1040A, OMB No. 1545-0085   ☐ 1040NR, OMB No. 1545-0089

☐ **1.** Your return is not signed. Please sign in the space provided. (If this is a joint return, both husband and wife must sign.)

☐ **2.** Please attach Form W-2, Wage and Tax Statement; Form W-2P, Statement for Recipients of Periodic Annuities, Pensions, Retired Pay, or IRA Payments; or Form W-2G, Statement for Certain Gambling Winnings, to support the entry of $ _____ for tax withheld. If you cannot get the forms, please attach an explanation of source of income and name and address of person or organization that withheld the tax.

☐ **3.** Please explain the entry of $ _____ for wages by sending us Form W-2 or a statement with name and address of person or organization that withheld tax.

☐ **4.** Please complete or clarify the filing status section of your return.

☐ **5.** Please complete or clarify the exemptions section of your return.

☐ **6.** Please complete the enclosed Form(s) _____ or Schedule(s) _____ to support your entry on line(s) _____ of Form 1040.

☐ **7.** Please explain your entry of $ _____ on line _____ of Form _____ or Schedule _____ and attach the appropriate form, schedule, or information to support the entry.

☐ **8.** Please fill in line(s) _____ on Form _____ or Schedule _____.

☐ **9.** When your tax is at least $1, you may designate that $1 be contributed to the Presidential Election Campaign Fund. When you file a joint return reporting tax of $2 or more, you and your spouse may each designate $1 for the fund. This does not increase your tax or reduce your refund. You did not indicate on your return whether you want any of your tax to go to

the fund. If you like you can make the designation now by checking the appropriate box or boxes on page 1 of your return.

☐ **10.** Please complete the enclosed Form 2210 (2210F) to support Underpayment of Estimated Tax Penalty written on page 2 of your Form 1040.

☐ **11.** The Form 5695 attached to your return is not complete. Please answer the question on line 1.

☐ **12.** Please provide taxpayer's date of death on Form 1040.

☐ **13.** The required Form 1310 is missing, or the Form 1310 attached does not contain enough information. Please complete, sign, and return the enclosed form. If you are an administrator or executor, also send a court certificate currently in effect showing your appointment as personal representative. If you are not court appointed, please mark box C as claimant, complete Schedule A and send a copy of the death certificate.

☐ **14.** Please send a court certificate or copy of the power of attorney that authorizes someone else to sign the attached return and that was in effect when the return was prepared.

☐ **15.** We are unable to determine the name of the person claiming the refund. Please type or print the name of the claimant.

☐ **16.** Your Schedule R is incomplete. Complete line 2a and any other lines that apply to you. If the amount for line 2a is zero, enter "0."

☐ **17.** Your Schedule RP is incomplete. Please enter the name of each public retirement system involved. Complete lines 2 and 5 and any other lines that apply to you. If the amount for line 2a is zero, enter "0."

over

Form 3531. Request for Missing Information to Complete Return. (cont'd)

□ **18.** We can process either Schedule R or RP, but not both. Please see the instructions to determine which schedule to file.

[ ] **19.** Your Schedule RP, Columns (a) and (b) have identical entries; however, community property laws do not apply in figuring the credit for the elderly. Please enter the total of all taxable and nontaxable income in the appropriate column for the person who received the income.

□ **20.** Please have your physician complete and sign the statement of permanent and total disability at the bottom of Form 2440.

□ **21.** Please enter the gross amount of unemployment compensation received on line 9a, Form 1040A, or line 19a, Form 1040.

□ **22.** We cannot determine which taxpayer is filing Form 5329. Please enter on Form 5329 the name and social security number of the taxpayer who has the Individual Retirement Arrangement and is required to pay the tax. If both taxpayers are required to pay the tax, each must file a separate Form 5329.

□ **23.** The Form 5329 attached to your return is not signed. Please sign it in the space provided.

□ **24.** On Schedule SE, please enter the name and social security number of the taxpayer owing self-employment tax. If both husband and wife have self-employment income, each must file a separate Schedule SE.

[ ] **25.** If a taxpayer is unable to sign the return, the signatures of two witnesses are required. Please sign the return again in the presence of two witnesses.

□ **26.** You may file a joint return and claim your spouse's exemption(s) if your spouse died within the tax year, and you did not remarry within the tax year. If you have a dependent child(ren), you may claim qualifying widow(er) status for the following 2 years. Please provide your spouse's name and social security number.

□ **27.** If you are filing a separate return (Filing Status 3), you must report only your own income, exemptions, deductions, and credits. If you want to combine your incomes, you must file a joint return (Filing Status 2).

□ **28.** Your return includes income or tax for more than one tax period or for more than one person (other than husband and wife). Since each person (or married couple) must file a separate tax return for each tax period, we have enclosed blank forms for you to complete.

[ ] **29.** Please show all income, credits, other taxes and payments as appropriate. If you are not required to file this year or if you don't expect to have to file in the future, please do so indicate.

□ **30.** Please let us know the taxable amount of your disability pension.

□ **31.** Please complete the enclosed Form 2441 to support the amount of $ _____ reported for child and dependent care. (This amount should have been reported on Form 2441 instead of on Schedule _____.)

□ **32.** Your return indicates Form _____ is due. Please complete the enclosed Form _____.

□ **33.** Please fill in lines 1 through 9 on Schedule A to support the amount shown on line 10, Schedule A.

□ **34.** Please complete Schedule B of Form 3468 to support the entry on line 18, page 1 of Form 3468.

□ **35.** Your social security number or your spouse's social security number is missing or does not show nine digits.
In the space provided on your return, please write your correct social security number exactly as it appears on your social security card or your spouse's, if applicable. If you do not have a number, please get Form SS-5, Application for a Social Security Number, from the Social Security Administration or the Internal Revenue Service, and file the application promptly with the Social Security Administration to avoid delay in receiving your number. Write "Number Applied For" in the spaces provided on your return for your social security number.

□ **36.** Your return does not show that you:
1. Subtracted the Work Incentive (WIN) Program Credit from salaries or wages reported on Schedule C or Schedule F, or
2. Adjusted your income or losses on Schedule E, Part II, by the amount of the WIN credit shown on Form 4874.
If the WIN credit is for wages or salaries reported on either Schedule C or F, enter it on Schedule C, line 29c, or Schedule F, line 32c, and subtract it from the salary or wage deduction. If the WIN credit applies to salaries or wages included in figuring income or losses reported on Schedule E, Part II, increase the income or decrease the loss on Schedule E by the amount of the WIN credit shown on Form 4874.

□ **37.** Your return does not show that you subtracted the jobs credit reported on Form 5384 from your deduction for the salaries and wages you paid. You should show the credit on Schedule C, line 29b, or on Schedule F, line 32b. Either enter the credit on the appropriate schedule and subtract that amount from your wage deduction, or attach an explanation when you reply.

□ **38.** Please indicate the tax period covered by your return.

□ **39.** _____
_____
_____
_____
_____
_____
_____

Form 4743. Questionnaire—Taxes.

Form 4743 (Rev. November 1981)	Department of the Treasury — Internal Revenue Service **Questionnaire - Taxes**	OMB No. 1545-0397 Expires 12/31/82
Taxpayer(s) name(s) and address		In reply refer to
		Tax year

Please furnish the following information to support the taxes deducted on your Federal income tax return for the above year. If you need more space, please attach extra sheets and label each column as shown below. Also attach documents such as receipts and canceled checks *(photocopies are acceptable)* to substantiate the taxes paid. We will return the documents as soon as we are through with them.

Thank you for your cooperation.

Kind of tax	To whom paid	Date paid	Amount paid	Is receipt or canceled check attached? Yes	No

1. Real estate taxes: Please show below the name of the owner of the real property at the time the taxes were paid.

Owner's name _____

If the property was bought or sold during the year, please give the date, and show what division was made between the taxes levied on you and those levied on the other owner.

Date of purchase _____ or Date of sale _____

Total tax $ _____ Your portion of the tax $ _____

256 • APPENDICES

2. State and local income taxes: If, during the year being examined, you received a refund of any taxes deducted in a prior year, please show the amount refunded.

Amount of refund $ _____

3. Sales tax: If the amount you deducted is greater than the amount shown in the sales tax tables in the instructions you received with your return, please explain how you determined your deduction.

4. Are any special assessments included in the taxes you claimed? ☐ Yes ☐ No
If Yes, please explain the purpose and show the amount.

Declaration	Your signature	Date
I declare that I have examined the information on this form and, to the best of my knowledge and belief, it is true, correct and complete.	Spouse's signature if a joint return was filed	Date

Form **4743** (Rev. 11-81)

Form 4746. Questionnaire—Credit for Child and Dependent Care Expenses.

OMB Clearance No. 1545-0412
Expires 9-30-82

Form **4746** (Rev. Dec. 1981)	Department of the Treasury — Internal Revenue Service **Questionnaire — Credit for Child and Dependent Care Expenses** For Privacy Act and Paperwork Reduction Act Notice, see enclosed Notice 609.

Taxpayers' Names and Address	In Reply Refer To:
	Tax Year

Please furnish the following information to support the child and dependent care credit on your Federal income tax return for the above year. If you need more space, please attach extra sheets. Also attach supporting documents such as receipts and canceled checks. (Photocopies are acceptable.) We will return the documents as soon as we are through with them. Thank you for your cooperation.

1. Name of Qualifying Individual *(See explanation on back)*	Individual's Relationship to You	Individual's Date of Birth	Was this individual physically or mentally unable to care for self?	
			Yes	No·
A.				
B.				
C.				

2. Names and addresses of payees (persons or organizations you paid to perform child and dependent care services):	Payee's Taxpayer Identifying Number*	Payee's Relationship to You	Amount Paid
A.			
B.			
C.			

*Social security or employer identification number

3. Please indicate the place where dependent care services were performed:	Were Forms 942 Filed?	
	Yes	No
A.		
B.		
C.		

4(a) Indicate your marital status on the last day of the year in question: Single ☐   Married ☐

Married but not living with spouse ☐   Separated under a court decree ☐   Divorced ☐   Widow ☐ Widower ☐

(b) Please give the dates of any changes in your marital status during the tax year in question. Show also your income and your total dependent care expenses for each period.

(over)

Form **4746** (Rev. 12-81)

Joint return filers use column A for wife and column B for husband. All other filers use column C.	Joint Return		
	A (Wife)	B (Husband)	C (Other)
5(a) Were you either working or looking for work on all days for which you paid child and dependent care expenses? (Answer Yes or No)			
(b) If you answered No to 5(a), what was the total amount of payments for days when you were neither working nor looking for work?			
6(a) Did you work full time? (Answer Yes or No)			
(b) If you worked part time, how many hours a day did you work?			

Explanation of item 1:
A qualifying individual is one who lived in your house as a member of your family and is:

1. Your dependent under age 15 who can be claimed as an exemption; or
2. A dependent (or a person you could claim as a dependent, if it were not for the gross income test) who is physically or mentally incapable of caring for self; or
3. Your spouse, if physically or mentally incapable of caring for self.

Declaration I declare that I have examined the information on this form and, to the best of my knowledge and belief, it is true, correct, and complete.	Your Signature	Date
	Spouse's Signature (if a joint return was filed)	Date

Form 4746 (Rev. 12-81)

Form 4748. Questionnaire—Casualty or Theft Loss.

Form **4748** (Rev. Nov. 1981)	Department of the Treasury — Internal Revenue Service **Questionnaire-Casualty or Theft Loss**	OMB No. 1545-0403 Expires 9/30/82

Taxpayer's name and address	In reply refer to
	Tax year

Please furnish the following information to support the deduction for casualty or theft loss shown on your Federal income tax return for the above tax year. If you had more than one loss or need more space, please use the back of this form and number the items to correspond with those below. Attach documents, such as receipts and canceled checks, to substantiate the loss and the amount. *(Photocopies are acceptable.)* We will return the documents as soon as we are through with them. Thank you for your cooperation.

1. Describe property *(If automobile, show year, make, and body style)*

2. Were you the legal owner of the property? ☐ Yes ☐ No	3. On what date did you acquire the property?	4. How long was the property in your possession?	5. What was the cost? (Or other basis of determining value?)	6. On what date did the loss occur?

7. Describe nature of loss

8. Has any portion of the property been recovered?   ☐ Yes   ☐ No

9. Did you notify the police?   ☐ Yes   ☐ No   *(If Yes, please furnish a copy of the police report)*

10 Show fair market value of the property at time of loss and explain how you determined this value.

11 Show fair market value of the property immediately after loss and explain how you determined this value.

12. Was the property insured?   ☐ Yes   ☐ No
   If Yes, please show—

a. Name and address of insurance company	b. Maximum amount of coverage $	c. Amount of insurance compensation received $

(Please furnish a copy of the insurance settlement report.)

13. What amount have you spent to replace, repair, or restore the property? $
   (This amount should not include any expenditures for improving or expanding the property beyond its original condition.)

14. a. Has legal action been taken to recover any of the loss?   ☐ Yes   ☐ No
    b. If Yes, please show any amount you recovered or expect to recover $

DECLARATION I declare that I have examined this statement and, to the best of my knowledge and belief, it is true, correct, and complete.	Your Signature	Date
	Spouse's Signature If a Joint Return Was Filed	Date

Form **4748** (Rev. 11-81)

page 746.271
4/82

Form 4749. Questionnaire—Employee Expenses of Miscellaneous Deductions.

Form **4749** (Rev. November 1981)	Department of the Treasury — Internal Revenue Service **Questionnaire - Employee Expenses** **or Miscellaneous Deductions**	OMB No. 1545-0413 Expires 9/30/82
Taxpayer's Name and Address		In Reply Refer To
		Tax Year

Please complete this form for the following items deducted on your Federal income tax return for the year shown above. If you need more space, you may use the back of this form. When you return this form, please enclose supporting records, such as receipts and cancelled checks (photocopies are acceptable). We will return them promptly upon completing our examination of your return.
Thank you for your cooperation.

1.

Deductions for	Kind of Supporting Evidence Enclosed	Amount Paid
		$
		$
		$
		$

2. If you cannot furnish evidence to support a deduction, please show how you computed the amount deducted.

3. a. Were you reimbursed for any expenses listed above? ☐ Yes ☐ No

b. If Yes, please show the amount and explain how it was determined. $_____

c. Was this reimbursement included in the income reported on your return? ☐ Yes ☐ No

d. If you were not reimbursed, did your employer require you to furnish these items? ☐ Yes ☐ No

4. Explain how each item was related to your job.

5. If any of the deductions listed were for expenses not related to your employment, please give the reason for each of these expenses.

DECLARATION I declare that I have examined the information on this form, and to the best of my knowledge and belief it is true, correct, and complete.	Your Signature	Date
	Spouse's Signature *(If joint return)*	Date

For Privacy Act and Paperwork Reduction Act Notice, see back of form.

Form **4749** (Rev. 11-81)

E
List of Federal Tax Forms

This is a list of federal tax forms most frequently used by taxpayers or their representatives.

A complete listing of federal tax forms can be purchased from the Superintendent of Documents, Washington, DC 20402. Ask for IRS Publication 676, Stock Number 048-004-01829-2.

W-2 (6-part form)
Wage and Tax Statement (For Use in Cities and States Authorizing Combined Form) Used to report wages, tips and other compensation, third-party sick pay, employee FICA tax, income tax withheld, state or city income tax withheld, and to support credit shown on individual income tax return.

W-2P
Statement For Recipients of Periodic Annuities, Pensions, Retired Pay, or IRA Payments Used to report annuities, pensions, and retirement pay; Federal and state income tax withheld.

W-3
Transmittal of Income and Tax Statements Used by employers and other payers to transmit wage and income tax withheld statements (Forms W-2 and W-2P).

W-4
Employee's Withholding Allowance Certificate Filed by employee with employer so that proper amount of income tax

can be withheld from wages. Also used by employee to certify that he or she had no liability for income tax for preceding taxable year and anticipates that no liability will be incurred for current taxable year (qualifying employee will then be exempt from Federal income tax withholding).

W-5
Earned Income Credit Advance Payment Certificate Used by employee to request employer to furnish advance payment of earned income credit with the employee's pay.

706
United States Estate Tax Return Used for the estate of a deceased United States resident or citizen.

709
U.S. Quarterly Gift Tax Return Used to report gifts in excess of $3,000 (or, regardless of value, gifts of a future interest in property). (For gifts made before 1-1-82.)

709-A
United States Short Form Gift Tax Return Used by married couples to report nontaxable gifts of $6,000 or less per donee. (For gifts made before 1-1-82.)

712
Life Insurance Statement Used with Form 706 or Form 709.

940
Employer's Annual Federal Unemployment Tax Return Used by employers to report FUTA tax. A two-part set containing an original and duplicate copy of Form 940, with instructions for preparation.

941c
Statement to Correct Information Previously Reported Under the Federal Insurance Contributions Act Used to correct FICA wage, and FICA tax reports previously submitted by employers.

943
Employer's Annual Tax Return for Agricultural Employees Used by agricultural employers to report FICA and income taxes withheld.

990

Return of Organization Exempt From Federal Income Tax (Except Private Foundation) Used by organizations exempt under IRC section 501(a) and described in section 501(c) other than private foundations. (An information return.)

Schedule A (Form 990)
Organization Exempt Under 501(c)(3) (Supplementary Information) Used by organizations described in IRC section 501(c)(3) (other than private foundations filing Form 990-PF).

990-C
Exempt Cooperative Association Income Tax Return Used by Farmers' Cooperative Marketing and Purchasing Associations exempt under IRC sec. 521.

990-PF
Return of Private Foundation or Section 4947(a)(1) Trust Treated as a Private Foundation Used by private foundations and section 4947(a)(1) trusts. (An information return.)

990-T
Exempt Organization Business Income Tax Return Used by exempt organization with unrelated business income (under section 511 of the IRC).

1040
U.S. Individual Income Tax Return Used by citizens and residents of the United States to report income tax. Also see Form 1040A and Form 1040-EZ.

Sch. A (Form 1040)
Itemized Deductions. Used to report itemized deductions (medical and dental expenses, taxes, contributions, interest and miscellaneous deductions).

Sch. B (Form 1040)
Interest and Dividend Income Used to list gross dividends (if in excess of $400), any interest from an All Saver's certificate, and other interest income (if in excess of $400) received; and to ask questions about Foreign Accounts and Foreign Trusts.

Sch. C (Form 1040)
Profit or (Loss) from Business or Profession Used to compute profit (or loss) from business or profession.

Sch. D (Form 1040)

Capital Gains and Losses Used to report details of gain (or loss) from sales and exchanges of capital assets to compute the alternative tax and to compute post-1969 capital loss carry-overs.

Sch. E (Form 1040)

Supplemental Income Schedule Used to report income from rents, royalties, partnerships, small business corporations, estates, trusts, etc.

Sch. F (Form 1040)

Farm Income and Expenses Used to compute profit (or loss) from farming.

Sch. G (Form 1040)

Income Averaging Used to determine whether tax computed under the averaging provisions is the most advantageous method.

Sch. R&RP (Form 1040)

Credit for the Elderly Used to compute the credit for the elderly for individuals 65 or over and individuals under 65 having public retirement system income.

Sch. SE (Form 1040)

Computation of Social Security Self-Employment Tax Used to compute self-employment income and self-employment tax.

1040A

U.S. Individual Income Tax Return Used by citizens and residents of the United States to report income tax.

1040-ES

Declaration of Estimated Tax for Individuals This declaration provides a means for paying currently any income tax (including self-employment tax, but not the minimum tax on items of tax preference) due in excess of the tax withheld from wages, salaries, and other payments for personal services. It is not required unless the total tax exceeds withholding (if any) and applicable tax credits by $200 or more. (The threshold is $100 for 1981 declarations.)

1040-EZ

Income Tax Return for Single Filers with no Dependents The simplest income tax return, limited to certain taxpayers.

1040NR

U.S. Nonresident Alien Income Tax Return Used by all nonresident alien individuals who file a U.S. tax return, whether or not engaged in a trade or business within the United States. Also used as required for filing nonresident alien fiduciary (Estate and Trust) returns.

1040X

Amended U.S. Individual Income Tax Return Used to claim refund of income taxes, pay additional income taxes, or designate dollar(s) to a Presidential Election Campaign Fund.

1041

U.S. Fiduciary Income Tax Return (For Estates and Trusts) Used by a fiduciary for domestic estate or domestic trust. (An annual return.)

Sch. D (Form 1041)

Capital Gains and Losses Used to report details of gain (or loss) from sales or exchanges of capital assets.

Sch. K-1 (Form 1041)

Beneficiary's Share of Income, Deductions, Credits, etc. Used to report each beneficiary's share of the income, deductions, credits, and items of tax preference from the estate or trust.

Sch. J (Form 1041)

Trust Allocation of an Accumulation Distribution (IRC Section 665) Used for domestic complex trusts.

1065

U.S. Partnership Return of Income Used by partnerships as an information return.

Schedule K-1 (Form 1065)

Partner's Share of Income, Credits, Deductions, etc. Used to show partner's share of income, credits, deductions, etc. A four-part assembly—Copy A is filed with Form 1065, Copy B is for partnership records, and Copy C is given to each partner. The last part is instructions for the partner.

1087-DIV

1087-INT

1087-MED

1087-MISC

1087-OID
Persons receiving Forms 1099-DIV, 1099-INT, 1099-MED, 1099-MISC, or 1099-OID who are not the actual owners of that income, but received it as a nominee on behalf of another person, should file a similar Form 1087 to designate the actual owner of that income.

1096
Annual Summary and Transmittal of U.S. Information Returns Used for summarizing and transmitting reports on Forms 1087-DIV, 1087-INT, 1087-MED, 1087-MISC, 1087-OID, 1099-BCD, 1099-DIV, 1099F, 1099-INT, 1099L, 1099-MED, 1099-MISC, 1099-NEC, 1099-OID, 1099-PATR, 1099R, and 1099-UC.

1099-DIV
Statement for Recipients of Dividends and Distributions Used to report dividends and distributions.

1099F
Statement for Certain Fishing Boat Crew members Used by fishing boat owners or operators to report payments to crew members of proceeds from sale of catch or distributions in kind.

1099-INT
Statement for Recipients of Interest Income Used to report interest income.

1099L
U.S. Information Return for Distributions in Liquidation During the Calendar Year Used to report a distribution of $600 or more made during the year to a shareholder.

1099-MED

Statement for Recipients of Medical and Health Care Payments Used to report payments totalling $600 or more during the year to a physician or other supplier or provider of services under health, accident and sickness insurance plans or medical assistance programs.

1099-MISC

Statement for Recipients of Miscellaneous Income Used to report rents, royalties, prizes and awards (but not for services rendered).

1099-NEC

Statement for Recipients of Nonemployee Compensation Used to report fees, commissions, or any other compensation for services rendered in the course of the payer's business when the recipient is not treated as an employee. Also includes expenses incurred for use of an entertainment facility when such use is treated as compensation.

1099-OID

Statement for Recipients of Original Issue Discount Used to report original issue discount.

1099-PATR

Statement for Recipients (Patrons) of Taxable Distributions Received from Cooperatives Used to report patronage dividends.

1099R

Statement for Recipients of Total Distributions from Profit Sharing, Retirement Plans, and Individual Retirement Arrangements Used to report total distributions from profit sharing, retirement plans, and individual retirement arrangements.

1116

Computation of Foreign Tax Credit-Individual, Fiduciary, or Nonresident Alien Individual Used to support the foreign tax credit claimed for the amount of any income, war profits, and excess profits taxes paid or accrued during the tax year to any foreign country or U.S. possession.

Sch. A (Form 1116)
Schedule of Foreign Taxable Income and Foreign Taxes Paid or Accrued Used as an attachment to Form 1116, Computation of Foreign Tax Credit—Individual, Fiduciary, or Nonresident Alien Individual, to support the foreign tax credit claimed when income has been derived from or taxes have been paid to more than one foreign country or U.S. possession.

1120
U.S. Corporation Income Tax Return Used by a corporation to report income tax.

Sch. D (Form 1120)
Capital Gains and Losses Used by a taxpayer who files either Forms 1120, 1120-DISC, 1120F, 1120-H, 1120L, 1120M, 1120-POL, 990-C, or certain Forms 990-T, to report details of gain (or loss) from sales or exchanges of capital assets, and to figure the alternative tax.

Sch. PH (Form 1120)
Computation of U.S. Personal Holding Company Tax Used to compute personal holding company tax; filed with the income tax return of every personal holding company.

1120-DISC
Domestic International Sales Corporation Return Used for a tax year relating to a DISC.

Sch. K (Form 1120-DISC)
Shareholder's Statement of DISC Distribution Used to report deemed and actual distributions from a DISC to shareholders.

Sch. N (Form 1120-DISC)
Export Gross Receipts of the DISC and Related U.S. Persons Used to report gross receipts of the DISC and certain related persons.

1120F
U.S. Income Tax Return of a Foreign Corporation Used by foreign corporations to report income tax.

1120S
U.S. Small Business Corporation Income Tax Return

Used by qualifying small business corporations that make the election prescribed by IRC section 1372.

Sch. D (Form 1120S)
Capital Gains and Losses Used by qualifying small business corporations that make the election prescribed by IRC section 1372 to report details of gains (and losses) from sales or exchanges of capital assets and to figure the tax imposed on certain capital gains.

Sch. K-1 (Form 1120S)
Shareholder's Share of Undistributed Taxable Income, etc. Used by shareholders, a three-part assembly—Copy A is filed with Form 1120S, Copy B is given to each shareholder, and Copy C is for corporate records.

1120-W (Worksheet)
Corporation Estimated Tax Used as a worksheet by corporations to compute estimated tax liability; not required to be filed. Corporations should keep it for their records.

1120X
Amended U.S. Corporation Income Tax Return Used by corporations to amend a previously filed Form 1120.

1139
Corporation Application for Tentative Refund Used by corporations which have certain carry-backs and desire a quick refund of taxes.

1310
Statement of Person Claiming Refund Due a Deceased Taxpayer Used by a claimant to secure payment of refund on behalf of a deceased taxpayer.

2106
Employee Business Expenses For optional use to support deductions from income tax for travel, transportation, outside salesperson or educational expenses (except moving expenses).

2119
Sale or Exchange of Principal Residence For use by individuals who sold their principal residence. Also used by those individuals 55 or older who elect to exclude gain on the sale of their principal residence.

2120

Multiple Support Declaration Used as a statement disclaiming as an income tax exemption an individual to whose support the taxpayer and others have contributed.

2210

Underpayment of Estimated Income Tax by Individuals Used to furnish an explanation to avoid penalty for underpayment of estimated tax.

2220

Underpayment of Estimated Tax by Corporations Used by a corporation to determine whether it paid enough estimated tax, whether it is subject to the penalty for underpayment of estimated tax, and how much penalty it may owe for any underpayment.

(If additional tax is due, a computation schedule is provided.)

2350

Application for Extension of Time to File U.S. Income Tax Return Used by U.S. citizens and certain resident aliens abroad, who expect to qualify for special tax treatment to obtain an extension of time for filing an income tax return.

2440

Disability Income Exclusion Used to compute amount of disability income excluded from income tax.

2441

Credit for Child and Dependent Care Expenses Used to support credit for child and dependent care expenses. (To be attached to Form 1040.)

2555

Deduction From, or Exclusion of, Income Earned Abroad Used by U.S. citizens and certain resident aliens who qualify for deductions from, or exclusion of, earned income from sources outside the U.S. (To be attached to Form 1040.)

2688

Application for Extension of Time to File U.S. Individual Income Tax Return Used to apply for an additional extension of time to file Form 1040.

2758
Application for Extension of Time to File U.S. Partnership, Fiduciary, and Certain Exempt Organization Returns Used to apply for an extension of time to file Form 1065, Form 1041, and certain exempt organization returns.

2848
Power of Attorney and Declaration of Representative Used as an authorization for one person to act for another in any tax matter (except alcohol and tobacco taxes and firearms activities).

3468
Computation of Investment Credit Used by individuals, estates, trusts, and corporations claiming a regular or business energy investment credit and any small business corporation, partnership, estate, or trust that apportions the investment credit property among its shareholders, partners, or beneficiaries.

Schedule B (Form 3468)
Computation of Business Energy Investment Credit Used by individuals, estates, trusts, and corporations to figure a business energy investment credit. The energy credit is then entered on Form 3468. Schedule B is also used by any small business corporation, partnership, estate, or trust that apportions the business energy property among its shareholders, partners, or beneficiaries.

3903
Moving Expense Adjustment For optional use to support deductions from income for expenses of travel, transportation (including meals and lodging) and certain expenses attributable to disposition of an old residence and acquisition of a new residence for employees moving to a new job location.

4136
Computation of Credit for Federal Tax on Gasoline, Special Fuels, and Lubricating Oil Used by individuals, estates, trusts, or corporations, including small business corporations and domestic international sales corporations, to claim credit for Federal excise tax on the number of gallons of gasoline, special fuels, and lubricating oil used in business.

4137

Computation of Social Security Tax on Unreported Tip Income   Filed by an employee who received tips subject to FICA tax but failed to report them to his or her employer.

4255

Recapture of Investment Credit   Used by individuals, estates, trusts, or corporations to recapture the regular or energy investment credit taken on property disposed of before the end of the useful life used in computing the credit. The tax must be increased if the credit allowed is more than the credit allowable at the time of disposition.

4466

Corporation Application for Quick Refund of Overpayment of Estimated Tax   Used to apply for a "quick" refund of overpaid estimated tax. (Must be filed before the regular tax return is filed.)

4562

Depreciation   For use by individuals, estate and trusts, partnerships, and corporations claiming depreciation.

4625

Computation of Minimum Tax—Individuals   Used by individuals who have items of tax preference in excess of $10,000, or minimum tax liability deferred to the current year.

4626

Computation of Minimum Tax—Corporations and Fiduciaries   Used generally by corporations and fiduciaries to compute minimum tax when tax preferences are more than $10,000.

4684

Casualties and Thefts   For use by all taxpayers for reporting gains and losses from casualties and thefts.

4726

Maximum Tax on Personal Service Income   Used by individuals and certain fiduciaries to determine whether it is more advantageous to figure tax by using maximum tax on personal service income.

4782

Employee Moving Expense Information   Used by employers to show employees the amount of any reimbursement or payment made to an employee, a third party for the employee's benefit, or the value of services furnished in-kind, for moving expenses during the calendar year.

4797

Supplemental Schedule of Gains and Losses   Used to report details of gain (or loss) from sales, exchange, or involuntary conversions (other than casualties and thefts) of noncapital assets and involuntary conversions of capital assets other than casualties and thefts held for more than one year.

4798

Capital Loss Carry-over   Used by an individual to figure the capital loss limitation if pre-1970 losses are involved, and any capital loss carry-over from the current taxable year to the following taxable year.

4835

Farm Rental Income and Expenses and Summary of Gross Income From Farming or Fishing   Used by landowner (or sublessor) to report farm rental income based on crops or livestock produced by the tenant where the landowner (or sublessor) does not materially participate in the operation or management of the farm.

4868

Application for Automatic Extension of Time to File U.S. Individual Income Tax Return   Used to apply for an automatic 2-month extension of time to file Form 1040.

4874

Credit for Work Incentive (WIN) Program Expenses Used by individuals, estates, trusts, and corporations claiming the WIN credit.

4952

Investment Interest Expense Deduction   Used by an individual, estate, or trust to compute the deduction limitation for interest expense on funds borrowed to purchase or carry property held for investment.

4970
Tax on Accumulation Distribution of Trusts   For use by a beneficiary of a domestic or foreign trust to compute the tax attributable to an accumulation distribution.

4972
Special 10-Year Averaging Method   Used to determine the income tax on the ordinary income portion of lump-sum distributions.

5329
Return for Individual Retirement Arrangement Taxes   Used to report the various individual retirement arrangement taxes under IRC sections 408(f), 409(c), 4973, and 4974.

5330
Return of Initial Excise Taxes Related to Pension and Profit-Sharing Plans   Used to report excise taxes imposed by IRC sections 4971, 4972, 4973(a)(2) and 4975.

5500
Annual Return/Report of Employee Benefit Plan   Used to report on deferred compensation plans and welfare plans that have at least 100 participants.

Sch. A (Form 5500)
Insurance Information   Used as an attachment to Forms 5500, 5500-C, 5500-K and 5500-R to report information about insurance contracts that are part of a qualified deferred compensation plan.

Sch. B (Form 5500)
Actuarial Information   Used to report actuarial information with respect to a defined benefit plan. It is attached to Form 5500, 5500-C, 5500-K, and 5500-R.

Sch. P. (Form 5500)
Annual Return of Fiduciary of Employee Benefit Trust   Used as an attachment to Forms 5500, 5500-C, 5500-G, 5500-K and 5500-R to satisfy reporting requirements under IRC section 6033(a) and start statute of limitations under IRC section 6501(a).

Sch. SSA (Form 5500)
Registration Statement Identifying Separated Partici-

pants with Deferred Vested Benefits Used as an attachment to Forms 5500, 5500-C, 5500-K, and 5500-R to list the employees who separated from employment and have a deferred vested benefit in the employers plan of deferred compensation.

5500-C
Return/Report of Employee Benefit Plan Used to report on deferred compensation plans and welfare plans that have fewer than 100 participants, none of whom is an owner-employee.

5500-G
Annual Return/Report of Employee Benefit Plan for Government and Certain Church Plans Used to report on government pension benefit plans and church pension benefit plans (not electing coverage under IRC section 410(d)).

5500-K
Return/Report of Employee Pension Benefit Plan for Sole Proprietorships and Partnerships Used to report on H.R. 10 (Keogh) plans that have fewer than 100 participants and at least one owner-employee participant.

5500-R
Registration Statement of Employee Benefit Plan Used to report on deferred compensation plans and welfare plans that have fewer than 100 participants. This form is filed for plan years when Form 5500-C or 5500-K is not required to be filed.

5544
Multiple Recipient Special 10-Year Averaging Method Used to determine income tax on the ordinary income portion of lump-sum distributions received by a multiple recipient.

5558
Application for Extension of Time to File Certain Employee Plan Returns Used to request an extension of time to file Forms 5500, 5500-C, 5500-K, 5500-G, 5500-R, and 5330.

5695
Residential Energy Credit Used by individual taxpayers to claim a credit against their tax for qualified energy-saving property.

5884

Jobs Credit   Used by individuals, estates, trusts, and corporations claiming a Targeted Jobs Credit, and any small business corporation, partnership, estate, or trust which apportions the credit among its shareholders, partners, or beneficiaries.

6251

Alternative Minimum Tax Computation   Used by individuals, estates, and trusts to report tax preference items for capital gains and adjusted itemized deductions and to compute their alternative minimum tax liability.

6252

Computation of Installment Sale Income   Used by taxpayers other than dealers, who sell real or personal property, and receive any payment from the sale in a tax year after the year of sale.

6765

Credit for Increasing Research Activities   Used by individuals, estates, trusts, and corporations to claim a credit for increasing research activities for a trade or business.

7004

Application for Automatic Extension of Time to File Corporation Income Tax Return   Used by corporations and certain exempt organizations to request an automatic extension of 3 months to file the corporate income tax return.

7005

Application for Additional Extension of Time to File Corporation Income Tax Return   Used only by corporations and certain exempt organizations that have previously been granted an automatic 3-month extension on Form 7004 and are now requesting an additional extension.

Treasury Department Form 90-22.1 (9-78)

Report of Foreign Bank and Financial Accounts   Filed by any individual, trust, partnership, or corporation that has a financial interest in, or signature authority or other authority over, bank, securities, or other financial accounts in a foreign country, that exceeded $1,000 in aggregate value at any time during the calendar year.

F
List of Federal Tax Publications

You can order these free publications, and any forms you need, from the IRS Forms Distribution Center for your state. The address is in the instructions to your tax return. Or you can call the Tax Information number listed in your phone book under *United States Government, Internal Revenue Service.*

Spanish Language Publications

G
List of Tax Havens

In 1981 the IRS kindly described jurisdictions that have one or more characteristics common to tax havens beyond self-promotion (or "tax aggression," as the Service called it). The characteristics are: (1) low or relatively low taxes, (2) secrecy, (3) active financial facilities, (4) modern communication facilities, and (5) lack of currency controls. The havens listed by the Service are:

Anguila	Liechtenstein
Antigua	Luxembourg
Bahamas	Montserrat
Bahrain	Netherlands Antilles
Bermuda	Nevis
British Antilles	Panama
British Virgin Islands	Singapore
Cayman Islands	St. Kitts
Costa Rica	St. Lucia
Dominica	St. Vincent
Hong Kong	Switzerland
Liberia	

H
Tax Data Organizer

These forms will help you gather the information necessary to prepare your own federal tax returns, or to present information to a professional tax preparer, in an effective way, each year. It is very helpful (as well as interesting) to attach a copy of the prior year's return. Preparers find it useful, also, to list recurring items (like receipts of dividends and interest) alphabetically so that changes can be readily identified from one year to the next.

I. PERSONAL DATA

YOUR NAME_____SOCIAL SECURITY NO._____

SPOUSE'S NAME_____SOCIAL SECURITY NO._____

ADDRESS_____ZIP_____

YOUR OCCUPATION_____SPOUSE'S OCCUPATION_____

Your date of birth: Legally blind?
Spouse's date of birth: Legally blind?

Dependent Children
Names and ages of your children under 19, regardless of the amount of their income, provided you furnished more than one-half of their support:

_____   _____   _____   _____

Names of your children 19 or over, regardless of the amount of their income, provided you furnished more than one-half of their support and they were full-time students for at least five months during the year:

_____ _____ _____ _____

Other Dependents
Other individuals with less than $1,000 who received more than one-half of their support from you:

Names	Relationship	Months lived in your home	Amount you furnished for support	Amount furnished by others including the dependent

• FILING STATUS

☐ Single
☐ Married filing joint return (even if only one had income)
☐ Married filing separate return
☐ Head of household (with qualifying person. If he or she is your unmarried child, enter child's name _____)
☐ Qualifying widow(er) with dependent child (Year spouse died 19____)

II. INCOME

AMOUNT

• WAGES, SALARIES, and OTHER COMPENSATION, etc. (Attach Forms W-2 or Forms 1099)

• INCOME FROM TIPS

• DIVIDENDS and OTHER CORPORATE DISTRIBU-TIONS (Attach any Forms 1087-DIV and 1099-DIV received. Show amounts withheld after June 30, 1983.)

SHARES   COMPANY

_____

- INTEREST (Attach Forms 1087-INT, 1099-INT, and 1099-OID. Show amounts withheld after June 30, 1983.)

NAME of PAYER

_____

All Saver's Certificate Interest

_____

- SALES, EXCHANGES, REDEMPTIONS, ETC., of SECURITIES (Attach brokers' confirmations)

Shares or Par Value	Description	Date Acquired	Date Sold	Cost Basis	Gross Sales Price

- In case of loss, did you purchase or contract to acquire "substantially identical" securities as those sold within 30 days prior to or 30 days after the sale?
- Attach a list of securities or other property that became worthless during the calendar year, and describe the manner and date of acquisition and how the cost was determined.
- SALES, EXCHANGES, ETC., of OTHER PROPERTY (If not purchased, give details of acquisition)

Description	Date Acquired	Date Sold	Cost Basis	Gross Sales Price

- Attach details regarding sales of property for which you will be paid in installments.

Give full details regarding the following kinds of income:

AMOUNT

- ALIMONY RECEIVED

- ANNUITIES and PENSIONS (Show amounts, if any, withheld)

- COMMISSIONS and FEES

- RENTS (Include date of acquisition, kind, location, and cost of rental property, total rent received, and an itemized list of repairs and expenses)

- ROYALTIES

- PROFIT or LOSS from BUSINESS or PROFESSION
(Itemize receipts and expenses. Give full accounting
details of business or profession)

- RECEIPTS from PARTNERSHIPS, ESTATES, or
TRUSTS (Attach Schedules K-1s or other statements)

- STATE or LOCAL TAX REFUNDS

- INCOME from FOREIGN SOURCES (Including taxes
withheld)

- MISCELLANEOUS INCOME (Include cancellation of debts, gambling winnings, prizes, "bargain purchases," and any other receipts of cash or
property, including barter, that *might* be considered income. List details)

AMOUNT

III. DEDUCTIONS AND CREDITS

• MEDICAL and DENTAL EXPENSES
    MEDICINE and LEGAL DRUGS   AMOUNT

Reimbursements received from insurance or
Medicare

ALL OTHER MEDICAL and DENTAL EXPENSES

Hospitalization, health insurance, and/or
Medicare—gross premium

Transportation or travel required for medical
treatment (Actual expenses or mileage)

Doctors, nurses, hospital, eyeglasses, X ray,
therapy, lab fees, dentists, etc. (Itemize)

Reimbursements received from insurance or
Medicare

• INTEREST PAID

Mortgage interest (home or cooperative apartment)

Loans, charge accounts, credit cards, taxes,
etc. (Itemize)

• CONTRIBUTIONS

ORGANIZATION	AMOUNT
Total cash contributions for which you have receipts or canceled checks	
Other cash contributions for which you have no receipts or canceled checks (Itemize)	
Noncash contributions (Give details of manner in which made, date acquired, and tax cost basis)	
Out-of-pocket expenditures for charities (Give details)	

• CONTRIBUTIONS to POLITICAL CANDIDATES or COMMITTEES

• Do you wish to designate $1 of your taxes for the Presidential Election Campaign Fund?

• TAXES	AMOUNT
State and local income—amounts withheld	
State and local income—estimated payments	
State and local income—paid on last year's taxes	
Real estate	
General sales (Including large purchases like autos)	
Personal property	
Business taxes (Itemize)	
Other (Give details)	

- LOSSES from FIRE, STORM, COLLISION, or OTHER CASUALTIES or THEFT (List losses, in excess of $100, not compensated for by insurance or otherwise; should be supported by documentary evidence) _____
- BAD DEBTS (If a debt owed you became uncollectible during the calendar year, attach a description of [a] what the debt was; [b] the debtor's name and family relationship, if any; [c] when the debt was created; [d] when the debt became due; [e] what efforts were made to collect; [f] how the debt was determined to be uncollectible) _____
- CHILD- or DEPENDENT-CARE EXPENSES (Expenses paid to enable you—and, if married, your spouse—to be gainfully employed, if paid for the care of [a] a dependent under 15, [b] a dependent physically or mentally disabled, or [c] a disabled spouse) _____
- ALIMONY and SEPARATE MAINTENANCE PAYMENTS

_____

- TAX PREPARATION FEES

_____

- MISCELLANEOUS DEDUCTIONS (List details regarding expenses incurred in connection with
income-producing property, such as safe deposit
rental or fees, tools, supplies, or other expenses,
in connection with earned income and *any* other
expense that you believe might be a deductible
income tax item) _____

DEDUCTIONS, CREDITS AND OTHER DATA

- HOME-OFFICE EXPENSES (List details, including
allocation of utilities, etc.)

AMOUNT

_____
_____
_____
_____
_____
_____
_____

- UNREIMBURSED BUSINESS TRAVEL and ENTERTAINMENT EX-
PENSES (List full details, including dates, parties entertained, business
relationship, etc.)

_____
_____
_____

- CONTRIBUTIONS to PENSION PLANS (List full details)

_____

- RESIDENTIAL ENERGY CREDITS (Home-energy-
conservation expenditures for insulation, storm
windows and doors, caulking and weatherstrip-
ping, and clock thermostats; alternative-energy-
equipment expenditures for installing new solar,
wind, or geothermal energy equipment in principal residence) _____

• FOREIGN ACCOUNTS and FOREIGN TRUSTS
Did you, at any time during the taxable year, have any interest in or signature or other authority over a bank, securities, or other financial account in a foreign country (except in a U.S. military banking facility operated by a U.S. financial institution)?

Were you the grantor of, or transferor to, a foreign trust during any taxable year, which foreign trust was in being during the current taxable year (even if you have no beneficial interest in the trust)?

CREDITS AND OTHER DATA

• CREDIT for the ELDERLY (For certain persons 65 or over)

Amount, if any, of Social Security, military or other exempt retirement benefits, received during the year. (May also be used to increase sales-tax deduction) $_____

• ADDITIONAL INFORMATION (Attach full details of foreign bank accounts, new home purchase or sold, job-hunting expenses, moving expenses incurred for new job, sick pay received, etc.)

AMOUNT

_____

_____

_____

_____

_____

_____

_____

_____

_____

• CREDITS for ESTIMATED TAXES PAID and CREDITS from PRIOR YEARS

_____

_____

_____

_____

Glossary

Defined below are some terms that tax professionals often use. These are not legal definitions—which usually employ other technical legal terminology. In most cases these terms are more fully explained in the text and are gathered here simply for ready reference.

Accelerated cost recovery system (ACRS)   The automatic recovery (through tax deductions) of the costs of depreciable assets over periods shorter than and unrelated to the actual expected lives of the assets. ACRS generally applies to assets placed in service after 1980 and is in contrast to the old methods of utilizing rapid depreciation deductions by allocating higher deductions to the first years of use of depreciable assets.

Accounting methods and periods   Tax accounting is generally accomplished by either of two methods: *(a)* accrual or *(b)* cash basis. Accounting periods may be *(a)* by calender year or *(b)* by fiscal year, which is any other twelve-month period, if books have been kept that way. (The first or last fiscal year may be less than twelve months.)

Adjusted basis   The cost basis of property reduced (e.g., for depreciation) or increased (e.g., for capital improvements) for purposes of computing gain or loss. *See also* **Basis.**

Adjusted gross income Gross income reduced, for individuals only, by specified above-the-line expenses (certain employee expenses and trade or business expenses, alimony, long-term capital gain deductions, Keogh and IRA contributions, and so forth). Adjusted gross income is used to calculate limits on medical and charitable deductions.

At risk The sum of cash, property, and borrowing that the taxpayer personally risks in an investment.

Away from home Away from one's main business location or tax home, rather than away from one's residence. Reasonable travel expenses (for meals and lodging) in the pursuit of a trade or business are deductible if they are incurred away from home.

Bad debts Uncollectible debts, whether or not related to business (though tax treatment will differ regarding business and nonbusiness bad debts).

Basis The tax cost of property, used to calculate gain or loss. Basis is subject to adjustments and to special rules if the property was not purchased by the taxpayer.

Bequest A gift of personal property by will; not subject to income tax when received (though subject to inclusion in the gross estate of the decedent for estate tax purposes).

Boot Property or cash received in an otherwise nontaxable exchange.

Capital gain or loss The profit or loss from the sale or other disposition of property that qualifies as a capital transaction. Capital gains and losses are subject to reduction, for purposes of taxation, if the property disposed of was held long term (over one year, under current rules). A capital transaction requires, first, a capital asset (most kinds of property, except inventory held for sale to customers; accounts receivable; and certain other designated assets) and, second, a sale or exchange thereof. See also **Holding period, Long-term capital gain or loss.**

Carry-backs and carry-overs The transfers of one year's tax events, which yield deductions or credits, backward or forward to another tax year.

Collapsible corporation A corporation that, under specific tests, is considered to be established for one business opportunity and that is to be promptly liquidated in an attempt to realize capital gains rather than ordinary operating income.

Conduit rule The theory that trusts or estates are fundamentally passages, or conduits, for distributions that retain their character. Distributions are treated by the beneficiaries as they would have been treated had they been retained by the trust or estate.

Constructive ownership or receipt Ownership of property or receipt of income that is not actual but, nevertheless, is so treated for tax purposes, because the taxpayer can exercise control or demand over the property or income.

Corpus Principal, rather than income, of a trust or estate.

Credit The amount that may be subtracted directly from a tax liability because of payments previously made, or, by legislative grace, regarding special expenses, or by the taxpayer's tax condition.

Deduction The amount that may be subtracted from gross income or, in the case of individual taxpayers who itemize, from adjusted gross income to arrive at an amount upon which income tax is based. Deductions similarly are granted in the calculation of estate taxes.

Deficiency The amount by which a calculated tax liability is underpaid.

Dependent A relative of the taxpayer for part of a tax year or a member of the taxpayer's household for the whole year who is supported by the taxpayer. A dependent must meet mechanical tests regarding support, gross income, relationship, citizenship, and filing status in order to provide the taxpayer with a dependency exemption.

Depreciation Steady reduction in the value of property because of wear and tear or obsolescence over a period of time (longer than a year), for which a deduction is allowed. *See also* **Accelerated cost recovery system.**

Devise   A gift of real property by will; not subject to income tax when received (though subject to inclusion in the gross estate of the decedent for estate tax purposes).

Distributable net income (DNI)   All the ordinary income of an estate or trust, less certain expenses, distributed or distributable to beneficiaries. Tax-exempt income is included in DNI, capital gains or losses and lump-sum payments of inheritances, bequests, or devises are not.

Dividend   A distribution, whether or not in cash, by a corporation to its shareholders out of its current or accumulated earnings and profits.

Employee   A worker who is subject to an employer's will and control, particularly in regard to methodology; generally distinguished from an independent contractor who is engaged to achieve a result only.

Excess itemized deductions   The amount by which itemized deductions exceed the zero bracket amount (formerly the standard deduction).

Exemption   An allowance for status or dependency—for which adjusted gross income is reduced by a fixed amount.

Fair market value   The price of property that would be agreed upon by a willing seller and a willing buyer, neither of whom must buy or sell and each of whom has full knowledge of the necessary facts.

Fiscal year   Annual accounting period that is not concurrent with a calendar year. *See also* **Accounting methods and periods.**

Flower bonds   Certain series of Treasury bonds, issued before March 4, 1974, that may be used to pay federal estate taxes at par, despite lower market value.

Grantor trust   A trust in which control over principal or income is retained by the grantor to an extent sufficient to cause the grantor to continue to be treated, for tax purposes, as owner of the principal and income.

Holding period   The length of time property is held or

deemed to be held for tax purposes; used to determine treatment of capital transactions, wash sales, and other transactions. *See also* **Long-term capital gain or loss.**

Imputed interest   An amount that is considered to be interest, taxed as such to the seller and deductible as such by the buyer, under a deferred payment contract that is made without provision for interest or with provision for interest at less than a "test" rate.

Income averaging   An elective method of computing income taxes by spreading unusually high taxable income received in one tax year as if it were received evenly over the current year and the preceding four years.

Income in respect of a decedent   Income earned, but not received, by a decedent at the time of death.

Inheritance   Property acquired from a person who dies without a will; not subject to income tax when received (though subject to inclusion in the gross estate of the decedent for estate tax purposes).

Installment method   The mode of reporting gain on an installment sale that taxes the profit on the sale proportionately in the years in which the installment payments are received.

Investment credit   A direct credit of 10 percent of the cost of qualified investment in depreciable personal property (and certain other property). The credit may be reduced if the expected life of the property is short. It is subject to certain limitations and may be carried back or forward. Contributions to employee stock ownership plans may earn an extra 1 percent credit.

Involuntary conversion   The transformation of property, because of theft, destruction, condemnation, or requisition (or threat of imminent public seizure), into similar property or cash.

Long-term capital gain or loss   The gain or loss from the sale or exchange of a capital asset with a holding period, currently, of more than one year. For individuals, net long-term gains are subject to a 60 percent capital gains deduction, net long-term losses are reduced by 50 percent. *See also* **Capital gain or loss, Holding period.**

Minimum tax Additional tax on certain kinds and amounts of preferred items of income. For individuals, there is a regular minimum tax (on various "tax preference" items) or an alternative minimum tax (primarily on long-term capital gains) that is applicable if it exceeds the regular income tax.

Net operating loss The net loss from operating a trade or business (and certain other losses). The unused portion of a net operating loss may be carried back to be applied against income reported in prior years or (if not utilized by carry-backs) carried forward to future years; used under specific computational rules.

Nonresident alien A person who is neither a citizen nor a resident of the United States.

Personal holding company A corporation held by no more than five owners to retain investments or personal service contracts and the income produced therefrom. Such an incorporated pocketbook is subject to specific tests which, if met, will cause the imposition of punitive taxes on the amount of personal holding company income (as defined) that remains undistributed.

Puts and calls Options to sell or buy stock or commodities at set prices, within fixed times under specified rules. The exercise or failure to exercise such options are subject to special tax rules regarding the nature of gains or losses and holding periods.

Recapture The repayment, under specified rules, of tax deductions or credits because of the occurrence of an event contrary to the assumption upon which such tax advantages were previously based. (For example, the sale of depreciable personal property prior to the end of its useful life may give rise to taxable ordinary income to replace the earlier depreciation deductions claimed.)

Residence Physical presence in a particular place united with family, social, or cultural connections; an elusive term, dependent in large measure on the taxpayer's intention to make a place a residence. An intention to make a place a legal, permanent abode is not required. One may have more than one residence at a time (but only one domicile). Tax regulations distinguish between a resident and a transient, but say that "a mere floating intention" to return to a prior residence someday will not avoid residence in a taxpayer's current location.

Short sale The agreement to sell borrowed stock or other securities that must subsequently be purchased (or otherwise replaced) in order to cover the sale. Gain or loss is calculated when the transaction is covered, and special rules regarding determination of holding periods apply to short sales.

Short-term capital gain or loss The gain or loss from the sale or exchange of capital assets with a holding period of one year or less. *See also* **Capital gain or loss, Holding period.**

Small business corporation (1) A corporation that, upon liquidation, may yield either capital gain or ordinary loss to its shareholders; subject to specific qualifying rules regarding shareholders, stock, and income (a "Section 1244 Corporation"). (2) A corporation through which income, losses, and other characteristics are passed to the shareholders proportionately and which pays no tax at the corporate level; subject to specific qualifying rules regarding shareholders, stock, and income (a "Subchapter S Corporation").

Step-up The increase in basis of property, generally because it is acquired from a decedent or because a taxable gain is recognized on its transfer.

Straight-line A method of depreciation by which the depreciable cost is deducted evenly over the useful life of property in equal annual amounts.

Subchapter S *See* **Small Business Corporation** (2) above.

Substituted basis Basis that is determined by reference to the basis of other property or another owner (e.g., as the result of a tax-free exchange or the receipt of a gift).

Surviving spouse For tax purposes, a widow or widower whose spouse died within the two years before the current tax year, who has not remarried, and who maintains a dependent child at home. A surviving spouse may file a return using joint rates.

Tacking Increasing the holding period of property by adding the time other property was held or the time another person held the property (e.g., as the result of a tax-free exchange or the receipt of a gift).

Taxable Income For individuals, adjusted gross income less personal exemptions, unused zero bracket amount, and itemized deductions in excess of the zero bracket amount; for corporate taxpayers, gross income less all deductions. Tax, before any credits, is calculated on taxable income. *See also* **Adjusted gross income.**

Trade or business Any activity or pursuit genuinely carried on for livelihood or profit.

Wash sale The sale of stock or securities within a period starting thirty days before and ending thirty days after the acquisition of identical or substantially identical stock or securities. A loss on a wash sale will not be recognized.

Windfall profit An unexpected or unearned profit. A temporary windfall-profits tax is imposed on excess-crude-oil profits received by certain producers.

Zero bracket amount The marginal bracket at which the tax rate is zero. The zero bracket amount, in lieu of a standard deduction, is an amount of income that is not subject to tax. (Currently the zero bracket amounts range from $1,700 to $3,400, depending on the status of the taxpayer.)

Index